A REAL RIGHT TO VOTE

◯ How a
◯ Constitutional
⬭ Amendment
◯ Can Safeguard
◯ American
◯ Democracy

RICHARD L. HASEN

PRINCETON UNIVERSITY PRESS
Princeton and Oxford

Published by Princeton University Press
41 William Street, Princeton, New Jersey 08540
99 Banbury Road, Oxford OX2 6JX

press.princeton.edu

All Rights Reserved

ISBN 978-0-691-25771-6
ISBN (e-book) 978-0-691-257723

British Library Cataloging-in-Publication Data is available

Editorial: Bridget Flannery-McCoy and Alena Chekanov
Production Editorial: Jill Harris
Text Design: Heather Hansen
Jacket Design: Heather Hansen
Production: Erin Suydam
Publicity: Kate Hensley and Kathryn Stevens
Copyeditor: Leah Caldwell

This book has been composed in Arno Pro with Helvetica

Printed on acid-free paper. ∞

Printed in the United States of America

10 9 8 7 6 5 4 3 2 1

For the American People,
who have always deserved, and still deserve, a real right to vote

CONTENTS

Acknowledgments   ix

Introduction. Why We Need a Real Right to Vote   1

Chapter 1. Courts Are Not Enough   19

Chapter 2. An Amendment for Political Equals   41

Chapter 3. Expanding the Right to Vote?   67

Chapter 4. Deescalating the Voting Wars   91

Chapter 5. Safeguarding American Democracy   112

Chapter 6. How to Get a Real Right to Vote   132

*Appendix. Draft Versions of a Constitutional Amendment
Affirmatively Protecting the Right to Vote*   153

Notes   159

Index   215

ACKNOWLEDGMENTS

I have been considering the ideas in this book for a long time and had thought I knew what I would include in a proposal for a constitutional amendment guaranteeing a right to vote. But once I started writing, I realized that there are many twists and turns, and quite a few pitfalls, both in drafting such a proposal and in defending it. I have benefitted greatly from the generosity of readers who saved me from many embarrassing mistakes and helped me strengthen my arguments and prose. Any errors that remain are solely my responsibility.

Thanks to David Ettinger, Jared Hasen-Klein, Justin Levitt, Steve Kay, Alex Keyssar, Nate Persily, and Rick Pildes, who read and gave detailed comments on the manuscript. Thanks also to Angela Baggetta, Matthew Campbell, Travis Crum, Jacqueline De León, Joey Fishkin, Bill Frucht, Pam Karlan, Lori Klein, Michael McDonald, David Pozen, Jamie Raskin, Kal Raustiala, Rob Richie, Kathleen Unger, Lauren van Schilfgaarde, Neil Weare, and Brenda Wright for useful comments and suggestions. I also received helpful comments when I presented an early version of these ideas as the 2023 Emroch Lecture, "A Constitutional Right to Vote: Why We Need It and How to Get It," at the University of Richmond School of Law.

The term "A Real Right to Vote" first appeared in a law review article, Kareem Crayton and Jane Junn, *Five Justices, Section 4, and Three Ways Forward in Voting Rights,* 9 Duke Journal of Constitutional Law and Public Policy, 113, 147 (2013).

I appreciate the tremendous support of UCLA Law. Thanks to the stellar librarians who helped me on this project: Shangching Huitzacua, Sherry Leysen, Elyse Meyers, and Brian Raphael. Thanks as well to Gennifer Birkenfeld-Malpass, Sam Hall, and Sammy Zeino for exemplary research assistance, and to Ben Austin-Docampo for first-rate administrative assistance.

Bridget Flannery-McCoy, ably assisted by Alena Chekanov, has been a thoughtful and judicious editor at Princeton University Press. In her understated way, Bridget pushed me effectively to improve the manuscript both in terms of its readability as well as in the soundness of the argument. The book is much stronger thanks to her wisdom and care. Leah Caldwell meticulously copyedited the manuscript, and Jill Harris ably coordinated production. Thanks as well to my agent Mel Flashman, assisted by Ali Lake, in assuring that this project ended up in a strong and supportive home.

And as always thanks to my wife, Lori Klein. Lori supports me in everything I do, and offers not only encouragement but also the benefit of her good judgment. I am so grateful for her partnership and love.

Portions of chapter 1 draw from my chapter, *Election Reform: Past, Present, and Future,* in the Oxford Handbook of American Election Law (Eugene Mazo, ed., Oxford: Oxford University Press, forthcoming 2024). Portions of chapter 5 draw from Richard L. Hasen, *Identifying and Minimizing the Risk of Election Subversion and Stolen Elections in the Contemporary United States,* 135 Harv. L. Rev. F. 265 (2022). Both are reprinted with permission.

A REAL RIGHT TO VOTE

Introduction

WHY WE NEED A REAL RIGHT TO VOTE

Throughout U.S. history, too many Americans have been dis-enfranchised or faced needless barriers to voting. And the blame for these weak voting rights falls in large part on the U.S. Constitution that never has contained, and still does not contain, a general affirmative right to vote.

Among other groups, African American voters and women were mostly disenfranchised from the very founding of the United States solely on the grounds of their race or gender. Sometimes these disenfranchised Americans looked to the constitution and the courts for a legal argument recognizing their right to vote. That is what Virginia Minor did in the 1870s.

Minor described herself in a court filing as "a native born, free, white citizen of the United States, and of the State of Missouri, over the age of twenty-one years, wishing to vote for electors for President and Vice-President of the United States, and for a representative in Congress, and for other officers, at the general election held in November, 1872." Missouri officials would not let her vote because of a provision in the state constitution limiting the franchise to otherwise eligible male citizens.[1]

Minor argued in an 1874 Supreme Court case, *Minor v. Happersett*, that her disenfranchisement by Missouri violated the then-recently-ratified Fourteenth Amendment of the U.S. Constitution, which barred states from making or enforcing "any law which shall abridge the privileges or immunities of citizens of the United States." Voting, she contended, was just such a privilege of citizenship, and Missouri therefore could no longer disenfranchise women after the Fourteenth Amendment's passage.

The Supreme Court agreed that women were citizens of the United States, but it held that the Fourteenth Amendment did not require enfranchising women because voting was not a "privilege" of citizenship. Voting rights instead were left up to each state. The all-male Supreme Court was "unanimously of the opinion that the Constitution of the United States does not confer the right of suffrage upon any one, and that the constitutions and laws of the several States which commit that important trust to men alone are not necessarily void."[2]

Minor's lawsuit was unsuccessful, but her efforts were not in vain. Her case came in the middle of a decades-long struggle to end voting discrimination against women by amending the constitution. It was an important step along the way. As historian Ellen Carol Dubois explained, in *Minor v. Happersett*, "the Supreme Court had essentially vitiated federal control over voting," leaving states "with almost full control over the franchise. Suffragists began to refocus on amending state constitutions to grant women suffrage rights." As women gained the right to vote state by state, they built momentum toward a national constitutional amendment expressly prohibiting gender discrimination in voting.[3]

Even with the ratification of the Nineteenth Amendment in 1920 barring discrimination in voting "on the basis of sex" throughout the United States, the Supreme Court refused to read the amendment as fully guaranteeing a right to vote regardless of gender. In a 1937 case, *Breedlove v. Suttles*, the court held it would be constitutional to exempt only women from paying a poll tax in order to be able to vote: "In view of burdens necessarily borne by them for the preservation of the race, the State reasonably may exempt them from poll taxes." When the court overturned the constitutionality of the poll tax in state elections in a 1966 case, *Harper v. Virginia State Board of Elections*, it did not overturn that aspect of *Breedlove* allowing men to face a burden to voting that women did not.[4]

State and local voting laws still sometimes discriminate on the basis of gender. Some states, for example, require that voters provide photographic identification from a limited list of acceptable documents, such as a driver's license, before voting. Women are more likely than men to change their names upon getting married, and that can create problems in states with stringent voter ID laws when the name on an older form of acceptable identification does not match the name contained in a state's voter registration database. Women face a greater risk than men of disenfranchisement under these laws, which studies have shown do not stop any serious amount of voter fraud.[5]

The issues are even more severe for transgender voters. Consider the plight of Henry Seaton, a transgender man who went to vote for the first time upon turning eighteen in a suburb of Nashville, Tennessee, where a photo identification for voting is required. According to an NBC News report, "Seaton showed his state ID. But the poll worker gave him a confused look and called over another poll worker to look at Seaton's identification. Then, in front of the Nazarene church where he was supposed to vote, the poll workers asked him about what they saw as a discrepancy between his ID and his appearance." "I had to out myself as transgender," Seaton told NBC News. His ID still said he was a "female."[6]

Nationally, according to an analysis by the Williams Institute at UCLA, approximately "414,000 voting-eligible transgender Americans live in the 31 states that both (1) primarily conduct their elections in person at the polls, and (2) have a voter ID law. Nearly half of these, or 203,700 individuals, do not have an ID that correctly reflects their name and/or gender. Of voting-eligible transgender people who live in states with voter ID requirements, 64,800 live in the states with the strictest voter ID laws." Further, "Black, indigenous, or people of color, young adults, students, people with low incomes, people experiencing homelessness, and people with disabilities are overrepresented among" transgendered voters lacking acceptable forms of identification in some states.[7]

Discrimination in voting hardly is confined to issues of gender or gender identity. In the middle of the COVID-19 pandemic during the 2020 presidential election season, when many people thought it was safer to vote by mail, Texas voters sued their state, claiming that its law allowing only those over the age of sixty-five to vote by mail without providing an excuse for not voting in person violated the Twenty-Sixth Amendment, which bars age discrimination in voting for those at least eighteen years of age. The U.S. Court of Appeals for the Fifth Circuit held there was no violation, reasoning that because there was no constitutional right to vote by mail (even in the middle of a pandemic), there was no problem with the state offering an easier (and healthier) way of voting to just older Texans.[8]

For much of American history, African American voters were formally denied the vote, and other racial and ethnic groups faced disenfranchisement as well. Today, well after the passage of the Fifteenth Amendment and the 1965 Voting Rights

Act, minority voters still sometimes face extra hurdles in voting. For example, Native Americans who live on reservations faced special burdens with voting during the pandemic because of the great distances to travel both to physical polling places and to areas with regular postal service. But courts often have not recognized that these special burdens require accommodations to assure that these voters have the same access to the ballot as everyone else.

Or consider a Kansas law requiring that those registering to vote to show documentary proof of citizenship, such as a birth certificate or naturalization papers, before state officials would accept the registration. Most people do not walk around with such papers or have easy access to them when they come across an opportunity to register. About thirty thousand Kansans were denied the ability to register until a lawsuit put an end to the practice. Kansas's then-Secretary of State Kris Kobach sought to defend the law on the grounds that it would prevent a great deal of illegal noncitizen voting, offering scant evidence of fraud that he termed "the tip of the iceberg." But a federal district court found that the amount of illegal noncitizen voting in Kansas was an "icicle," and the law therefore would disenfranchise tens of thousands of eligible Kansans for no good reason.[9]

The suit by Kansas voters followed a now-familiar pattern ever since the constitution was amended to bar certain forms of explicit discrimination, such as those based on race or gender. A state enacts a restrictive voting rule and voters have to rely upon the courts to strike it down or limit it. Voters often can show that these laws do not prevent a lot of voter fraud, instill voter confidence, or do much of anything that helps secure election integrity. But many courts these days are hardly protective of voting rights, and without robust protection of voting rights in the U.S. Constitution, far too often these voters end up losing. The disenfranchised Kansans were lucky they had good lawyers and a reasonable judge.

There has to be a better way than waiting for the government to impose new voting restrictions and then suing over them to an uncertain judicial result. That way is to pass and ratify a constitutional amendment affirmatively guaranteeing all eligible voters their right to vote.[10]

☑ ☑ ☑

The angst this country endures each presidential election cycle over whether we can hold free and fair elections is the product of a dysfunctional, decentralized, partisan election system administered under a national constitution that does not adequately protect voters' ability to vote and to have each eligible ballot fairly and accurately counted.

Many of the discriminatory laws described above were adopted in states with Republican legislatures and election officials. Whether it is regulating voting by students, by minorities such as Native Americans, or by former felons who (at least in theory) have had their voting rights restored, Republicans have too frequently imposed registration and voting barriers, sometimes out of a belief—often wrong—that making it harder for people to vote will give their party electoral advantage. They claim that these laws are necessary to prevent fraud and promote voter confidence, but they do neither. Instead, these laws require some people, often people of color, to put in tremendous efforts just to freely cast a ballot. Effort that could have been put into campaigning or get-out-the-vote drives is wasted on something that should be guaranteed to every eligible American voter.[11]

Democratic states generally do better at protecting the right to vote, though in earlier generations many southern Democratic states were the worst vote suppressors (and even today some Democrats enact voting rules meant to stifle competition within the party). It seems that in every generation there will be some who think that voting restrictions are worth pursuing to try to limit voting by people likely to vote for the other side.

Further, Democratic legislatures and election officials sometimes enact policies or administer elections in ways that raise legitimate concerns about the integrity of the election system. Voter rolls are sometimes bloated with the names of voters who have died or moved, either because the system is run inefficiently or because Democrats worry they might remove eligible voters if they are too aggressive about keeping their registration lists clean, thus hurting their party's chances. California recently loosened its rules to allow the unlimited collection of absentee ballots (also known as "mail-in" or "vote-by-mail" ballots). The state did so despite evidence that this third-party ballot collection, sometimes derided as "ballot harvesting," raises a real, if rare, risk of election fraud. Democrats, too, operate on the mistaken theory that making voting easier inevitably helps Democrats.[12]

In addition to state divisions over proper voting rules, we now face new challenges. When Donald Trump emerged on the political scene during the 2016 election season, he introduced a whole new set of concerns about the resilience of the U.S. election system. He stoked Republican fears about election fraud and convinced many of his supporters, despite all evidence to the contrary, that the system was "rigged" against Republicans and against Trump in particular. The matter caused a national crisis in 2020, when Trump lost in his presidential reelection bid to Democrat Joe Biden and falsely claimed that Democrats stole the election from him.[13]

Trump came far closer than many people realize to blocking Biden from assuming the presidency by exploiting weaknesses in the set of uniquely American rules for choosing the president via the Electoral College. This risk of election subversion remains real and serious, although the risk somewhat lessened in 2022 with the defeat of election denialist candidates in swing states and the passage of new federal legislation governing the counting of Electoral College votes.[14]

Throughout all of these skirmishes, in what I have called "the voting wars," courts have been called upon to assure that we have fair elections. Yet courts have not been the great protectors of voting rights that we might hope for, even as they did what was necessary to thwart Trump's attempts to subvert the 2020 election. Indeed, in recent years courts have been the last place that voting rights activists have wanted to be to protect the right to vote, because the conservative Supreme Court has been actively hostile to both constitutional claims and to many claims under federal statutes, most importantly the Voting Rights Act.[15]

Part of the reason for the lack of success in voting rights claims before the judiciary is the constitution itself. Many Americans assume that the constitution includes an affirmative right to vote, but shockingly, it does not. It stipulates no right of any person to vote for members of the House of Representatives, the Senate, or the president. The United States stands in marked contrast with many other countries whose constitutions affirmatively guarantee the right to vote.

Article I guarantees a popular vote for the House of Representatives, but the provision enfranchises only those who are qualified under state law to vote for the state's most numerous legislative house. The Seventeenth Amendment extended the same rule for Senate elections. Voting rights therefore depend in part upon state law, not a federal constitutional guarantee.[16]

Many of the protections that some Americans enjoy today for voting rights come not directly from the text of the constitution but rather from a generous reading of the Fourteenth Amendment in Supreme Court opinions from the 1960s, during the period known as the Warren Court. These precedents, emerging when Earl Warren was the chief justice of the United States, protected most citizen, adult, resident, nonfelons from certain forms of disenfranchisement.[17]

These precedents are important but are not enough. They leave a great deal of room for discriminatory voting laws that do not directly disenfranchise people but instead burden their right to vote. They leave some people who should be eligible to vote unprotected or underprotected. And we currently face an ultra-conservative Supreme Court supermajority that gives every benefit of the doubt to states that pass laws intended to make it harder to vote. Even worse, there are worrying signs that some of the earlier Warren Court voter-protective precedents are in danger of being overturned.

The current court's chary protection of voting rights is much more in line with the bulk of the court's history than with that short period of the Warren Court. People must stop thinking of the Warren Court as representing the Supreme Court's typical approach to voting rights; it was the anomaly. It was the Supreme Court in 1874 that told Virginia Minor that she had no constitutional right to vote because she is a woman, despite the passage of the Fourteenth Amendment. As we will see in the next chapter, it also was the Supreme Court in 1903 that told Jackson W. Giles, an eligible African American voter, that it could do nothing to assure that he could vote in Alabama, despite the passage of the post–Civil War Fifteenth Amendment barring discrimination in voting on the basis of race.

In some ways, the current Supreme Court majority is more dangerous than earlier Supreme Court majorities because it has not just been skimpy with constitutional protection of voting rights. It has also read Congress's power to protect voters' rights very narrowly. Even though a half-dozen provisions in the constitution empower Congress to protect voting rights, such as provisions in the fourteenth and fifteenth amendments providing that Congress "shall have power to enforce" each amendment "by appropriate legislation," the conservative majority is much more protective of states' rights to run elections as they see fit than of Congress's constitutional prerogatives, even if the states are disenfranchising voters. It has been unwilling to treat Congress as an equal branch of government entitled to proactively protect voters.

It was this Supreme Court majority in 2013 that struck down a key part of the Voting Rights Act in *Shelby County v. Holder*. The voting law, overwhelmingly enacted and reenacted by bipartisan congresses and presidents, mandated federal oversight of states and localities with a history of racial discrimination in voting. The law was remarkably effective in protecting minority voters from discrimination, but the court held there was not enough evidence of current discrimination in those states covered by the law to justify continued federal oversight. With federal oversight gone, discrimination unsurprisingly quickly reemerged.[18]

Today, protectors of voting rights essentially play defense, leading to a flood of litigation each election cycle between the political parties over the minutiae of registration and voting rules. Some egregious voting rules get rolled back, but many do not. Often the judges deciding the cases break down on ideological and party lines, with judges running as or appointed by Republicans being more protective of states' rights and more hostile to voting rights legislation than judges running as or appointed by Democrats.

The litigation almost never fully resolves disputes. When a law is struck down, a legislature often enacts a new or revised version of it, and the litigation starts anew. New campaign finance rules and a hyperpolarized political system create incentives to pursue as much election litigation as possible. Democrats sue when voting restrictions are severe and even when they are not. Republicans, too, often sue when states or localities loosen rules to make it easier for voters to register and vote. If politics these days is a game of inches, then election litigators are the ones scuffling in play after play. It is a vicious cycle with no ending or realistic resolution.[19]

☑   ☑   ☑

This book is about a proposed constitutional amendment providing an affirmative right to vote, which would be the Twenty-Eighth Amendment to the constitution, assuming no other amendments are ratified first. It is about how an amendment can more fully protect voting rights than the current constitution, make elections more secure, and deter election subversion.

The basis for an amendment is the concept of political equality. In a modern democracy, the people should rule, and the primary way they do so is by voting for president, members of Congress, and state and local leaders. Among those people who meet basic citizenship, residency, and adulthood eligibility requirements, voter registration and voting should be easy in a system designed to assure integrity and prevent fraud. Each voter's ballot should be weighted equally and fairly counted.

The idea of such an amendment is not new. Some supporters of the original Fifteenth Amendment after the Civil War wanted a broad law protecting the voting rights of more Americans. People considered an amendment affirmatively guaranteeing a constitutional right to vote again starting in 1959, when the civil rights movement was getting going, and yet again after the disputed presidential election of 2000. Those efforts have not yet borne fruit. We have always needed an affirmative right to vote in the constitution, but current fights over voting and voting rules make the matter more urgent.

An affirmative constitutional right to vote would put voting rights advocates in a much better position. It would provide much more direct protection for voting rights and shift the burden of proof in the courts so that states would have to come forward with real and compelling reasons to make it harder to vote. It would make it more difficult for courts to reject voting rights claims.

In addition to assuring that all voters are treated equally and do not face undue burdens on voting, a constitutional right to vote would protect the right to have ballots equally and fairly counted. It would protect minority voters from discrimination more directly than the Fifteenth Amendment. It would facilitate systems for automatic voter registration and national voter identification. It would give Congress broad powers to protect voting rights and instruct courts not to unduly interfere with those powers. These provisions would create a system where eligible Americans each have the same opportunity to participate in the political process and to elect representatives of their choice.

But a constitutional right to vote would also deescalate the voting wars and decrease the amount of election litigation by simultaneously protecting voter access and assuring election integrity. It would be written clearly enough that it would be hard for the Supreme Court to ignore its commands and continue to thwart voter protections, and it would enhance Congress's powers to protect voters if the Supreme Court continues to resist. A system of automatic voter registration coupled with voter identification could minimize the need for litigation, assure that all eligible voters will be able to cast a vote, and deter election fraud by those who exploit the current system. And it would do so without mandating a federal takeover of the election process.

A constitutional right-to-vote amendment would also thwart election subversion and safeguard American democracy. An explicit guarantee of the right to vote for president, for example, would moot and obviate any attempt to get state legislatures to override the voters' choice for president though the appointment of alternative slates of electors, as Trump and his allies tried to do in 2020. Rules that guarantee not only the right to vote but the right to have that vote fairly and accurately counted would provide a basis for suing election officials who seek to disrupt the integrity of election systems. Leaks of voting system software or an administrator's lack of transparency in counting ballots could become constitutional violations that voters could remedy by suing.

In short, a constitutional right to vote would protect core voting rights while simultaneously dealing with some of the particular pathologies of the electoral system that have served to make the United States a laggard rather than a world leader on the question of democracy. It is possible to promote election integrity and fairness for voters while preserving much of our decentralized system for running elections.[20]

☑   ☑   ☑

Readers who have gotten this far into this introduction and who are sympathetic to its mission are nonetheless likely to think that calls for a constitutional amendment are futile. The skepticism is well founded.

After all, even when Democrats controlled the presidency, the House of Representatives, and the U.S. Senate in 2021 and 2022, they could pass neither a comprehensive set of voting reforms known as the "For the People Act," nor the "John R. Lewis Voting Rights Advancement Act," to update the Voting Rights Act and reverse the Supreme Court's *Shelby County* decision. While those bills passed the House and got a bare majority vote in favor in the Senate, they could not overcome the Senate filibuster, and at least two Democratic senators, Joe Manchin of West Virginia and Kyrsten Sinema of Arizona, refused calls to eliminate the filibuster to pass the legislation.[21]

Moreover, passing a constitutional voting rights amendment would be much harder than enacting legislation. It would require two-thirds affirmative votes of both houses of Congress and ratification by three-quarters of the state legislatures. The last voting-related amendment to be ratified was the Twenty-Sixth Amendment (lowering the voting age to eighteen) in 1971, before most of the current U.S. population was born. Since then, American politics has become much more polarized, and the prospects of any constitutional amendment gaining supermajority support in both Congress and the states seems fanciful—much less one on as charged a subject as voting rights.[22]

For three reasons, however, I believe that pursuing a constitutional right-to-vote amendment makes sense, especially now. First and foremost, movements for constitutional amendments take a long time and pay important dividends as the amendment progresses. The Nineteenth Amendment, protecting women's right to vote, is a good example; it took decades of political organizing and coalition building to get the amendment passed. Along the way, state after state passed constitutional amendments that enfranchised women. Indeed, by the time of the Nineteenth Amendment's ratification in 1920, women's suffrage was a reality in thirty states. State action built a groundswell of support for women's suffrage that eased the ultimate passage of the Nineteenth Amendment, thereby locking in its gains for future generations in case of attempted backsliding or a failure of an amendment to pass on the national level.[23]

Second, a constitutional right to vote could actually promote the voter integrity that Republicans and conservatives say they favor. For example, provisions for automatic voter registration coupled with unique voter identification numbers will clean up the voting rolls and make double voting significantly harder. Further, increasing turnout can also work to the benefit of Republicans and conservatives, especially with the Republican Party's recent turn toward courting working-class voters.

Third, an amendment would deter election subversion, something in the interest of all democracy-supporting Americans. We face new dangers of stolen elections and an urgent need to safeguard our democracy.

There are many forms such an amendment could take, and later in this book I sketch out two possibilities. First I present a basic version that provides the key protections for those who should already be enfranchised by those Warren Court precedents (citizen, adult, resident, nonfelons) and that creates a rational voter registration and identification system. Second, I consider a more robust version that could go beyond these basic provisions to enfranchise felons who have completed their sentences and residents of U.S. territories such as Puerto Rico; eliminate the Electoral College and replace it with a national popular vote for president; and change the composition of the Senate to reflect one-person, one-vote concepts otherwise accepted in U.S. politics and law.

It will be up to those who lead a popular movement toward a new constitutional right-to-vote amendment to decide whether to go basic and appeal more widely across the political spectrum, or to go more robustly toward political equality and enfranchisement at the risk of alienating some potential political allies. The end of this book discusses those tradeoffs more fully.

☑   ☑   ☑

I make the case for a constitutional right to vote through stories of how different states have made it harder for different populations to vote over the last few decades. The focus is as much on what is broken as how it can be fixed.

Chapter 1 examines the inconsistent role of the courts in protecting voting rights. Beginning with an example of Texas discriminating against military voters, and the Supreme Court's rare rejection of that discrimination, it shows how most of the time the Supreme Court has failed to be a broad protector of voting rights, and that instead it has been the people, through advocacy for passage of constitutional amendments, who have stepped up for enfranchisement.

Just as chapter 1 shows how Texas made it hard for military voters, chapter 2 describes how that state has long gone after student voters, and, in particular, students at its largest Black college, Prairie View A&M University. The attacks on student voting undermine a core value of current American democracy: political equality. The chapter explores the key provisions of a proposed constitutional amendment that promotes political equality by granting fully equal voting rights to all citizen, adult, resident, nonfelons.

Chapter 3 then turns to potential expansions within a constitutional right to vote: to felons who have completed their sentences, to residents of at least some U.S. territories, and through changes in how we elect the president and members of the U.S. Senate. This book's appendix offers a few versions of the potential constitutional right to vote, considering the various permutations.

Although political equality is the primary motivation for passage of a constitutional amendment containing an affirmative right to vote, the amendment also would serve two other major purposes. First, as chapter 4 explains, a constitutional amendment would reduce litigation and polarization over the voting process itself, deescalating the voting wars. Second, as detailed in chapter 5, an affirmative right to vote in the constitution would make it harder for unscrupulous politicians to subvert election results and turn election losers into winners.

Chapter 6 concludes the book by grappling with the "how to get there" question. It looks at prior efforts to place an affirmative right to vote in the constitution and how earlier voting rights amendments passed. It considers why red states might support a constitutional right to vote, a key question given that amending the constitution requires supermajority support from both houses of Congress and ratification by three-quarters of state legislatures. The chapter explains that a constitutional right to vote would not federalize American elections, and it would come with benefits for red states. The chapter debunks the common wisdom that turnout increases invariably help Democrats, and it shows that a constitutional right to vote can help Republicans win elections as much as it can help Democrats. A constitutional amendment also would lessen the risks of election fraud and limit voter confusion.

Still, in today's polarized society getting any constitutional amendment through both Congress and state legislatures, much less one that could have an effect on who is elected to office in those bodies, is going to be a hard slog. There is no sugarcoating the difficulties of the task ahead.

But even the attempt to pursue a constitutional amendment would have great benefits for democracy. Continued Republican intransigence to a constitutional right-to-vote amendment could embolden Democrats to take more aggressive statutory steps to protect the right to vote, potentially generating new conflict with the Supreme Court that could in turn generate further democratic reform.

The status quo is unsustainable and dangerous to our democracy. Pursuing a constitutional amendment protecting the right to vote is the most sensible way forward, even if it takes more than our generation to get there.

Chapter 1

COURTS ARE NOT ENOUGH

Sergeant Herbert N. Carrington was one of the lucky few whose right to vote was protected by the Supreme Court.

In 1946, an eighteen-year old Carrington enlisted in the military in his home state of Alabama. When the army transferred him to a job in White Sands, New Mexico, in 1962, he moved with his family to nearby El Paso, Texas. Yet when he tried to register to vote in the Republican Party primary in Texas he was surprised to learn he was ineligible. The state constitution prohibited from voting any military members who were not Texas residents before joining the service.[1]

Carrington sued directly in the Texas Supreme Court in 1964, arguing among other things that his disenfranchisement violated the Equal Protection Clause of the Fourteenth Amendment of the U.S. Constitution, a provision barring states from denying "any person within its jurisdiction the equal protection of the laws."[2]

The Texas high court denied his petition, pointing to a 1959 Supreme Court case, *Lassiter v. Northampton County Board of Elections*, that rejected an equal protection challenge to a North

Carolina law establishing a literacy test for voting. *Lassiter* held that so long as the state had a rational reason for denying classes of voters the franchise, and the law was not being put in place for racially discriminatory reasons or administered in a racially discriminatory way, this disenfranchisement was constitutionally permissible. "The ability to read and write," the Supreme Court in *Lassiter* held, "has some relation to standards designed to promote intelligent use of the ballot."[3]

And just as North Carolina could decide that those who could read or write English might make better voting decisions and therefore be better voters, the Texas Supreme Court held that Texas could disenfranchise military personnel on grounds that "in the nature of their sojourn at a particular place [they] are not, and cannot be, a part of the local community in the same sense as its permanent residents." The argument was that these military personnel were just passing through and not residents with sufficient ties to the community. The court called the disenfranchisement "not unreasonable" and "nondiscriminatory."[4]

Carrington sought relief from the U.S. Supreme Court, raising his equal protection claim once again. In defending its state constitution, Texas argued that "it has a legitimate interest in immunizing its elections from the concentrated balloting of military personnel, whose collective voice may overwhelm a small local civilian community."[5]

Without discussing any tension with its *Lassiter* decision, the Supreme Court in *Carrington v. Rash* struck down the Texas law as a violation of the Equal Protection Clause. The right to vote, the court wrote in a 7–1 opinion, "cannot constitutionally be obliterated because of a fear of the political views of a particular group of bona fide residents." Justice John Marshall Harlan, dissenting for himself alone, argued that the Equal Protection

Clause, enacted after the Civil War, was "not intended to touch state electoral matters."[6]

It is hard to overstate how lucky Carrington was in getting the Supreme Court to strike down his disenfranchisement. His lawsuit came during the only period in the entire 235-year history of the Supreme Court when it was hospitable to broad constitutional voting rights claims. The so-called Warren Court, lasting from the mid-1950s to the late 1960s under Chief Justice Earl Warren, saw a broad expansion of voting rights thanks mainly to its capacious reading of the Equal Protection Clause.[7]

The Warren Court enfranchised not just Carrington but also people like Morris Kramer. He was a thirty-one-year-old bachelor stockbroker who lived with his parents and who had been barred from voting in a local New York school board election by state law that limited voting for school board members to those who were parents of school-aged children or an owner or renter of taxable property in the district. The state said it was trying to limit the right to vote in the local election to those primarily interested in its outcome.[8]

The Supreme Court in the 1969 case *Kramer v. Union Free School District No. 15* noted that that the law disenfranchised "the following persons (unless they are parents or guardians of children enrolled in the district public school): senior citizens and others living with children or relatives; clergy, military personnel, and others who live on tax-exempt property; boarders and lodgers; parents who neither own nor lease qualifying property and whose children are too young to attend school; parents who neither own nor lease qualifying property and whose children attend private schools." It held that the law was not "sufficiently tailored to limiting the franchise to those 'primarily interested' in school affairs," even assuming that New

York had a compelling state interest in so limiting the franchise.[9]

Herbert Carrington and Morris Kramer, both, perhaps not coincidentally, white men (and Carrington in the military no less), fared better than many others who had previously brought their claims of disenfranchisement to the Supreme Court over time, including most importantly Virginia Minor and Jackson W. Giles. Their cases perpetuated the disenfranchisement of millions of women and African American voters despite constitutional amendments that appeared to protect their rights.[10]

We already saw in the introduction how the court rejected Virginia Minor's claims to gender equality in voting, deciding that the question of enfranchisement was a matter for the states rather than federal constitutional law. Minor's case came before the passage of the Nineteenth Amendment, which barred discrimination in voting on the basis of sex. In contrast, Jackson Giles's case came to the Supreme Court after passage of the Fifteenth Amendment, which barred discrimination on the basis of race, and the court still refused to help him.

From before the founding of the United States and through the Civil War in the 1860s, southern colonies and states had enslaved African Americans, and, along with some Northern states, had denied them the right to vote. In 1857, the court in the infamous case of *Dred Scott v. Sandford* held that that African American slaves and their descendants, even if free, were not citizens of the United States and therefore not entitled to the rights of citizens. Without citizenship there was certainly no right to vote.[11]

In the aftermath of the Civil War, Congress passed the Reconstruction Amendments: the thirteenth (in 1865), abolishing slavery except as a condition of criminal punishment; the fourteenth (in 1868), guaranteeing that states protect the privileges and immunities of citizenship and prohibiting states from denying any persons within the state due process or equal protection of the laws; and the fifteenth (1870), barring racial discrimination in voting. One might have thought that those amendments would have led to the quick enfranchisement of African Americans—or, at least, African American men—but it was not to be.[12]

Jackson Giles alleged in his 1903 case that despite the passage of the Reconstruction Amendments decades before, Alabama continued to disenfranchise thousands of African Americans while regularly affording white male Alabama citizens the right to vote. Without disputing that the Fifteenth Amendment expressly barred discrimination in voting on the basis of race, a majority of the justices on the all-white Supreme Court refused to grant relief to Giles, in part because it would be impossible for courts to enforce a rule requiring the state of Alabama to register African American voters and allow them to vote.[13]

The ruling recognized the ineffectiveness of the Fifteenth Amendment without federal enforcement, and it perpetuated the continued disenfranchisement of African American voters under the conditions of Jim Crow in the American South. It came in the middle of nearly a century of race-based disenfranchisement and white supremacy between the end of the Civil War and the beginning of the civil rights movement.[14]

It was not until the passage of the Voting Rights Act in 1965 that the federal government began to enfranchise African American and other minority voters effectively. Although the Supreme Court at first upheld the act against constitutional challenge and repeatedly interpreted its provisions broadly to protect minority voting rights, by the early twenty-first century, the court had pulled back. In the 2013 *Shelby County v. Holder*—a crucial case that I will return to later in this chapter—the court held that Congress no longer had the power to force states with a history of discrimination to get federal approval before making changes in their voting rules. As we shall see, the implications of this ruling were quite broad in terms of the court reining in Congress's power to protect voting rights. Further, in a series of cases interpreting section 2 of the act, the court read its voter protective provisions narrowly, undercutting the power of racial minorities to challenge restrictive voting rules and assure fair representation in legislative bodies.[15]

Things have remained bleak for other voters seeking enfranchisement via the courts. The Supreme Court in 1973 refused to recognize that disenfranchisement of felons who had completed their sentences violated the constitution. The court in 2000 rejected the claim of residents of Washington, D.C., that they had the right to vote for members of Congress. Lower courts similarly rejected voting rights claims brought by U.S. citizens living in U.S. territories such as Puerto Rico. The Supreme Court also upheld an Arizona law barring the third-party collection of mail-in ballots, a prohibition that made it harder for Native American voters living on reservations a chance to cast a ballot. The court has never overruled its *Lassiter* opinion, which allows some literacy tests as prerequisites for voting. It is only a congressional statute, part of the Voting Rights Act, that prevents states from once again imposing English reading and writing requirements for voting. Congress can reverse statutes by simply passing a new bill rather than going through the arduous process for creating a new constitutional amendment.[16]

From that moment in time in the 1960s, we could see what it would mean for a Supreme Court to muscularly protect voting rights, as the court did for Carrington, Kramer, and some others, such as students, who were often discriminated against in college towns by local residents unhappy with the choices students might make at the ballot box. Those decisions established that when a state disenfranchises those who are citizens, adults, residents, and nonfelons, the disenfranchisement is likely to be held unconstitutional by the courts under the Fourteenth Amendment's Equal Protection Clause. As a matter of doctrine, the Warren Court established the legal principle that a voting rule disenfranchising voters who are citizen, adult, resident, nonfelons must satisfy "strict scrutiny," showing a court that a voting law is "narrowly tailored" to satisfy a "compelling state interest"—a standard that is very hard for states to meet. (It is sometimes said that "strict scrutiny" is strict in theory but fatal in fact, yet there are some rare cases in which the court has upheld laws judged under this onerous standard.)[17]

The idea that claims of outright disenfranchisement would be subject to a close judicial look has mostly survived as the Supreme Court turned more conservative in recent decades, although there are worrying signs these precedents could be in danger. Moreover, the courts never extended close judicial scrutiny to rules that do not explicitly or formally disenfranchise voters but instead put up roadblocks that make it systematically harder for some Americans, such as poor Americans, to vote or to register to vote.

The shift in judicial attitudes leaves the protection of voting rights to the whims and preferences of a majority of Supreme Court justices. There is no question that since the end of the Warren Court, the court has pulled back on its protection of voting rights. For example, in the case of *Bush v. Gore*, which ended the disputed presidential election of 2000, the court affirmed that the constitution does not guarantee *anyone* the right to vote for president. The court explained that under a provision in Article II of the constitution allowing each state to appoint presidential electors "in such Manner as the Legislature thereof may direct," states at any time could take back their power to appoint presidential electors directly in future elections. It is only when a state gives voters the right to vote does the requirement that voters receive equal treatment come into play. (The court in *Bush* held that the recount conducted in Florida violated this requirement of equal treatment.)[18]

Similarly, in 2008, the court in *Crawford v. Marion County Election Board* allowed states to pass more onerous voting rules, such as strict voter identification laws, without proof that such laws serve any interests in preventing fraud or promoting voter confidence. This case followed a pattern of the court deferring heavily to states when they said, but did not prove, that their onerous laws were needed to protect against fraud.[19]

The arc of the moral universe may bend toward justice, but the Supreme Court's cases have not bent uniformly toward greater enfranchisement. Think more of a one-time pendulum swing than a one-way arc. Right now, with a deeply conservative Supreme Court, the pendulum is swinging back to where it was before the Warren Court—away from voting rights.

☑   ☑   ☑

It is not surprising given the age and structure of the U.S. Constitution and a focus on past practice that courts have not led the way on the protection of voting rights; at the time of the constitution's ratification, many states limited voting rights to white, male property owners.

Unlike the constitutions of many other advanced democracies that expressly protect the right to vote, the U.S. Constitution is silent. We have nothing like section 3 of the Canadian Charter of Rights and Freedoms, providing that "every citizen of Canada has the right to vote in an election of members of the House of Commons or of a legislative assembly and to be qualified for membership therein," or like Article 38 of the Basic Law of the Federal Republic of Germany, which provides that when it comes to election of the Bundestag (or parliament), "Any person who has attained the age of eighteen shall be entitled to vote."[20]

The original constitution said remarkably little about voting. It provides (in Article I, section 2) that when representatives are elected to the U.S. House of Representatives, the qualifications for voters in that race have to be the same as the qualifications that the state has set for voting for "the most numerous branch of the state legislature." That provision appears to guarantee popular election for the House, but it does not enfranchise anybody in particular, leaving voter qualification questions to the states. Senators, under the original constitution, were chosen by state legislatures, not the people in a direct election. Nor does Article II of the constitution give anyone the right to vote for the U.S. president. It instead gives states the power to appoint presidential electors "in the manner as the Legislature thereof may direct," a provision that some argue opens the pathway for election subversion as state legislatures potentially overturn the will of the voters to vote for president. This is in some ways unsurprising. As the leading historian of the right to vote, Alex Keyssar, wrote: "Few, if any, of the late eighteenth-century framers would have supported even a white male approximation of universal suffrage, and most were inclined to view voting as a privilege rather than a right; there was no way, thus, that a 'right to vote' could have been inscribed in our fundamental law, as it has been in many constitutions written in the twentieth century. Moreover, for pragmatic political reasons—having to do largely with the politics of constitutional ratification—the framers decided to let individual states define the breadth of the franchise, which the states commonly did in their own constitutions."[21]

Looking across American history, it has been not the Supreme Court but the people who have been the main protectors of voting rights. After the Supreme Court refused to recognize enslaved African Americans as citizens, and after the Civil War freeing the slaves, Congress passed and states ratified a series of amendments ending slavery, guaranteeing citizenship for those born in the United States, and barring discrimination in voting on the basis of race.

After the Civil War, in debating what would become the Fifteenth Amendment, Congress considered but rejected passage of a broad amendment that would have come closer to recognizing an affirmative right to vote. As Keyssar explains, the center of the Republican Party was not united around this broader amendment: "What opponents of a broad amendment rejected in the end was the abolition of discrimination based on nativity, religion, property and education. They wanted to retain the power to limit the political participation of the Irish and Chinese, Native Americans, and the increasingly visible clusters of illiterate and semiliterate workers massing in the nation's cities." The debate ended with a compromise in the Fifteenth Amendment that did not broadly protect voting rights but instead phrased the right in the negative, barring discrimination in voting on the basis of race. The negative phrasing proved to be a common model for future amendments.[22]

When the Supreme Court in *Giles* refused to enforce the Fifteenth Amendment, the struggle for civil rights continued for decades. It was the people's representative, Congress, that passed the 1965 Voting Rights Act that finally put power behind the promise of the Fifteenth Amendment's probation on race discrimination in voting.[23]

After the court in *Minor* in 1874 rejected a claim that the con-stitution already enfranchised women, women and men came together in a common struggle and passed the Nineteenth Amendment in 1920 barring discrimination in voting on the basis of sex. It took decades from the first organized attempts at gender equality in voting until it became part of the constitu-tion. The women's suffrage movement engaged in coalitional politics to build support state-by-state; coalition building was complicated by concerns among southern states that enfran-chising women would inadvertently lead to greater voting rights for African Americans.[24]

The Seventeenth Amendment, ratified in 1913, gave voters who were qualified to vote under state law a right to vote di-rectly for U.S. senators, overturning Article I's earlier provision giving state legislators the right to choose senators. The direct election of senators was a Progressive-era reform, proposed alongside other reforms such as a failed proposal to abolish the Electoral College. But while the Seventeenth Amendment, like Article I before it, afforded some degree of popular sovereignty, it deferred to the states to set voter qualifications. The Seven-teenth Amendment enfranchised no one in particular.[25]

The next set of election reforms via constitutional amend-ment came five decades later in the 1960s, amid the rise of the modern civil rights movement. The Twenty-Third Amendment, which gave Washington, D.C., three Electoral College votes, began in the Senate as a more ambitious proposal from moderate Republican Senator Kenneth Keating that would also have led to potential representation for District of Columbia residents in the House of Representatives. Senator Keating's proposal got paired with Senator Spessard Holland's proposal to ban the use of poll taxes in state elections. Both measures got folded into a piece of must-pass continuity of Congress legisla-tion. When the measure passed the Senate and reached the

House—where it faced significant opposition from Southern Democrats for its inclusion of the poll tax provision—Manny Celler, the chair of the House Judiciary Committee, stripped the proposal down to an amendment only for D.C. representation in the Electoral College. It passed by voice votes in both houses of Congress, and states ratified the measure nine months later in 1961.[26]

The Twenty-Fourth Amendment, barring the use of poll taxes in federal elections, emerged as the civil rights movement gained steam. At the time, only five southern states still required some form of payment to be eligible to vote. The unlikely champion of the measure in the Senate was Senator Holland, a segregationist who long fought to repeal the poll tax as an objectionable wealth-related condition for voting. John Kowal and Wilfred Codrington III point out that although the poll tax was a measure primarily aimed at preventing African Americans from voting, by the time Holland advocated for an amendment, demographic change meant that poor whites were more likely to be disenfranchised by the tax than African Americans. The measure repealing poll taxes nonetheless faced severe opposition from Southern Democrats, who saw it as an attack on white supremacy, and it took some parliamentary maneuvering to get the measure out of Congress in 1962.[27]

Civil rights groups viewed the proposed poll tax amendment as a diversion from more sweeping voting rights and civil rights protections and did not support it. As Bruce Ackerman and Jennifer Nou explain, "The National Association for the Advancement of Colored People (NAACP) opposed the Twenty-Fourth Amendment precisely because it threatened to condemn further civil rights initiatives to the tender mercies of a minority veto by the states under Article Five of the Constitution, which requires ratification by three-fourths of the states."[28]

Once Congress approved the measure, ratification in the states took seventeen months, and only two southern states, Florida and Tennessee, were among the ratifying states. Two years after the 1964 ratification, the Warren Court in *Harper v. Virginia State Board of Elections* held that the Equal Protection Clause of the Fourteenth Amendment barred poll taxes in state elections as well.[29]

The Twenty-Sixth Amendment, extending the franchise to eighteen- to twenty-one-year-olds, passed during the Vietnam War, when eighteen-year-old males were being drafted into military service. Many conservatives and liberals had long united behind a franchise extension to include young soldiers in an appeal to patriotism and military service, supporting those putting their lives and safety at risk while fighting for the United States as disenfranchised adults. But progress on an amendment had stalled.[30]

Congress extended voting rights to age eighteen by statute in a section of a 1970 amendment to the Voting Rights Act. But the Supreme Court ruled in *Oregon v. Mitchell* that the age extension was unconstitutional as applied to state elections. This created great confusion about how the upcoming 1972 elections were going to be conducted, with eighteen- to twenty-one-year-olds having only the right to vote in federal, but not state, elections. Congress quickly passed the Twenty-Sixth Amendment in 1971, and a supermajority of states ratified it in four months (with some states ratifying on the same day Congress voted), the fastest ratification in U.S. history.[31]

☑   ☑   ☑

Each amendment to the U.S. Constitution protecting voting rights was an improvement on the past, and Warren Court voting decisions under the Equal Protection Clause were noteworthy expansions, but even together they are not nearly enough. Especially in the hands of a Supreme Court hostile to broad protection of voting rights and one that could well consider overturning or weaking some of the key voter-protective court precedents, voting rights remain in peril.

We should not simply assume that those Warren Court precedents protecting the right to vote are so sacrosanct that they would not be overturned by the Supreme Court. A court that could overturn precedent and allow states to ban abortion despite the 1973 decision in *Roe v. Wade* and despite decades of decisions upholding the practice could overturn voting cases such as *Carrington* and *Kramer*. It could also hold additional key parts of the Voting Rights Act unconstitutional or continue whittling away at its vitality through chary statutory interpretation.[32]

The potential vulnerability of past voting rights decisions is more than theoretical. Consider, for example, a series of Warren Court cases including *Baker v. Carr* and *Reynolds v. Sims* that came to establish the "one-person, one-vote" rule. These cases hold that when states or local bodies draw district lines for Congress, a state legislature, or a local body, the districts must have approximately equal numbers of people in them. Chief Justice Warren later called *Baker* the most important decision of his tenure, a remarkable statement given that this period also included other landmark decisions such as *Brown v. Board of Education*, requiring integration of schools, and *Miranda v. Arizona*, establishing the right of criminal defendants to receive a warning of their right to remain silent. The one-person, one-vote rules prevent a kind of extreme gerrymandering, where small rural areas may have disproportionate power when district lines are drawn on the basis of geography rather than population.[33]

A 2016 case, *Evenwel v. Abbott*, exposed a possible way to dilute *Baker* and *Reynolds*. There, the Supreme Court rejected an argument that the one-person, one-vote rule requires drawing lines with an equal number of *voters*, rather than *people* in them. (Adopting the argument would have favored more rural Republican areas, with fewer noncitizens and children.) The Supreme Court held that the state did not have to choose to equalize the number of voters to comply with the one-person, one-vote rule. But the court left open the question whether, although a state was not required to draw lines on the basis of equal voters rather than people, a state could permissibly do so.[34]

Crucially, two of the Supreme Court's most conservative justices, Samuel Alito and Clarence Thomas, cast doubt on the one-person, one-vote rule overall, suggesting that states could go back to the practice of drawing district lines with unequal populations. And since that ruling, more justices have joined the court who may agree with them; justices such as Brett Kavanaugh, Neil Gorsuch, and Amy Coney Barrett, who fashion themselves as "originalists" focused on the "original public meaning" of the constitution, are unlikely to embrace Warren-era conceptions of "living constitutionalism" in which the meaning of constitutional provisions may change over time in line with current social values. This puts the whole series of Warren Court voting rights precedents in danger unless respect for precedent carries the day.[35]

If the one-person, one-vote rule could be subject to rethinking down the line, who knows what other damage the Supreme Court might do to voting rights?

☑ ☑ ☑

It would be bad enough if the Supreme Court turned back Warren Court precedents that expand voting rights for citizen, adult, resident nonfelons. But the court stands poised—and already has shown—it can do further damage to voting rights by reading Congress's broad voting-related lawmaking powers narrowly.

To understand the harm the court can do in this context, consider the structure of the constitution. Congress has the power to act only when the constitution enumerates that power; the Tenth Amendment reserves all other power to the states or the people. Some of Congress's enumerated powers are very specific, such as the powers in Article I, section 8 to declare war, coin money, establish a post office, and provide and maintain a navy. Other powers are broad or vague, such as the power to "make all laws which shall be necessary and proper for carrying into execution the foregoing powers."[36]

When it comes to Congress's power over voting rights, most of the election-related amendments to the constitution include a specific section stating that "the Congress shall have power to enforce this article by appropriate legislation." Justice Ruth Bader Ginsburg saw in those sections a vast reservoir of congressional lawmaking power:

> The Constitution uses the words "right to vote" in five separate places: the Fourteenth, Fifteenth, Nineteenth, Twenty–Fourth, and Twenty–Sixth Amendments. Each of these Amendments contains the same broad empowerment of Congress to enact "appropriate legislation" to enforce the protected right. The implication is unmistakable: Under our constitutional structure, Congress holds the lead rein in making the right to vote equally real for all U.S. citizens. These Amendments are in line with the special role assigned to Congress in protecting the integrity of the democratic process in federal elections.[37]

Unfortunately, Justice Ginsburg wrote those words in a dissenting opinion that therefore did not carry the weight of law.

Her holistic analysis of Congress's power in the constitution to take "lead rein" on voting rights appeared in her dissent in *Shelby County v. Holder*, the 2013 case in which the court held that Congress no longer had the power under the Fifteenth Amendment to require states and localities with a history of racial discrimination in voting to get federal approval—or "preclearance"—before making changes to their election rules. Before the court in *Shelby County* killed off this provision, these jurisdictions had the burden of demonstrating to the U.S. Department of Justice or to a three-judge federal court in Washington, D.C., that a proposed new voting law would have neither the purpose nor the effect of making minority voters worse off.[38]

Preclearance had proven to be extremely valuable in protecting minority voters, and the Supreme Court had repeatedly upheld the provision against claims by covered states that it exceeded Congress's powers and infringed on state sovereignty protected by the Tenth Amendment. In the 1966 case *South Carolina v. Katzenbach*, for example, the Warren Court agreed preclearance was strong medicine but wrote the provision was justified by a century of resistance to African American enfranchisement. The court held that this part of the Voting Rights Act was well within Congress's powers to enforce the Fifteenth Amendment's ban on racial discrimination in voting.

The court in *Katzenbach* emphasized that the measure was both geographically targeted to those jurisdictions where racial discrimination in voting had been a problem, and temporally limited, as the law would sunset after five years if not renewed by Congress. As originally enacted in 1965, preclearance applied to much of the Deep South and a bit beyond: Alabama, Georgia, Louisiana, Mississippi, South Carolina, and Virginia, along with many counties in North Carolina and one in Arizona.[39]

Racism unsurprisingly did not disappear immediately after passage of the Voting Rights Act, and Congress repeatedly renewed the preclearance provision to protect minority voters. In the 1970s, Congress tweaked the formula used to determine the jurisdictions covered and applied it to any state or locality that before the act had used a "test or device" for voting, such as a literacy test, and had low voter turnout in 1964, 1968, or 1972. This brought Alaska, Arizona, and Texas and counties in California, Michigan New York, and South Dakota under the act as well.[40]

Congress repeatedly extended the duration of the preclearance requirement, most recently in 2006 when it extended the law for another twenty-five years. It did not, however, alter the coverage formula, which meant that jurisdictions covered by preclearance were still determined using data from the 1960s and 1970s. Changing coverage would have been a politically delicate maneuver, because it would have required identifying which new jurisdictions were engaged in racial discrimination in voting and which had improved enough in protecting minority voting rights so they no longer needed federal supervision.[41]

Congress's choice not to reassess the coverage formula proved to be fatal. In the years since the renewal of the Voting Rights Act in 1986, the Supreme Court had undergone a states-rights federalism revolution. This conservative shift in judicial philosophy had made the court more skeptical overall about Congress's power to regulate state conduct.[42]

It was clear early on that this revolution was going to spill over into voting rights. As Congress considered the 2006 amendments to the Voting Rights Act, including a reauthorization of preclearance, I testified with other law professors before the Senate Judiciary Committee about the threat of the court holding the preclearance provision of the Voting Rights Act unconstitutional. We urged Congress to update the coverage formula or take other steps to demonstrate it was taking seriously the court conservatives' concerns about what they viewed as congressional overreach. But leaders in Congress worried about upsetting the delicate bipartisan coalition supporting the status quo, and the 2006 amendments passed without such changes.[43]

In 2009, the Supreme Court heard the first post-2006 challenge to the continued constitutionality of preclearance. In *NAMUDNO v. Holder*, the court ducked a decision on the constitutional question, but the 8–1 opinion plainly signaled that the law was in danger of being struck down. The court suggested the measure was now in serious constitutional doubt, a warning sent clearly to Congress to fix the coverage formula. Justice Clarence Thomas alone dissented, viewing preclearance as unconstitutional, even if Congress tried to fix it.[44]

Congress did not act even after *NAMUDNO*'s warning, and in 2013 the Supreme Court issued its 5–4 decision in *Shelby County*, holding unconstitutional the coverage formula used to determine which jurisdictions were subject to preclearance. The court, in an opinion by Chief Justice John Roberts, ruled Congress had not provided recent evidence of sufficiently widespread intentional discrimination in voting by states covered by preclearance, and this failure to update the formula offended the states' rights to "equal sovereignty," a concept the court did not well define but likely stemmed from the Tenth Amendment's reservation of power in the states. It held that the Voting Rights Act had to rely upon more recent data to be justified as permissible under Congress's enforcement powers.[45]

The court tried to portray its decision as minimally invasive, not striking down preclearance itself but merely the coverage formula. Once again, only Justice Thomas was willing to kill preclearance as a whole. Yet Chief Justice Roberts and the rest of the conservative justices in the majority knew full well that striking down the coverage formula effectively dismantled preclearance—preclearance cannot operate without a valid coverage formula and the political impediments that made coming up with a new coverage formula in 2006 were present—or indeed, even greater—than in 2013.[46]

Justice Ginsburg's dissent explained that because the preclearance provision had been such a good deterrent to unconstitutional conduct, there was not likely to be much evidence in the preclearance states of intentional discrimination in voting. "Throwing out preclearance when it has worked and is continuing to work to stop discriminatory changes," the justice wrote, "is like throwing away your umbrella in a rainstorm because you are not getting wet." She and the other liberal justices believed that, given Congress's broad powers to enforce the Fifteenth Amendment and other voting amendments, the court should defer to a rational judgment by Congress about targeting legislation to where voting rights concerns were the greatest.[47]

Shelby County marked a new era in how the court approached both voting rights and Congress's power to enforce the various amendments to the constitution protecting those rights. Far from recognizing "the special role assigned to Congress in protecting the integrity of the democratic process in federal elections," as Justice Ginsburg's dissent suggested, the court has treated Congress like a regular litigant appearing before a trial court that has to produce an adequate evidentiary record. It has not treated Congress as a coequal branch of government entitled to exercise its own judgment as to what laws are constitutionally required to protect voting rights under Congress's enforcement powers.[48]

Shelby County made it clear how difficult it would be to get bold voting rights legislation through the Supreme Court. With a court that not only fails to protect voting rights on its own but that could also well stymie congressional efforts to provide that protection, we need a more direct path toward full enfranchisement.[49]

One other avenue of congressional power remains somewhat more promising, at least in federal elections. Article I, section 4 gives Congress broad powers to "make or alter" state rules for conducting congressional elections. As constitutional law scholar Franita Tolson has shown, this power in the "Elections Clause" was historically understood quite broadly, and a Supreme Court taking history seriously (as many of the justices purport to do) would accept such a broad understanding of congressional power. But in the hands of a Supreme Court majority skeptical of both voting rights and of Congress's power over the states generally, there is reason to worry that Congress's Elections Clause power will wither just as its power to enforce voting-related amendments has. In our polarized polity, even getting meaningful voting rights legislation through Congress has proven difficult, meaning that much of Congress's power under the Elections Clause remains untapped.[50]

☑ ☑ ☑

The time has come to add an amendment to the U.S. Constitution affirmatively protecting the right to vote. Voters in the United States can no longer depend upon the negative protections of voting rights in the constitution itself, or the Supreme Court's interpretation of those rights, or Congress's attempts to protect those rights when it is subject to what is essentially a Supreme Court veto.

In the past, some have argued that pushing such a constitutional amendment could be counterproductive, because it might imply that the constitution does not already robustly protect voting rights through the Fourteenth Amendment's Equal Protection Clause and the voting-related amendments. The argument had some appeal following the voter-protective decisions of the Warren Court era and even in the years after, when more conservative Supreme Court majorities did not appear to have much appetite for overturning such holdings and clung more seriously to *stare decisis*, or respect for precedent.[51]

But today, there is far more reason to worry about the fate of those Warren Court precedents, and there already is a Supreme Court majority that does not believe the constitution robustly protects voting rights. While an attempt to amend the constitution to include an affirmative right to vote carries some risk of a negative implication, this concern is outweighed by the political and social benefits that such an attempt would bring. In short, there is little downside to pushing for a constitutional right to vote, and especially little risk when it comes to Supreme Court backlash. We already have the backlash without any widescale efforts to add the amendment.

The right to vote is too important to leave in the hands of a Supreme Court that has shown itself increasingly hostile to voting rights. Most of us would not be as lucky as Sergeant Carrington or Morris Kramer before the Supreme Court. The time has come to play offense and not just defense.

The struggle for a constitutional right to vote, even if it takes decades and ultimately does not succeed, will have benefits for American society and politics. We need to consider what the contents of such an amendment would look like, what the amendment would do, and how to try to pass it. We cannot afford to avoid this struggle.

Chapter 2

AN AMENDMENT FOR POLITICAL EQUALS

When the state of Texas defended its disenfranchisement of military voters in the *Carrington* case, it made two arguments. One stressed the supposed transitory nature of military service and soldiers' ostensible lack of ties to the community. The other maintained that the state "has a legitimate interest in immunizing its elections from the concentrated balloting of military personnel, whose collective voice may overwhelm a small local civilian community."[1]

The two arguments are radically different. Texas's first claim—that only residents of a community should be entitled to vote for leaders of that community—is quite commonplace and accepted in the United States and around the world. Any set of voting rules must recognize some limitations on the franchise, such as allowing only people who live in an area to choose its representatives.

Texas's second claim—that the state may exclude some residents from voting because of how they might vote and affect public policy—is more controversial and complex. Even today, despite its rejection by the U.S. Supreme Court during the

Warren Court era, the argument still holds sway among some people.[2]

This second argument should be considered illegitimate in a twenty-first century participatory democracy. Elections should be about the division of power among political equals, and a state should not be allowed to disenfranchise otherwise eligible voters because of how they might vote and change public policy. This political equality principle must be at the core of any constitutional amendment protecting the right to vote.

Texas's resistance to student voting over many decades shows the continued inclination of some to limit the franchise because of how people might vote. As we will see, the long-running battle against student voting in Texas's Waller County is best explained not by a concern that students fail to meet the legal residency requirements. Instead, it appears derivative of that second argument Texas made in *Carrington*: voting restrictions driven by fear that these mostly African American students might have preferences different from nonstudent residents and that they could elect representatives who would enact their views into law and policy.

Basic principles of political equality reject the legitimacy of imposing voting restrictions based upon how people might vote. Only a constitutional amendment that protects the political equality of all voters can fully counter illegitimate attempts to shape the electorate.

☑   ☑   ☑

Let's return to Texas's first claim that it could use military employment as a proxy or shortcut for residency status. State and local governments almost always require residency as a condition for voting. I may have a great interest in who is elected governor in Michigan, for example, and I may even donate to a Michigan gubernatorial candidate's campaign, but as a resident of California without ties to Michigan, no one seriously contends that I have the right to vote for Michigan's governor. Without some form of a residency requirement, elections could be swamped by people who are not part of the geographic community in which an election is taking place.[3]

The problem with Texas's residency argument in *Carrington* was not about the concept of residency as a condition for voting, but about its implementation. Roughly speaking, residency for voting means that a person lives primarily in the particular area where the person intends to stay an indefinite period rather than move elsewhere. It is a question of fact about each voter's location and intent. In a 1964 elections case unconnected to *Carrington*, the Texas Supreme Court explained that "neither bodily presence alone nor intention alone will suffice to create the residence, but when the two coincide at that moment the residence is fixed and determined. There is no specific length of time for the bodily presence to continue."[4]

Under this definition, many soldiers living in Texas were hardly transients—they were longtime Texas residents who had the same interests and concerns as nonsoldiers living in Texas. They cared about their roads, schools, taxes, police, and everything else affecting what it meant to live in their community. Sergeant Carrington had moved to Texas with his family, set up his home, and even ran a side business in El Paso. He was hoping to vote in a local election taking place two years after his arrival in Texas about issues related to his everyday life. He was disenfranchised only because he served in the military.[5]

Texas's blanket rule against voting by members of the military (except those who were Texas residents before enlisting) swept in not just the short-timers passing through on military assignment. It also covered those people, such as Sergeant Carrington, who had developed or had started developing roots in the community. The Texas Supreme Court referred to military members as people traveling through on "sojourns," but that description was inaccurate for many of the soldiers stationed on U.S. military bases in Texas, who had lived in Texas for years and intended to stay there indefinitely. The U.S. Supreme Court ultimately concluded that Texas's rule was just too crude to separate bona fide residents who happened to be in the military from those soldiers who were stationed there temporarily.[6]

Texas's second argument in favor of its discriminatory voting rule was not about whether members of the military in fact intended to remain in Texas but about whether it was fair to let those soldiers who intended to remain vote in elections where their vote could change election results that might lead to different policy choices. Texas's argument in *Carrington* coupled an empirical claim with a normative one: the empirical claim was that members of the military have different preferences on public policy issues than nonmilitary members, and with an influx of military voters, public policy could change toward the preferences of those military voters. The normative claim was that this change in public policy would be bad, and that Texas had a "legitimate" reason to stop voters who work for the military from "overwhelm[ing]" the preferences of other local residents.[7]

The Warren Court blasted this second argument, describing it as founded on "a fear of the political views of a particular group of bona fide residents." Although the Supreme Court flatly declared that "'fencing out' from the franchise a sector of the population because of the way they may vote is constitutionally impermissible," these kinds of arguments continue to be persuasive to some people, even if they remain implicit: sometimes arguments ostensibly about bona fide residency mask policies motivated simply by a desire to exclude some people from the franchise because of how they may vote. Given *Carrington* and cases like it, states like Texas are no longer going to publicly admit they are excluding people from voting based upon how they might vote. They might instead hide behind excuses like strict interpretations of residency rules to exclude these people from voting. Disenfranchisement because of how people might vote persists today despite the U.S. Constitution and despite the court's statements in *Carrington* and other, similar cases.[8]

☑   ☑   ☑

Consider Texas's long fight against college students voting in light of Texas's two arguments in *Carrington*. In 1973, a federal appeals court struck down a Texas statute that told Texas election officials to presume—absent evidence to the contrary—that students living in a college town were not residents of that town. Five years later, students at Prairie View A&M University, the oldest Black university in Texas, sued Leroy Symm, the tax assessor-collector of Waller County, Texas, where the university is located, because he appeared to be still applying such a presumption against student residency. He would not register Prairie View students to vote unless they had a promise of postgraduate employment in the county, had parents living in the county, or were married and living with a spouse in the county.[9]

Symm testified "that students and servicemen fall within the same category, and that neither are residents, as a general rule, of the place where they are stationed or attending school, and in making this determination of residency, he applie[d] this assumption." He refused to register most students at the university.[10]

Citing *Carrington* and other equal protection voting cases from the Supreme Court, a three-judge federal district court held that Symm's practice of treating most Prairie View students as nonresidents violated the Twenty-Sixth Amendment's prohibition of voting discrimination on the basis of age. The Supreme Court affirmed the district court's ruling without a written opinion, confirming that Symm's treatment of student voters was unconstitutional.[11]

Texas's battle against student voting has continued for many years, and some Texas counties tried different strategies to exclude student voters. In 2004, the secretary of state of Texas, Geoffrey S. Connor, issued an advisory opinion admonishing Texas counties they could not use special questionnaires to determine whether students, such as those at Prairie View, counted as residents and could be registered to vote. Rebuffing the proposal, Connor concluded that such questionnaires were impermissible: "No more or less can be required of college students during the voter registration process than any other Texas voter. In particular, no Texas county voter registrar may require an affidavit or questionnaire in addition to the information required on the application for a voter registration certificate. A person who has reached the age of majority is presumed able to make a factual statement about voting residence. Moreover, the student is presumed to be in the best position to make such factual statements about the residence of the student."[12]

Today, Texas remains one of the few states that does not accept student identification as a permissible form of identification to vote. Texas is also one of the few states that does not allow people to register to vote online or to change registrations when they move within a state. Students, who tend to move a lot and who often do not have driver's licenses that could be used as identification for voting, continue to face special burdens to voting in Texas and elsewhere.[13]

☑   ☑   ☑

In 2018, Waller County sheriffs arrested a staffer of Mike Siegel, a Democrat who was challenging incumbent Republican Representative Michael McCaul for the local congressional seat. The staffer, Jacob Aronowitz, was trying to deliver a letter to the Waller County courthouse that complained about a decision made by local election officials that risked excluding Prairie View students who lived in campus dorms from voting in the congressional district. Aronowitz took a picture of himself delivering the letter as proof of delivery, and this action apparently disturbed the clerk receiving the letter.

Waller County Sheriff Captain Manny Zamora said that Aronowitz "had been told to leave. He agitated and perhaps accosted the female that was there working . . . and that's what we were responding to." Aronowitz was arrested and authorities reported he was going to be charged with failing to identify himself to law enforcement officials, though Aronowitz through his attorney said he did identify himself. A few days later, perhaps spurred by the attention generated by the arrest, the Texas secretary of state intervened to ensure that Prairie View students living in the dorms could vote in the congressional election.[14]

Aronowitz was never charged. As he told me: "No charges were ever actually filed, much less dropped. When they took me under arrest, they didn't provide a basis or probable charge at that time either. When media attention and public outcry

came their way during my first few hours of arrest, they interrupted and stopped the intake process in progress, returned my
belongings, and then released me after a short and rather surreal
exit interview." This is just the kind of low-level harassment
meant to deter people from helping students vote.[15]

That same year, students at Prairie View A&M again sued
Waller County, this time claiming officials made early voting
easy in other, whiter parts of the county, but offered limited
opportunities at the university. A *Texas Tribune/VoteBeat* report related the story of one of the plaintiffs in the lawsuit, Jayla
Allen, who was suing over the discrimination. When her
grandfather was a student at the university in the 1970s, he was
disenfranchised. When her parents attended in the mid-1980s,
county officials still resisted registering students to vote in the
county. "When her older sister was there in the early 2000s,
the local district attorney flagrantly threatened to prosecute
Prairie View A&M students who voted in Waller County, er-
roneously claiming they weren't legitimate residents."[16]

Unlike the earlier successful lawsuits brought by Prairie View
students, this time Waller County prevailed. Federal district
judge Charles Eskridge, a Donald Trump appointee, found that
Waller County had engaged in past discrimination against Black
residents and students at Prairie View, but it no longer did so
and it did not limit voting opportunities for the students. After
noting that "no other comparably sized county in Texas places
a precinct polling place for early voting directly on, or immediately adjacent to, a college campus in the way that Waller
County has for" Prairie View, the judge went out of his way to
praise the county along with the students: the students "can
draw considerable satisfaction from the fact that their determined pursuit for recognition of their voting rights was the

likely catalyst to this singular accomplishment. But at the same time, it's a matter of great credit to Waller County."[17]

The remarks giving credit to Waller County rang hollow to some. "The court's decision is another reminder that the full promise of freedom and full citizenship remains unfulfilled for Black Prairie View A&M University students in Waller County," said John Cusick, assistant counsel at LDF, which represented the students.[18]

Some likely remembered the 2015 notorious arrest and jailing of Prairie View alumna Sandra Bland on a traffic violation, and her subsequent suspicious death—ruled a suicide—in a Waller County jail three days later. Bland's death was one of the catalysts for the Black Lives Matter movement. Bland, a Chicago resident, was returning to Prairie View to start a summer job at the school.[19]

With Texas government under Republican control, and a student vote trending Democratic, the continued resistance to student voting is hardly surprising. African American voters are also the most reliable Democratic voters—according to one survey, 76 percent of African American Texans identify as Democrats and only 9 percent as Republicans—and that, too, likely played into the calculus to make voting harder for students at the historically Black Prairie View A&M. It is hard to see Texas's resistance to student voting as anything other than that second argument in *Carrington*: that people may be excluded from voting because of how they might vote.[20]

The struggles of students to vote, despite the passage of the fourteenth and twenty-sixth amendments and despite numerous Supreme Court and lower court rulings affirming equal treatment in voting, demonstrate that more needs to be done. There are many, similar stories about hurdles put in front of

African American voters and many others, as the next chapter explains. The existing tools we have to protect full political equality in the United States are inadequate.

☑ ☑ ☑

The debates over military and student disenfranchisement in Texas nicely demonstrate two competing conceptions of the purpose of voting. The first—the equal power conception—is that voting is about the division of power among political equals. This links up with the Warren Court era cases such as *Carrington* and *Kramer*. The second—the best-choice conception—is that voting is about making the "best" choices for society. This second conception links up with Texas's argument in *Carrington* about excluding military voters because of how they might vote. Excluding those voters, Texas claimed, would preserve the power of nonmilitary residents. In essence, Texas argued in favor of disenfranchising a portion of the population to allow what it viewed as the real or deserving residents of an area who choose the area's leaders. In this view, longtime local residents have more of a stake and more knowledge of local issues and therefore are more deserving of the right to vote.

Although *Carrington* emphatically rejected the best-choice conception of the purpose of voting, elsewhere the court has embraced it. Recall the 1959 Supreme Court decision in *Lassiter* holding that the disenfranchisement of otherwise eligible voters who were also illiterate in the English language promotes "intelligent use of the ballot." The court has never repudiated *Lassiter*—the issue has been put on hold because the Voting Rights Act, by statute, now bans literacy tests—and some justices could well embrace *Lassiter* down the line should a similar issue return to the Supreme Court. Literacy tests themselves

could even return in the United States if a state tried to reim-
pose them by arguing that the statute was no longer constitutional, much as opponents of the preclearance portion of the
Voting Rights Act successfully argued about the act's coverage
formula in *Shelby County*.[21]

Despite *Lassiter*, the equal power conception of voting, as embodied in those Warren Court voting decisions of the 1960s, has
seeped into American public consciousness and deserves explicit
recognition in the constitution. The one-person, one-vote principle of the redistricting cases such as *Reynolds v. Sims* is no longer
as controversial as it was when rural counties had much more
power in state legislatures. Even in the 2016 *Evenwel* case, as described in the last chapter, the debate concerned whether it was
appropriate to draw districts with equal numbers of people or
equal numbers of voters, not about whether the principle should
be jettisoned altogether (though two justices appeared open to
questioning the one-person, one-vote principle itself). Today,
with the exception of the Electoral College and composition of
the U.S. Senate (anomalies that I return to in the next chapter),
we use the one-person, one-vote principle across American legislative elections without controversy.[22]

A constitutional right to vote should embrace the equal-
power conception of voting. For shorthand I refer to this conception as the principle of "political equality." Why is political
equality so central to a constitutional right to vote? If you and I
are political equals, I have no more power to deny you a vote if
you cannot read and write in English, are not in the military, or
are a college student than you have the power to tell me I cannot
vote if I cannot read Spanish, pass a test on basic concepts of
budgeting and taxation, or regularly watch TikTok videos. In
other words, among a group of political equals we cannot impose tests for voting or look to a person's status to determine

who gets the franchise because such a question cannot be fairly determined by only a subset of the group of political equals. Allowing some political equals to exclude others unfairly empowers some members of the community over others. A voluminous literature among democratic theorists supports this idea of universal suffrage among political equals.[23]

The strongest argument for the alternative best-choice conception of voting is that democracy depends upon informed decision-making, or else demagogues or incompetent leaders may be selected by voters or voters may adopt bad policies through ballot initiatives and direct democracy. Informed decision-making is of course better than uninformed decision-making, and we should do everything we can to encourage informed voting. (Indeed, I wrote an entire book, *Cheap Speech*, premised on the idea that we need to give voters better access to reliable information about how to vote in a social media era filled with election-related disinformation.[24])

But as laudable as the goal of informed decision-making is, history shows that any attempt to limit the franchise to those who are most likely to be best informed—or using that ground as a pretext for limiting power of likely political opponents—can lead to pernicious, discriminatory results. In the past, Americans have lived under systems in which only white, male property owners could vote, because they supposedly were the best informed or the only ones with sufficient stake in election outcomes. Later systems excluded nonwhite voters, women, military voters, students, federal employees, and nonparents. Today most of us would recognize these exclusions of classes of people from the franchise as morally wrong, whether or not they are precluded by the constitution. These exclusions also are against international law and norms within advanced democracies.[25]

It is no doubt true that preventing the exclusion of some portion of the population from voting, such as military members or students or women or African Americans, could affect voting outcomes, but in a democracy where we are all equal, that is a feature and not a bug. Election results should reflect the will of all eligible voters, and there is no way to say in advance of the voting itself that the exclusion of a particular group of voters, such as soldiers or students, would lead to better public policy. In other words, deciding who is entitled to vote based upon how they might vote is inherently illegitimate. The best public policy is the one reflecting the will of the people, usually through their representatives chosen by the people in a fair election.[26]

This basic premise about democracy has wide support among U.S. citizens, and a right-to-vote amendment would assure, in the words of election scholar Richard Briffault, that the right to vote is "an American right" and not a "state-granted" one. A recent survey of citizens found substantial agreement on granting all adult, law-abiding U.S. citizens the right to vote. This universal suffrage is not embodied in the constitution, but it should be. It is especially important to do so because universal citizen suffrage is not unanimously accepted and voting restrictions remain, some of which could be accepted by a future Supreme Court. In that same recent survey, a considerable minority of survey respondents expressed support for disenfranchising citizens who do not pay income taxes, suggesting another reason for enshrining voting protections in the constitution.[27]

☑ ☑ ☑

Once we have agreed that political equality demands equal voting rights, the question then is how best to ensure such equality.

As the examples in this book show, the existing constitutional structure does not adequately promote political equality or protect voting rights. The solution is a constitutional amendment affirmatively protecting the right to vote.

Designing a constitutional right to vote requires setting rules beyond those addressing who formally gets the franchise to also cover the mechanisms for conducting elections. After all, a state could formally accept the principle of equal voting rights for all citizens but then impose unequally burdensome registration or voting rules as a pretext for disenfranchising groups of voters. This indirect disenfranchisement should be prohibited too.

Commentators sometimes justify such hurdles under the same best-choice conception of voting. In response to arguments that some states' voter registration requirements are onerous and lead to fewer people registering to vote, conservative columnist Jonah Goldberg has argued that such restrictions actually lead to better outcomes. "Voting should be harder, not easier—for everybody," Goldberg wrote in a 2005 newspaper column. "If you are having an intelligent conversation with somebody, is it enriched if a mob of uninformed louts, never mind ex-cons and rapists, barges in? People who want to make voting easier are in effect saying that those who previously didn't care or know enough about the country to vote are exactly the kind of voters this country needs now."[28]

Given these objectionable arguments to impose hurdles to voting to weed out voters who do not "care" enough or "deserve" to vote, a constitutional right to vote must consider not just the eligibility requirements themselves, but how voting rights are protected and elections implemented.

A constitutional right to vote is premised on the idea that voting is about the division of power among political equals. But this standard leads immediately to another question: Who

should count among "political equals?" States routinely disenfranchise felons, children, those found to be mentally incompetent, noncitizens, and nonresidents.

In the next chapter, I consider whether people in some of
these categories should have their voting rights protected in the
U.S. Constitution. For example, it is possible to draft a constitutional provision guaranteeing former felons (or even current
felons) the right to vote. I argue in favor of reenfranchising former felons who have completed their prison time and parole.
There are other contentious choices as well. An amendment
could include voting rights for people living in U.S. territories
such as Puerto Rico. These are complicated issues in some U.S.
territories and begin with questions about the right of self-
determination of people living there.

A voting rights amendment also could tackle the two main
U.S. institutions that still do not abide by the one-person, one-
vote principle of equal voting power: the Electoral College for
choosing the president and the malapportioned U.S. Senate.
But such expansions would make an already controversial proposal for a constitutional right to vote even more controversial
and less likely to be accepted, even in the medium term, among
more conservative voters and in Republican states. Ultimately,
I argue for these reforms to be considered separately from a
constitutional right to vote.

For this reason, I begin with what I term a "basic" version of
the constitutional right to vote, one that would continue to let
states exclude noncitizens, nonresidents, children, and former
or current felons, and which would not change voting rights for
U.S. territories or abolish the Electoral College or change the
Senate. I then turn in the next chapter to more fulsome versions
of the amendment that expand these categories of voting and
explore what we would gain by considering these seriously.

(Examples of the different versions of the amendment appear in this book's appendix.)

In deciding which version of a right-to-vote constitutional amendment to support, advocates will have to make tradeoffs between the versions of the amendment that are more politically possible and versions that are more consistent with the goals of promoting political equality. I return to this issue in chapter 6.

☑ ☑ ☑

By using the term "basic," I do not mean to suggest that such a right embodied in the constitution would be small, or inconsequential, or easily evaded. To the contrary, passage and ratification of the basic version of the amendment would be a monumental accomplishment that would profoundly change the nature of voting rights and elections in the United States. The fuller versions of the amendment would do even more.

☑ ☑ ☑

A basic constitutional right to vote should have these six elements:

(1) all citizen, adult, resident, nonfelons shall have the right to cast a ballot in all elections, including for president and vice president, and to have that ballot fairly and accurately counted;

(2) all votes in any election will be equally weighted, except for the weighting of votes across states permitted by the Electoral College in choosing the president and vice president;

(3) all eligible voters will be automatically registered to vote and provided with a unique identification number to allow them to vote as they move from state to state;

(4) states must provide equal and not unduly burdensome voting opportunities for all voters, measured by ease of voting, and must have substantial reasons, backed by real and significant evidence, for imposing necessary restrictions on, or placing impediments to, casting a ballot; and

(5) voters must have a fair opportunity to participate in the political process and to elect representatives of their choice regardless of the voters' race, ethnicity, or membership in a language minority group.

(6) Congress has broad power to protect voting rights and this power is not subject to narrow judicial interpretation.

Let me go through each of these in turn to explain the basics of these six provisions, saving for later chapters some of the details and complications.

(1) A Positive Right to Vote

The first provision of the proposed amendment is the most fundamental. It guarantees the rights of citizen, adult, resident, nonfelons the right to vote and to have that vote fairly and accurately counted. This provision applies to all elections, federal, state, and local, including those for president and vice president.[29]

This provision adds an explicit, positive right to vote to the constitution. As we have seen, the constitution generally frames voting rights in the negative and prohibits discrimination in voting on the basis of certain prohibited categories, such as race. This new amendment, in essence, would codify the Warren Court era rulings recognizing the right to vote as fundamental for this class of voters and locks it in so that a hostile Supreme Court cannot continue to water down voting rights.[30]

The amendment also gives voters the right to claim a constitutional violation if their votes are not being fairly and accurately counted, a provision important for the prevention of election subversion. Due process protections in the fifth and fourteenth amendments should already provide such a guarantee of a fair and accurate count, but placing such a right expressly in the constitution makes it more difficult for courts to deny the standing of voters to sue for a fair and accurate count.[31]

This provision also makes a major change to the rules in Article II of the constitution for conducting presidential elections and to the Supreme Court's interpretation of that article in the 2000 case, *Bush v. Gore*. In *Bush*, the court interpreted the provision in Article II allowing state legislatures to set the manner for assigning a state's presidential electors as granting states the power to appoint presidential electors directly, without a vote of the people. The amendment would require each state to conduct a popular vote for assigning the state's presidential electors. This provision not only serves the goal of political equality, but limits the potential for election subversion.[32]

Such an amendment would not upset the Electoral College system *between* states; it would only affect how Electoral College votes are assigned *within* states. It would not stop states from assigning some of their Electoral College votes by (equally weighted) congressional district, as Maine and Nebraska currently do. Nor would it stop a state from assigning its Electoral College votes proportionally within a state based on the popular vote, or from using ranked-choice voting for choosing how to assign Electoral College votes within a state. Each of these methods treats voters' voting power equally (although gerrymandered congressional districts do raise the risk of unfair allocation of some Electoral College votes assigned by district).[33]

(2) Equal Weighting of Votes

This provision would explicitly put into the constitution the Warren Court's one-person, one-vote principle. It is necessary, despite rulings such as *Reynolds v. Sims*, because a future Supreme Court could overrule those cases and determine that the original public meaning of the Equal Protection Clause of the Fourteenth Amendment (or Article I as applied to congressional elections) does not require the drawing of districts with roughly equal populations.[34]

States and local governments would not have the power to create systems of their own, analogous to the Senate, in which each state is entitled to two senators regardless of population. Nor could states design other means of dividing voting power that give more voting power to some voters over others.[35]

States would have some flexibility in deviating from perfect equality for good reasons, such as to keep city boundaries together. The same standards that the courts currently use to apply to state and local redistricting, rather than the strictest federal standard, would control.[36]

The provision would carve out voting for president and vice president, which the constitution has always required to be conducted on a state-by-state basis through the Electoral College. That system weights the votes of voters in states with smaller populations as greater than voters in states with large populations. As noted, however, within each state, the votes for president must be equally weighted.[37]

The provision does not require an explicit carve-out for Senate elections, because Senate elections are conducted statewide, not in districts. As I will explore further in the next chapter, the weighting issue with the Senate arises thanks to the constitutional requirement that each state be assigned an equal number of senators.[38]

(3) Automatic Voter Registration and Unique Voter Identification Numbers

This provision helps to implement the right to an equal vote. Voter registration and identification requirements are among the biggest sources of dispute in current election litigation. By making the government bear the burden and costs of registering all eligible voters and requiring the government to provide all eligible citizens unique voter identification numbers that would be used to help voters register across states and prevent double voting, elections may be run more securely with less litigation and greater voter confidence. And, of course, easing the path to voter registration promotes political equality by removing a hurdle from voters.[39]

Some states may not want to set up the procedures for automatic voter registration and may prefer to leave the registration question to the federal government. States would have the option to set up their own systems or leave it to the federal government. This means that the provision would not require a "federal takeover" of elections, as some conservatives fear.

Democrats and those on the left have reflexively opposed all voter identification provisions. But such laws are ubiquitous in most other democracies because they are coupled with voter registration conducted by the government (and often using national identity cards, which the United States does not produce).

The real objection to these provisions as they have been implemented in the states is that they have put the onus on voters to get the right form of identification, which puts an undue burden on certain people, such as students, poor voters, and others. Under the amendment, the government would take on all of those costs and burdens as part of the system of setting up automatic voter registration systems. This will make the system work better across states (as people would have a single voter identification number used for their entire life, just as they have a single social security number) and ensure not only eased voter registration but also a more efficient and more secure voting system overall. States may give voters options to use a thumbprint or other biometric identification methods, if sufficiently reliable.

This registration/identification requirement and the next two provisions in the proposed amendment are unusual in the federal constitution, in that they include much more specific language about the mechanics of government action, including judicial review, than what we normally see in a constitutional amendment. This is far more specific, for example, than a vague right to "equal protection" or "due process" or the "privileges or immunities" of citizenship. Specificity is necessary, however, because neither state governments nor the courts can be trusted to fully protect voting rights through general or aspirational language about the right to vote. Texas's instance of discrimination against military and student voters, for example, would be much harder to accomplish with these provisions in place.

(4) Assuring Equal Voting Opportunities and Limiting Burdens on Voting Rights

This provision addresses two substantive points and gives a set of instructions to the courts. First, it requires states to offer equal voting opportunities to voters within states. Second, it requires that the voting opportunities be reasonable. It also provides a rule for how courts are to adjudicate claims that states have not complied with the amendment.

First, voters in a state must have roughly equal voting opportunities. This provision does not require states to have a certain number of days of early voting (or even require early voting at all). It does mean, for example, that if a state decides to have an early voting period, the opportunity for voters must be roughly the same. Any burdens on voting are measured on a per capita, not a per county, basis. That means that people in urban and rural voting areas should have similar wait times to be able to vote. That might lead to more hours for early polling places in areas with higher populations compared to sparsely populated areas. The provision does not allow a state to assign one early voting place per county, which puts a bigger burden on voters in larger counties and only gives the illusion of equality or uniformity.[40]

Second, the provision requires that voting not be unduly burdensome on voters and that impediments to voting be reasonably necessary. This requirement should again be measured not by a specific number of early voting days but by the overall ease with which voters may vote. These standards are unavoidably general, but they should be applied by courts using reasonableness and common sense in a way that puts a thumb on the scale favoring the enfranchisement and easy voting opportunities for eligible voters.

For example, one good rule of thumb for election day voting is that voters should not have to wait more than thirty minutes in line to cast a ballot, and a state's voting system should be designed to avoid long lines. Such a requirement will likely create incentives for states to create early in-person or mail-in voting opportunities, but such additional voting opportunities would not be specifically required. The key point would be avoiding undue burdens on the right to vote.

To make both of these provisions—equal voting opportunities and voting without undue burdens—a reality, courts would sometimes need to adjudicate the reasonableness of voting restrictions. This provision of the amendment tells courts how to adjudicate such claims. It provides that when a state passes a law that burdens voters unduly or treats classes of voters unequally, states must come forward with a strong interest for doing so, and show with actual evidence that its voting rule is reasonably tailored to meet that interest.[41]

This provision is necessary because of opinions such as *Crawford v. Marion County Election Board*, the 2008 case in which the Supreme Court allowed the state of Indiana to impose a strict photographic voter identification provision despite a complete lack of evidence that such laws either prevented an appreciable amount of fraud or promoted voter confidence. Too often, stated reasons for passing laws that burden some voters are but a pretext for the unstated motivation of trying to shape the composition of the electorate, in violation of the equal powers conception of voting.[42]

Saying that the state must come forward with real evidence that its challenged laws are reasonably necessary to promote the government's substantial state interest is not intended to subject all of a state's election laws to strict scrutiny. Applying strict scrutiny would make it too difficult for states to run elections with any kind of discretion. Instead, the state would have discretion within a range of reasonable alternatives to adopt certain voting rules that assure equality among voters and reasonable voting opportunities. A claim that five early voting days are not enough and ten are required would be difficult to sustain under this standard. Courts should focus on voter equality and reasonable, nonburdensome voting opportunities.

The more burdensome the law is on voters, the greater the state's proven interests would have to be to justify the rule. That standard is not all that dissimilar from current balancing under the so-called balancing test that courts currently use to address such claims (known as *Anderson-Burdick* balancing); the main difference is that under the new standard the state would have a new burden of proof to provide real evidence of substantial need to justify burdensome voting laws. This shift will protect voters much more than current law.[43]

(5) Constitutionalizing Protection of Minority Voting Rights

This provision would transform what currently appears as section 2 of the Voting Rights Act into a constitutional guarantee of equal treatment. This is perhaps the most controversial aspect of the basic amendment, and one that could lead to some conservative and Republican resistance.

This provision is necessary because the fourteenth and fifteenth amendments have not been properly interpreted by the Supreme Court to adequately protect voting rights, and because the very conservative court could one day determine that section 2 of the Voting Rights Act, because it is race conscious, itself now violates the Equal Protection Clause of the Fourteenth Amendment. Despite strides toward greater political equality, there simply remains too much discrimination in voting, especially against African American, Latino, Native American, and Asian voters, to leave the issue to a congressional statute that can be neutered by the Supreme Court.

This constitutional provision would enshrine the original intent of section 2 to provide meaningful protection for minority voters, rather than the watered-down version of section 2 that the Supreme Court has recently embraced.[44]

Some skeptics may be concerned about enshrining another provision regarding race and voting in the constitution, in addition to the Fifteenth Amendment, on the grounds that it might give special treatment to racial minorities that would be locked in over time. This concern is misplaced, because section 2 of the Voting Rights Act, on which this provision is based, is self-sunsetting as racial discrimination dissipates. For example, the requirement under section 2 that jurisdictions draw congressional or legislative districts in which minority voters can elect candidates of their choice requires proof that these jurisdictions continue to exhibit racially polarized voting, in which majority white voters and minority voters prefer different candidates for office and the white majority is usually able to elect its candidates of choice. As racially polarized voting disappears, this provision becomes less necessary and its application less common.[45]

(6) Congress's Broad Enforcement Powers

This provision directly takes on the Supreme Court's federalism revolution, and it clarifies that when Congress acts under its powers to enforce voting rights, it is fully equal with the Supreme Court. Rather than treating Congress like an ordinary litigant that has to produce enough evidence to satisfy the court that it has adopted "congruent and proportional" legislation to deal with state violation of voters' rights, the Supreme Court must accept congressional legislation protecting voting rights so long as it is rationally related to Congress's purposes.[46]

This decision would reverse the results in cases such as the Supreme Court's *Shelby County* case by giving Congress greater discretion to determine when states need federal supervision over voting to ensure that everyone's voting rights are adequately protected. It embraces Justice Ginsburg's approach to congressional power in her *Shelby County* dissent.[47]

☑   ☑   ☑

In sum, the basic version of a constitutional amendment protecting the right to vote would be a major step forward in advancing voting rights, one that would promote political equality and assure that the promise of earlier voting rights amendments is finally fulfilled. It also would limit skirmishes in the voting wars, as chapter 4 describes, and it decreases the chances of election subversion or stolen elections, as explained in chapter 5. These additional benefits should make the constitutional amendment more appealing to a wider spectrum of the American public.

The next chapter explores three areas where a constitutional right to vote could be even bolder, with more controversial proposals that may be more in line with the ideals of political equality but that would provoke a much harder political struggle.

Chapter 3

EXPANDING THE RIGHT TO VOTE?

No one in the fight over student voting in Waller County, Texas, disagreed with the idea that voting could be limited to bona fide residents of the county; the fight was about whether Texas election officials were using residency as a pretext to exclude student voters because of how they might vote.

Certain basic limitations on the franchise have pretty much universal acceptance in democracies around the world: residency, citizenship, and adulthood. It is also fairly universal to exclude from the franchise those who lack the mental capacity to make basic decisions about themselves and their lives.

The exclusion of noncitizens and nonresidents is justified on the grounds of defining the overall political community. Citizenship confers certain rights and responsibilities. It is a formal, legal way of delineating full membership in a community. Not all agree that citizenship conveys meaningful criteria for membership in a community. But there needs to be some workable dividing line for determining who is entitled to full rights, and citizenship is the way that countries typically do so, which makes sense as a rough first cut. More practically, any calls in a constitutional amendment to enfranchise noncitizens would be a total political nonstarter, enmeshing the fight for the amendment in immigration battles over citizenship and borders.[1]

Residency requirements are a commonsense way of determining who will vote in elections to represent distinct geographic constituencies: people who live in Omaha should be the ones who determine the leaders in Omaha and people who live in San Diego determine that city's leaders. Omaha residents would not want San Diego residents voting for their mayor and vice versa. Without a residency requirement, there would be no clear way of determining who should be entitled to exercise the franchise on the local and district level. And the ease with which residency may be established means that residency requirements are a minor barrier for those who intend to live in a particular area.[2]

Of course, states and localities can consider expanding the franchise even if the constitution does not require it. Some local school boards have allowed noncitizens to vote in local school board elections on the grounds that local parents, whether citizens or not, should have the right to determine leadership of schools educating the community's children. Some vacation areas give the franchise to vacation homeowners in certain local elections. These are choices best left up to local communities, given the considerable variation of views on the importance of citizenship and residency in the political community.[3]

The exclusion from the franchise of children and those lacking mental capacity reflects a different concern, about basic competency to make voting decisions. In the last chapter, we saw that among political equals, the imposition of literacy tests or other tests for voting are inappropriate because each of us as a political equal cannot exclude others based upon what we consider to be appropriate attributes for voting. But such an argument comes apart at the extremes. We would not expect a two-year-old to be able to make enough sense of the world to vote, nor someone suffering from an acute mental illness that prevents them from understanding the nature of the world and their choices and interests. They may be excluded not because of fear they might favor different interests than others, but because they cannot form rational thought to determine their interests. (Some have argued that parents should be given extra votes to represent the views of their children, but that issue goes beyond our discussion here.)[4]

On voting by minors, there is room for local experimentation. Some jurisdictions are considering lowering the voting age to sixteen on the grounds that sixteen-year-olds have enough experience and rationality to be considered political equals and to express their interests in the community. These choices, too, are best left to local design; the question whether the line should be at eighteen, sixteen, or even lower is not something on which there is likely to be full consensus. Using the legal age of adulthood seems a sensible dividing line on a national scale.[5]

As to lack of mental competency, the issue is trickier. Care must be taken both that those who have enough capacity are not disenfranchised, while also not allowing the enfranchisement of those certainly lacking capacity whose votes may be manipulated by others. There is plenty of discrimination against persons with mental disabilities. Fears of nursing home staff voting on behalf of a facility's residents with dementia, while often exaggerated, cannot be dismissed out of hand.[6]

But what about other limitations on the franchise, or rules that weigh some voters' votes more than others'? This chapter considers whether a constitutional right to vote should be extended to former felons and to voters living in U.S. territories such as Washington, D.C., and Puerto Rico, who often have no or limited voting rights. It also considers whether the U.S. Constitution's unequal weighting of votes for president (through the Electoral College) and the Senate (where every state gets two senators, regardless of population) violate principles of political equality and deserve to be changed in an amendment.

This discussion must consider not only the merits of the proposals, but also whether the addition of such changes would be so politically controversial as to render a constitutional amendment, already a longshot, an impossibility.

☑   ☑   ☑

"Through our office of election crimes and security, in conjunction with the attorney general's office and [the Florida Department of Law Enforcement], the state of Florida has charged, and is in the process of arresting, twenty individuals across the state for voter fraud," Florida Governor Ron DeSantis announced to hoots of approval from a small group of supporters at an August 2022 Florida press conference.[7]

DeSantis explained that the investigation was targeting former felons in heavily Democratic counties: Palm Beach, Broward, and Miami Dade. Florida voters had overwhelmingly supported a voter initiative, Amendment 4, to restore the right of former felons to vote once they had completed their sentences, but that restoration did not apply to those who had been convicted of murder or sexual assault (who had to go through a more onerous process to get their voting rights back). The people targeted in the new Florida probe had convictions for these crimes and allegedly had voted without restoration.

"And so they did not go through any process," DeSantis explained. "They did not get their rights restored. And yet they went ahead and voted anyways. That is against the law. And now they are going to pay the price for it. So they will be charged, they are being charged and arrested today, for election fraud. This is a third-degree felony in the state of Florida. They could face a $5,000 fine and up to five years in prison for illegally voting in our elections."

DeSantis, the future presidential candidate, was burnishing his credentials with a Republican Party base that had been primed for decades to believe that voter fraud, especially committed by Democrats, was a major problem in American elections. Never mind that the rate of voter fraud in the contemporary United States is quite rare and that when election crimes have happened, they appeared as likely to be committed by Republicans as Democrats. DeSantis had established a new office of "election crimes and security," with a budget over $1 million per year, that critics worried would be used to deter legitimate voting, especially by poor people and people of color who were more likely to vote for Democrats.[8]

But far from uncovering a major crime wave with dire implications for democracy in Florida, DeSantis appeared to be engaging in a politically motivated prosecution of confused former felons. His efforts appeared aimed not only to shore up his base but also to deter voting by other former felons who were eligible to vote once again, perhaps because they might vote for Democrats.

The *New York Times* explained that of the twenty people charged out of eleven million Floridians who voted in 2020, "the violations appeared inadvertent, with police body camera footage showing the people puzzled when officers showed up to arrest some of them. In Florida, a conviction of voter fraud requires proof of intent. Already, a judge in Miami has dropped the charges against one of the 20." Since that report, charges against at least three people were dropped while other defendants took a plea deal.[9]

One of those body cams covered the arrest of Tony Patterson, in Tampa. He was recorded saying: "What is wrong with this state, man? . . . Voter fraud? Y'all said anybody with a felony could vote, man." He further asked the officer arresting him: "Why would you let me vote if I wasn't able to vote?" "'I'm not sure, buddy,' the officer replied. 'I don't know.'"[10]

The *Tampa Bay Times* reported that of "the 19 people arrested, 12 were registered as Democrats and at least 13 are Black." Not among those pursued by DeSantis's special police force, or even mentioned by him, was a Trump supporter living in the affluent The Villages community outside of Orlando, who indisputably voted illegally twice in the 2020 elections, once in Florida and once, by mail, in New York. That white voter, Joan Halstead, got community service and a mandatory civics class. She moved to have her criminal record expunged. She was one of at least four voters in The Villages so charged.[11]

It was unsurprising that Patterson was confused about reenfranchisement. Many states disenfranchise felons upon conviction, and Florida had made it exceedingly hard for felons to get their voting rights restored, requiring a restoration order from the state's governor. Florida voters decided that such strict felon disenfranchisement laws were too draconian, and in 2018 they overwhelmingly passed Amendment 4, a ballot measure that would allow felons to be reenfranchised upon completion of the terms of their incarceration. The measure, which was expected to automatically reenfranchise over one million Floridians, garnered a 64.5 percent positive vote, including from an estimated 62 percent of Republican voters, according to a poll by the University of North Florida.[12]

Amendment 4 was consistent with a national trend to reenfranchise felons who have completed their sentences, one driven in part by perceived inequities in the criminal justice system. Black men in Florida were far more likely to be incarcerated and therefore disenfranchised. The Brennan Center for Justice reported that by 2016, more than one in five of Florida's Black voting age population was disenfranchised. According to the Marshall Project, a nonprofit newsroom focused on criminal justice, "Roughly 20 states passed legislation returning or expanding the right to vote to people on probation and parole or those with a felony conviction who have served their time since 2016."[13]

The Florida legislature, dominated by Republicans, resisted the reenfranchisement in Amendment 4, probably for the same reason that Texas election administrators resisted student voting: fear that former felons might vote for Democrats. Legislators enacted a new law after the passage of Amendment 4 that created new penalties for former felons who attempted to register to vote if they had not first paid all court fines and fees in connection with their convictions. The law was in line with a unanimous Florida Supreme Court advisory opinion determining that Amendment 4 required the payment of all outstanding fines in order for a felon's voting rights to be restored.[14]

But Florida had no central repository of information regarding what those fees were, and there was no easy way for former felons to know whether they owed such fees. Registering to vote without knowing if all fines were paid risked committing a new felony, with up to five years in jail. It was Kafkaesque and cruel.

A coalition of civil rights groups sued Florida, claiming that the legislature's law would be a trap for the unwary and would ensnare former felons unwittingly in new crimes. A federal district court agreed, holding that the law violated the Equal Protection Clause and Due Process Clause of the Fourteenth Amendment; the Twenty-Fourth Amendment barring the payment of poll taxes; and a federal statute (the National Voter Registration Act) protecting voter registration in federal elections.[15]

But the entire U.S. Court of Appeals for the Eleventh Circuit heard and reversed this ruling, with the judges siding 6–4 with the state of Florida. The judges split along the party lines of the president who appointed them, with all of the Republican-appointed judges on that court holding there were no constitutional or statutory violations and all of the Democratic-appointed judges dissenting. The majority wrote, among other things, that the Due Process Clause imposed no obligation on Florida to provide "felons with the *facts* necessary to determine whether they have completed their financial terms of sentence."[16]

Judge Jill Pryor wrote in dissent:

So what we know is that Florida imposes substantial, often exorbitant, financial obligations on people convicted of felonies—the overwhelming majority of whom are indigent—with no exceptions for those unable to pay. The State doesn't track [amounts due] and has no mechanism for providing people seeking to register under Amendment 4 with notice of what and how much, if anything, they owe. Florida doesn't seriously deny this. Instead, it responds that it's just too bad if people can't figure out on their own how much they owe, because the State has no obligation to tell them whether they're eligible to vote . . . or how much they would need to pay to get the right to vote back. And here's the kicker: people aren't entitled to know how much they

owe, Florida says, because they couldn't afford to pay it any-
way. No harm, no foul . . . this cavalier attitude is hard to believe, yet there it is in the record of this case for all to see.[17]

Thanks in part to the legislature's action and confusion, by
2020, only 67,000 former Florida felons had been registered to
vote, a small fraction of the estimated 1.4 million Floridians disenfranchised because of a prior felony conviction. The *New
York Times* estimated that at least three-quarters of former Florida felons owe a court debt, and between 70 and 80 percent are
indigent and unable to pay.[18]

Tony Patterson, arrested in Tampa, had a somewhat different
problem from those who had completed their sentences but did
not know if they owed any fees. He had a sex-crime-related
felony conviction. Amendment 4 did not automatically reenfranchise those convicted of sex-related crimes or homicides,
although that fact did not appear to be widely known. Felons
with these convictions had to instead go through the old
process of requesting restoration of rights from the governor.
Patterson apparently did not know this, and local election officials who sent him a voter ID card and registered him to vote
in the 2020 elections apparently did not realize Patterson was
still ineligible to vote.[19]

It all amounted to a lot of confusion for both former felons
and election officials. Prosecutors, having to prove that Patterson intentionally committed the voting crime, dropped the
charges after receiving some undisclosed information from local
election officials. Likely they figured that election officials, by
giving Patterson a voter ID and registering him to vote, had
made him reasonably think that he was allowed to vote. Patterson could have gotten up to five years in jail had the charges gone
forward. Two other ineligible felons caught by Florida's election

crime squad pleaded guilty and were sentenced to probation after the evidence showed that both had contacted election officials and were wrongly assured they were eligible to vote.[20]

Meanwhile, the publicity surrounding the arrests and DeSantis's election police reverberated beyond Florida. The Marshall Project reported that DeSantis's activity deterred voting in other states where former felons had had their voting rights restored. For example, Iris Gray was "convicted of fraudulent use of a debit or credit card, a Class C felony in Alabama. When Gray first heard about the news of the arrests in Florida, she couldn't bring herself to watch the videos. Though she is legally eligible to vote in Alabama, and officially registered, she does not plan to vote in the midterms. 'No, ma'am,' she told The Marshall Project in a phone interview. 'I'm not gonna vote.'"[21]

The confusion seemed intentional. If you were a former felon, why take the chance and register to vote? The logical conclusion is that the Republican-dominated Florida legislature and Republican governor Ron DeSantis were doing what they could to make it harder for former felons to register and vote, despite widespread public support for felon reenfranchisement. The Republican lawmakers probably feared that many of these former felons would vote for Democrats, especially given racial disparities in incarceration and support among people of color for Democrats. Early data about former felons who successfully registered to vote indicated that about 52 percent registered as Democrats, 22 percent as Republicans, and 25 percent without a party affiliation.[22]

☑ ☑ ☑

Felons have historically been disenfranchised in many American states, and efforts to get the courts to hold such disenfranchisement unconstitutional have so far been unsuccessful.

In the 1973 case *Richardson v. Ramirez*, the Supreme Court ruled that disenfranchising felons did not violate the Equal Protection Clause of the Fourteenth Amendment. The court held it permissible to disenfranchise felons because section 2 of the Fourteenth Amendment, which penalizes states in congressional representation when they disenfranchise some male voters, did not apply when those states disenfranchised felons. From this failure to penalize states for disenfranchising felons, the court inferred that the Equal Protection Clause did not protect felons from disenfranchisement. In later cases, the court held that felon disenfranchisement laws that states enacted for intentionally racially discriminatory reasons (such as by targeting crimes more likely to be committed by African Americans) could be found unconstitutional. But that holding knocks out only a small subset of laws disenfranchising felons, in part because proving discriminatory intent is hard.[23]

Lower court cases later rejected the argument that the Voting Rights Act required felon reenfranchisement, with some courts holding that if the federal statute actually did that, it would unconstitutionally exceed Congress's powers. And although voting rights legislation unsuccessfully put forward by Democrats in 2021 in the "For the People Act" would have restored some felon voting rights, it is doubtful that the current conservative Supreme Court would hold that Congress has the power to do so under its powers to enforce the fourteenth and fifteenth amendments.[24]

A new constitutional amendment could moot these problems. It would not matter whether existing constitutional provisions or federal statutes implicitly prohibit felon disenfranchisement; a new constitutional right to vote could explicitly enshrine felon reenfranchisement in the constitution. "Addition 1" in the appendix includes language as part of the proposed amendment. Given the recent experience with Florida's Amendment

4, the provision explicitly excludes the payments of fines and fees from requirements for reenfranchisement.

I must admit my thinking on this question has changed. My earlier view was that including felon reenfranchisement in a constitutional amendment was unnecessary because states were already moving in that direction; just since 2016, twenty states eased their rules on felon disenfranchisement. According to the National Conference of State Legislatures, two states and Washington, D.C., do not disenfranchise felons even while incarcerated; twenty-one states restore voting rights upon a felon's release; and sixteen more states restore rights sometime after parole or probation. Only in eleven states are there indefinite bans or greater restrictions on voting rights restoration.[25]

There is much to be said for letting the process play out in the states, and for building support for felon reenfranchisement on the local and state level before pushing for national change. Adding felon reenfranchisement into the broader constitutional right to vote also could be controversial and make the overall measure harder to pass.

But the events in Florida have convinced me that not all states can be trusted to do the right thing, even when the people of the state favor reenfranchisement. The relentless effort to quash reenfranchisement because of how former felons might vote goes against the norms of political equality discussed in chapter 2. Putting aside the strategic considerations, it now makes sense to place the reenfranchisement of felons within a constitutional right-to-vote amendment.

One can support the reenfranchisement of felons without expanding the franchise to others who are regularly excluded from voting in federal elections: noncitizens, nonresidents, children under the age of eighteen, and those so lacking in mental capacity that they cannot make rational decisions. These limitations, but not felon disenfranchisement, are common across countries and accepted in international law, and the reasons for leaving these groups disenfranchised are not pernicious ones related to how these voters might vote.

In the end, in defining the community of political equals, it makes sense to expand the vote to felons (who have completed their sentences) in order to reintegrate them into society and treat them as political equals once again.

☑   ☑   ☑

"Puerto Rico is one of the most corrupt places on earth. Their political system is broken and their politicians are either Incompetent or Corrupt. Congress approved Billions of Dollars last time, more than anyplace else has ever gotten, and it is sent to Crooked Pols. No good! [. . .] And by the way, I'm the best thing that's ever happened to Puerto Rico!"[26]

To use CNBC's term, President Donald J. Trump was using Twitter to "unload" on Puerto Rico in August 2019, just as Tropical Storm Dorian was approaching the island. The storm was the latest threat to Puerto Rico, which is a so-called unincorporated territory of the United States.[27]

Trump had been severely criticized for the federal government's response to Hurricane Maria, a Category 5 storm that pummeled Puerto Rico in September 2017. That storm was responsible for almost three thousand deaths, and it left much of the island without electricity for months. Maria led to a desperate humanitarian crisis that never would have been tolerated if it took place in one of the fifty states. The former president even denied that many people died, falsely saying the number of dead had been made up by the Democrats.[28]

Puerto Rico has no senators, no voting member of the House of Representatives, and no votes for president in the Electoral College. Given this lack of representation, it was unsurprising that the federal response was slow, or that Trump, known for his outrageous comments generally, could unleash his wrath on the people of Puerto Rico with no real consequences. Aides later said that Trump raised the idea of selling or "divesting" Puerto Rico after Maria's devastation. According to Miles Taylor, a former chief of staff with the Department of Homeland Security, Trump asked about swapping Greenland for Puerto Rico "because, in [Trump's] words, Puerto Rico was dirty and its people were poor."[29]

Puerto Rico is not alone in being populated with U.S. citizens who have no right to vote for president, senators, or members of the House. That status also includes residents of Guam, the Northern Mariana Islands, and the U.S. Virgin Islands. And, on the U.S. mainland, residents of Washington, D.C., have no senators or a voting member of Congress, even though their neighbors in Maryland and Virginia have both forms of representation. D.C. residents only received the right to vote for president in the 1960s thanks to the passage of the Twenty-Third Amendment.[30]

The situation in American Samoa is even worse; residents there are denied the right to vote for president, senator, and representative while in the territory and are considered "noncitizen United States nationals" lacking the "birthright citizenship" to which all other people born on American soil are entitled. When a resident of Puerto Rico, or of any of the other territories aside from American Samoa, moves to Florida, she can vote in all elections while a Florida resident. But when a resident of American Samoa moves to Florida, she is not entitled to vote because she does not have U.S. citizenship entitling her to register to vote.

Many of the territories have very high poverty rates. According to a 2021 op-ed by Karl Racine, the attorney general for Washington, D.C., and Leevin Camacho, the attorney general for Guam, in the fifty states "the national poverty rate hovers around 11.4%. At the state level, the poverty rates of the neediest states—Louisiana and Mississippi—are around 19%, according to the U.S. Census Bureau Dashboard." In contrast, "nearly 23% of Guamanians live in poverty, according to the 2019 Guam Statistical Yearbook. And in Puerto Rico and American Samoa, the poverty rates are 43.5% and nearly 60%, respectively." Increased representation for people living in these territories could vastly improve their standard of living.[31]

Racine and Camacho were writing shortly before oral arguments in a Supreme Court case called *United States v. Vaello Madero*. At issue was whether residents of Puerto Rico have a constitutional right to Supplemental Security Income (SSI), or disability payments, if they would be entitled to such payments while living in one of the fifty states. José Luis Vaello Madero moved from New York to Puerto Rico in 2013. As Justice Brett Kavanaugh explained in the court's 2022 opinion, "While he lived in New York, Vaello Madero received Supplemental Security Income benefits. After moving to Puerto Rico, Vaello Madero no longer was eligible for Supplemental Security Income benefits. Yet for several years, the U.S. Government remained unaware of Vaello Madero's new residence and continued to pay him benefits. The overpayment totaled more than $28,000." When the government tried to recoup the money, Vaello Madero resisted, arguing that denying him these benefits violated his right to equal protection under the Fourteenth Amendment.[32]

Justice Kavanaugh, in an 8–1 decision for the court, wrote that U.S. territories such as Puerto Rico both receive different federal benefits and also have different federal obligations (such as no obligation to pay federal income, estate, or gift taxes). Relying on a series of Supreme Court precedents, he concluded that the question of entitlement to these benefits was one left to Congress's discretion. Justice Sonia Sotomayor, whose parents were born in Puerto Rico, issued a lone dissent. She argued that denying SSI benefits to Puerto Rico residents lacked a rational basis required under federal law.[33]

Justice Neil Gorsuch issued a blistering concurring opinion. Although agreeing that under existing precedent the government should win, he also urged the Supreme Court in an appropriate case to overturn that set of century-old precedents commonly known as "the Insular Cases" that justified treating those born in American territories as second-class citizens (or in the case of American Samoa, not even citizens at all).[34] He wrote that the Insular Cases were based upon racist assumptions about the supposed inferiority of "alien races," and he argued that they rested on a "rotten foundation" unmoored to the text of the constitution. Justice Sotomayor agreed, writing in her dissent that the Insular Cases "were premised on beliefs both odious and wrong."[35]

It did not take long before an opportunity to review these cases arose. John Fitisemanu, born in American Samoa, moved and established residency in Utah. He was denied the right to register to vote in Utah as a "noncitizen national." The district court held that denying Fitisemanu the right to vote was unconstitutional, but the U.S. Court of Appeals for the Tenth Circuit reversed, finding itself bound by the Insular Cases. In a Supreme Court filing, Fitisemanu and his co-plaintiffs explicitly asked the court to consider overruling the Insular Cases. Both the Biden administration and the government of American Samoa opposed the petition.[36]

The Supreme Court in 2022 declined to hear the case, with no noted dissents. It takes four justices to agree to hear the case, so even if Justices Gorsuch and Sotomayor wished to hear it, they needed at least two more justices to agree. Also, they likely would not have wanted the court to take the case unless they knew there were at least three more justices willing to reverse the lower court. The denial of Fitisemanu's suit suggests we should not expect action on this issue any time soon by the Supreme Court.[37]

In a modern democracy that generally allows resident, adult, citizen, nonfelons to vote, the treatment of Americans in the U.S. territories is anomalous and an unjustified relic of a colonialist past. Either those born in a territory that is part of the United States should be citizens of the United States with all the rights and privileges of citizenship or they should not be citizens at all; the second-class status that the Supreme Court has long recognized is justified by neither constitutional text nor modern views of democratic theory.

Although the general reasons for treating these Americans as political equals is clear, figuring out how to put that into practice is not. To begin with, not everyone living in American territories wants to be treated as fully part of the United States. The government of American Samoa opposed Mr. Fitisemanu's lawsuit, and some Samoans do not want birthright citizenship, claiming that the legal change would upset the kind of communal land ownership arrangements that are legal under local law but that could be found to be race-based and in violation of the U.S. Constitution. A prerequisite to any change in legal status should be a fair voter referendum on status, one that would give options to gain equal rights, establish independence, or keep the status quo. If the people living in these territories want full citizenship and voting rights, the rest of us in the United States should find a way to make it happen.[38]

Perhaps surprisingly, for voting rights in Washington, D.C., and in Puerto Rico, a constitutional amendment establishing voting rights is unnecessary. Congress has the power to admit both areas as states into the United States, creating the fifty-first and fifty-second states. Assuming the residents of these areas want it, this change would entitle each area to congressional representation and two senators. Puerto Rico would also get Electoral College votes to help choose the president, a right D.C. already gained through the passage of the Twenty-Third Amendment. In 2020, 52 percent of Puerto Rico voters supported statehood in an advisory plebiscite, although some criticized the plebiscite's wording as unfair.[39]

Democrats have discussed statehood for both areas. Although statehood for Washington, D.C., has been supported mostly by Democrats, sixteen Republicans joined with 217 Democrats in 2022 in passing a bill that would give the people of Puerto Rico the chance to weigh in on whether to become a state. While there is little question that Washington, D.C., would be a safe Democratic state in the near term, the political valence of Puerto Rico is harder to gauge. Some have suggested that given the island's politics and culture, it could well be a Republican or swing state. A 2020 *Politico* article noted that "both major islandwide elected officials in Puerto Rico are registered Republicans, as is the sitting governor, who was installed by the island's Supreme Court. Puerto Rico's Legislature, which has made a mark in recent years by enacting conservative laws including restrictions on abortion and on expressions of gender identity, is led by registered Republicans in both its House and

Senate." Today, Puerto Rico's governor is a Democrat, but its nonvoting delegate in Congress is Republican.[40]

For the other American territories, it is not clear that they are large enough that Congress would seriously consider granting statehood (with populations ranging from a bit over 50,000 to a bit over 100,000 residents each); perhaps some other form of representation on the national level makes sense. But at the very least a constitutional right-to-vote amendment can assure that when those residents are living in a state, they can register to vote in those state elections. One possibility is to allow residents of American territories to vote for president, with their votes counted along with votes cast by voters in Washington, D.C. Further, if the Electoral College vote is abolished, as discussed below, to be replaced with choosing the president through a national popular vote, then otherwise eligible voters living in these territories should have the right to vote for president. See the variations in "Addition 2" in the appendix.[41]

☑ ☑ ☑

Sometimes political inequality in voting comes not in who votes, but in how those votes are weighed and counted. Nothing is more unequal in the weighting of votes in the United States than the Electoral College system for choosing the president and the equal state rules for the U.S. Senate.

Joe Biden received over seven million more votes than Donald Trump in the 2020 presidential election. But U.S. presidents are not chosen by a national popular vote. Instead, they are chosen through the Electoral College mechanism that assigns each state a number of votes based upon the number of representatives that they have in the House of Representatives plus the state's two senators. Under this state-by-state voting system, there were 538 votes up for grabs, and Biden beat Trump 306–232.[42]

That may sound like a blowout, but looking closer shows that Trump could have won the Electoral College vote with just a small shift of votes in a few swing states. A Pew Research Center analysis found that "Biden won Pennsylvania by just 1.2 percentage points, Wisconsin by six-tenths of a percentage point, Arizona by about a third of a percentage point, and Georgia by a quarter of a percentage point. In those four states combined, Biden beat incumbent President Donald Trump by fewer than 125,000 votes out of 18.5 million total votes cast." Or, to put it another way, Trump would have been reelected president if he would have gotten just 10,458 more votes in Arizona, 11,780 more votes in Georgia, 80,555 more votes in Pennsylvania, and 20,683 more votes in Wisconsin. This, in a country that cast over 158 million votes. (Trump's win in 2016 over Hillary Clinton also was exceedingly narrow.)[43]

Now we do not know if Biden would have beaten Trump by over seven million votes—or indeed beaten Trump at all—if the contest between the two of them were for the national popular vote. Campaigning strategies would have been different. Biden would have spent time racking up votes in Democratic-heavy California and New York rather than ignoring those states as safe wins where he easily captured California's fifty-five and New York's twenty-nine Electoral College votes. Trump would have concentrated more on Florida and Texas, where he was able to count on Florida's twenty-nine and Texas's thirty-eight Electoral College votes.

But the current system does show that it is possible for a candidate to be supported by millions more Americans and still lose an election thanks to the state-by-state contests in the

Electoral College. Indeed, as historian Alex Keyssar notes, this "has happened five times in our history, most recently in 2016, and it has come close to happening on numerous other occasions, including 2004." It is a system that benefits small states, which get disproportionate power. "In 2016, for example," Keyssar writes, "Wyoming cast one electoral vote for every 190,000 residents; in California, an electoral vote represented 680,000 people." Swing states also get the lion's share of attention from presidential candidates.[44]

It is emphatically not a system that mirrors the one-person, one-vote ethic of modern political life that has permeated the rest of the American political system since the Warren Court adopted that standard in the 1960s. It is instead one that focuses heavily on the rights of states, as states, rather than the equality of the people living in all of them.

Fortunately, I need not spend much more time here spelling out the fundamental inequalities of the Electoral College and why it has nonetheless endured despite its unpopularity. That case has been made carefully and persuasively many times, most recently by Keyssar in his 2020 book, *Why Do We Still Have the Electoral College?*, and by *New York Times* editorial writer Jesse Wegman, in his 2020 book, *Let the People Pick the President: The Case for Abolishing the Electoral College*.[45]

Keyssar focuses on the puzzle of why the Electoral College has endured despite its unpopularity over time. His answer is multifaceted, but it begins by explaining the difficulties of amending the constitution. Wegman contrasts two competing narratives of the Electoral College's role in U.S. politics. The conservative narrative, supporting the Electoral College, says that the founding fathers "got it mostly right" in designing an Electoral College system that "channel[ed] and constrain[ed] the people's voice in order to prevent a tyrannical majority from trampling the rights of minorities." The liberal narrative, opposing the Electoral College, "emphasizes the egalitarian ideal at the heart of the Declaration of Independence. We are all created equal, and we should govern ourselves that way." Pointing to the multiple amendments to the constitution expanding voting rights and the Warren Court's one-person, one-vote cases, Wegman declares that the liberal narrative, "by and large, has won out."[46]

Perhaps. But proposals to eliminate the Electoral College have not garnered bipartisan support; far from it. Given that in recent decades it has been Democratic candidates who have mostly won the popular vote (and sometimes lost the Electoral College vote), support for reforming the Electoral College these days is undoubtedly lopsided favoring Democrats.

Current Republican opposition to Electoral College reform is strong. When Republican U.S. Senator Rand Paul of Kentucky wrote an op-ed in his local newspaper arguing in favor of fixing the Electoral Count Act—an 1887 law that Donald Trump tried to exploit to subvert the results of the 2020 U.S. presidential election (more about that in chapter 5)—he argued that the fixes would help to preserve the Electoral College: "The Electoral College is emblematic of the benefits of federalism. The United States is a continental nation that includes multiple cultures, values and points of view. An individual cannot win the presidency by merely pandering to coastal population centers." He added: "The Electoral College guarantees that a president can only be elected (and re-elected) by appealing to a broad base of Americans. In short, the Electoral College is the Founders' answer to a potential tyranny of the majority."[47]

Including Electoral College reform within a constitutional right-to-vote amendment would make the measure considerably less likely to pass, and for this reason it probably should be kept out of an amendment and pursued separately. If it were to be included in the right-to-vote amendment, I include language in "Addition 3" to do so in the appendix.

As the next two chapters show, ending the Electoral College system would also have the benefit of decreasing election litigation and making election subversion harder. It is undoubtedly worthy of change as a matter of principle.[48]

The requirement that each state, regardless of population, be awarded two senators in the Senate is the other feature of the political system in the United States that violates the one-person, one-vote principle. Political scientist Jonathan Ladd believes that the Senate presents a bigger political inequality problem than the Electoral College: "The Electoral College is a constitutional nuisance that created big problems in 2000 and 2016 but poses fewer problems in the long run, even as it is now. . . . In contrast, the Senate is a massive democratic problem with no plausible solution within our constitutional framework." Here, Ladd is alluding to the fact that the constitution itself seems to prohibit changing the rules on composition of the Senate. Article V of the constitution provides that, in considering amendments to the constitution, "no state, without its consent, shall be deprived of its equal suffrage in the Senate." This means that perhaps the United States would have to ratify *two* constitutional amendments to abolish the Senate: one eliminating the rule on no amendments and the second actually amending the Senate rules. See "Addition 4" in the appendix.[49]

Ladd points out the inequality problems with the Senate. "California's 39 million people get two senators in Washington, while two Senators also represent states like Wyoming (578,000 people), Vermont (626,000 people), and Alaska (737,000 people). In 2013, the *New York Times* pointed out that the six senators from California, Texas, and New York represented the same number of people as the 62 senators from the smallest 31 states. (Florida has since passed New York to be the third-biggest state, but the pattern persists.)" He further notes that those people in states underrepresented in the Senate tend to be those with larger nonwhite populations: "The 10 biggest states (by 2018 Census estimates) all have nontrivial percentages of nonwhite voters, while the 10 smallest states mostly consist of rural, overwhelmingly white states."[50]

☑ ☑ ☑

There's no getting around it: two of the biggest political inequalities in the United States—the Electoral College and the Senate—have a great impact on public policy and do not reflect the will of the people. They would be clearly unconstitutional under current interpretations of the Equal Protection Clause if they were not expressly stated in the constitution. But they are perhaps the hardest parts of the constitution to change.

But hope is not lost. Enacting the basic version of a constitutional right to vote, or one that includes additional voting rights for former felons and U.S. residents, will improve political equality in the United States. And that improved situation could then set the stage for further reforms of the Electoral College and the Senate. It may be that not everything can be changed at once, but movement in the right direction could support further reform.

Chapter 4

DEESCALATING THE VOTING WARS

Voting during the 2020 election season that coincided with the COVID-19 pandemic was not easy for many people, but the burdens fell far more heavily on some classes of voters, such as some Native Americans living on reservations, than on others. The burden led to a flurry of lawsuits between those seeking to promote voting rights and those seeking to protect state prerogatives to keep registration and voting difficult for some of our most vulnerable citizens. The litigation cycles seemed endless.

In 2020, vaccines and therapeutics to lessen the effects of COVID-19 were still in their development and testing stages, and health authorities advised limiting face-to-face contact to deal with the airborne virus. Some primary elections were delayed, poll workers often worked behind plexiglass shields, and voters spread at least six feet apart to limit virus transmission. Getting poll workers to show up for work shifts was not easy, especially during some primaries that coincided with localized surges in infection.[1]

In this difficult public health atmosphere, many people sensibly preferred voting by mail rather than in-person. But states had their own rules for voting by mail, and some states made doing so harder than others. In Texas, only those voters over the age of sixty-five, out of the state for reasons like military service, or suffering from a disability that made getting to the polling place difficult were able to vote by mail. Courts in Texas ruled that fear of contracting the virus did not count as a disability, forcing many people to vote in person if they wanted to vote at all.[2]

Texas was an outlier, however, and many states did ease the rules for voting by mail during the pandemic. Some states, such as Nevada, even mailed ballots to every active, registered voter during the 2020 general election, eliminating the burden of applying for a mail-in ballot. These practices led to unsubstantiated claims of voter fraud from President Donald J. Trump, running for reelection, who called the plan an "illegal . . . coup." This was just one of his false claims about mail-in voting, a centerpiece of his conspiracy theories of a "rigged" election.[3]

What could be easier than getting a ballot in the mail and popping it back into a nearby mailbox, leaving it for collection by the local mail carrier, or dropping it at a dedicated ballot drop box? This change to mail-in voting during the pandemic made voting easier than it had ever been for many people.

But for some voters on Native American reservations, things were not so easy. To begin with, there were significant barriers to voter registration, and unregistered people did not get ballots mailed to them. According to a 2020 report by the Native American Rights Fund, "Voters surveyed from the Duck Valley, Pyramid Lake, Walker River and Yerington Tribes in Nevada identified travel distance as 'the single biggest obstacle to registering. Among those who were registered to vote, 10 percent stated that it was difficult for them to travel to register. Among [those] . . . not registered, a whopping 34 percent said that it would be difficult for them to travel to a place to register . . . " For voters in Nye County, Nevada, "The closest elections office is in Tonopah, 140 miles each way by road from the Duckwater Reservation. The Pahrump elections office is 303 miles each way by road. Travel time is at least five hours or ten hours, respectively, if the weather conditions permit." Polling places for in-person voting can also be very far away, without any available transportation.[4]

Registering for the first time by mail was possible, but in some circumstances required including a photocopy of valid identification, and photocopy machines were not easily accessible on all reservations. Even postal services were sometimes many miles away. There is no mail delivery on some reservations, with voters instead using post office boxes far from home. Some states will not send ballots to a post office box, and even when they do, things get complicated when post office boxes are in different counties or states, or when multiple families share the same post office box.[5]

Part of the reason for reliance on post office boxes is not just the lack of regular mail service but also the common lack of standard residential addresses. The lack of addresses stemmed in part from the lack of basic services, like paved roads, in many of these reservations. As the PBS News Hour explained, "For many Native Americans living on tribal reservations, a home address is not a standard number and street name, like 735 Bleeker Street. Instead, it's a series of instructions. 'They'll say something like, I live off highway 86 by milepost 125 and a half,' said Gabriella Cázares-Kelly, a member of the Tohono O'odham Nation and a Democratic candidate for Pima County recorder in Arizona."[6]

Unsurprisingly, the burdens of voting fell especially heavily on Native Americans during COVID-19 times. According to a report in *High Country Times*, South Dakota encouraged mail-in balloting for its June 2020 primary in response to the pandemic. "Although the state received almost 89,000 absentee ballots in the primaries—five times the number of absentee ballots cast in the June 2016 primaries—and voting increased across the state, voter turnout on the Pine Ridge Reservation remained low, at approximately 10%." Part of the reason for the low turnout on the reservation was the state's voter identification requirement: "During South Dakota's 2020 primary election, any voter who used an absentee ballot was required to mail in a ballot application accompanied by a photocopy of an acceptable photo ID card, or else have a public officer notarize the application. For people on the Pine Ridge Reservation, where businesses are often few and far between, producing a photocopy, or even finding a notary public, can pose significant barriers to applying for absentee ballots."[7]

To anyone following Native American voting rights, the disparate impact of COVID-19 was unsurprising. The Supreme Court in 1884 held that Native Americans were not entitled to the protection of the fourteenth and fifteenth amendments; they were not even conferred U.S. citizenship by Congress until the Snyder Act of 1924. Even in the best of times, securing voting rights for this population has proven exceptionally challenging. Recent testimony before a Senate Judiciary Committee subcommittee from Jacqueline De León of the Native American Rights Fund revealed significant acts of intentional racial discrimination against Native Americans. She offered examples of Native voters in South Dakota being forced to vote in a "repurposed chicken coop with no bathroom facilities and feathers on the floor." Professor Jean Schroedel, writing in her 2020 book, *Voting in Indian Country: The View from the Trenches*, observed that some of the stories of voter suppression and dilution in Indian country sounded like "they had come out of the

Deep South of the 1950s as opposed to Obama's America." She explained the motivation for examining Native American voting rights: "I became convinced that what happens in Indian Country is crucial to determining whether 'the arc of the moral universe' in the United States does indeed bend 'towards justice.' If there is no justice for those descended from the nation's original inhabitants, how can one claim there is justice for anyone else?"[8]

☑   ☑   ☑

A constitutional amendment guaranteeing the right to vote can do more than bring justice for Native American voters, although that itself is absolutely crucial. It can also lessen the chances of fraud and decrease the amount of election-related litigation. This deescalation of the voting wars is in everyone's interest.

A longstanding controversy over Native American voting rights in North Dakota shows how a constitutional right-to-vote amendment would have made things better, both in limiting disenfranchisement and in bolstering election integrity. The specificity and breadth of the basic constitutional amendment can lower the overall amount of election litigation in cases such as the fight over North Dakota voting rights. The amendment would require courts to carefully to balance the risks of fraud or other government interests with the right to vote protected by the amendment, with a thumb on the scale favoring voters.

☑   ☑   ☑

North Dakota was an increasingly red state, but in 2012 Democrat Heidi Heitkamp squeaked through to reelection to the U.S. Senate by only about three thousand votes. Heitkamp drew a great deal of support from Native American voters, who made up about 5 percent of the voting population in the state and whose voting preferences skewed Democratic.[9]

Soon after Heitkamp's 2012 victory, Republicans in the state legislature adopted a strict voter identification law. North Dakota is the only state that does not require voter registration; it requires voters only to adequately identify themselves as eligible North Dakota residents. Before 2012, a local election official could vouch for a voter lacking identification or the voter could sign an affidavit confirming the voter's identity. The 2012 voter identification measure passed, mostly along party lines, using a "hoghouse amendment" process that expedited legislative procedures and stifled debate.[10]

As Matthew Campbell of the Native American Rights Fund put it, "Integral to the new voter ID law was the requirement that an ID have a residential address, when the legislature was aware that many homes on reservations in North Dakota lacked residential addresses. Given the high levels of poverty for Native Americans in North Dakota, the lack of access to transportation, the cost of an ID, and the distance to travel to obtain a state ID, it was no wonder that the law had a discriminatory effect." Among other things, "the law did not allow the use of P.O. boxes to verify a voter's residency, even though lawmakers knew that many Native Americans (as well as other citizens) relied upon P.O. boxes."[11]

In 2015, the state made the law even stricter by removing the authority of the secretary of state to prescribe new acceptable forms of identification and barring the use of college IDs by students for voting.[12]

Native voters sued North Dakota under the Voting Rights Act and under the U.S. and North Dakota constitutions. In 2016, a federal district court found that the law likely violated the equal protection rights of Native voters guaranteed by the Fourteenth Amendment and temporarily barred its enforcement. The court found, among other things, that Native residents were about twice as likely to lack the right form of identification as non-Native residents, and that on average they had to travel about twice as far as non-Native residents to get to a driver's license office to obtain identification. As the court explained: "The undisputed evidence before the Court reveals that Native Americans face substantial and disproportionate burdens in obtaining each form of ID deemed acceptable under the new law."[13]

The district court held that even under the U.S. Supreme Court's 2008 opinion in the *Crawford* case, which upheld Indiana's strict voter identification law without requiring Indiana to produce any evidence that the law deters fraud, the North Dakota law was unconstitutional under the Fourteenth Amendment's Equal Protection Clause. The court found the law imposed a severe burden on Native American voters and found that "[t]here is a total lack of any evidence to show voter fraud has ever been a problem in North Dakota." It restored the use of affidavits or election official vouching to verify identity during the 2016 election. Thousands of Native American voters used these less burdensome methods to vote in North Dakota that year.[14]

North Dakota did not appeal the ruling. Instead, the North Dakota legislature adopted a new, although very similar, version of its voter identification law in 2017, and it sought permission from the district court to enforce it. Native voters sought a new injunction. The trial court partially enjoined the revamped law. Among other things, the court's order prevented use of the "current residential address" standard and required the state to accept tribal identifications.[15]

The U.S. Court of Appeals for the Eighth Circuit reversed the district court's grant of emergency relief, on a 2–1 vote, with the judges dividing along the party lines of the president who appointed them. The Republican-appointed majority relied upon the Supreme Court's decision in *Crawford* upholding Indiana's voter identification law, even absent evidence the law was necessary to prevent fraud.[16]

Writing in dissent, Judge Jane Kelly, the sole Democrat-appointed judge on the entire Eighth Circuit, noted the extent of the burden of the current residential address requirement: "The court does not dispute that the district court concluded (based on unrebutted evidence) that at least 69,616 eligible voters—including 4,998 Native Americans—currently lack the identification required to vote. That group comprises nearly twenty percent of the total number of individuals who vote in a regular quadrennial election in North Dakota. And the district court further found that roughly half of eligible Native American voters lack proper supplemental documentation, such that 'at least 2,305 Native Americans will not be able to vote in 2018 under the new law.'"[17]

Plaintiffs tried to get the U.S. Supreme Court involved on an emergency basis, but the court refused. Justice Ruth Bader Ginsburg, dissenting for herself and Justice Elena Kagan, cited a "severe" "risk of voter confusion" and stated that "the risk of disfranchisement is large."[18]

A different set of Native voters brought yet another lawsuit, this one filed just a few days before the 2018 elections, which the district court rejected as coming too late. Faced with no prospect for judicial relief before the impending election, the tribes and their allies sprang into action, with volunteers rushing to issue new tribal identifications with residential addresses that could be used for voting. The effort got about two thousand new identifications into the hands of Native voters just days before the 2018 election.[19]

This back-and-forth is common when states pass laws that suppress the vote. The suppressive law fuels a counterreaction that helps to assure that at least some people affected by the law can still vote. This may explain why sometimes there are not great adverse turnout effects from these laws. These laws are still pernicious even if they affect too few people to change election outcomes, because they often require Herculean efforts to help people vote by overcoming obstacles put in their way for no valid reason. The question should always be why the state saw a need to put unnecessary barriers in front of voters, not whether they will lead to different election outcomes. Courts taking voting rights seriously would protect the dignitary right of each voter to vote.

In 2019, the same Eighth Circuit panel again divided 2–1, siding with North Dakota in the latest lawsuit over these voting rules. Then, in 2020, as one of the cases brought by Native voters over voter identification was about to go to trial, the tribes settled with the state of North Dakota, agreeing to a consent decree that would require the state to accept certain forms of tribal identification for voting. It was a long and difficult struggle.[20]

☑ ☑ ☑

Imagine how different the controversy between the state of North Dakota and its Native American residents would have looked, how much more protection these voters would have received, and how much more secure elections would have been, had the basic version of the constitutional right to vote amendment been in place.

North Dakota would not have had to implement a voter registration requirement under the proposed amendment, but whether or not it did so, either North Dakota or the federal government would have had to undertake the task of identifying every eligible voter in the state and assigning that person a unique voter identification number. New numbers also would have been assigned to North Dakota residents upon turning eighteen, becoming citizens, or otherwise becoming eligible to vote. For voters moving into North Dakota from elsewhere, the voter identification number would have been assigned by another state or the federal government. In short, a state or the federal government would have assumed the burden of registering (or, in North Dakota's case, at least identifying) every eligible voter, including bearing all of the costs of verifying identity, such as the costs for obtaining a birth certificate.

This process would have established a person's identity for purposes of voting, but North Dakota could still have required proof of residency in the state to show voter eligibility. In doing so, North Dakota still would not have been able to pass a law that had the effect of treating some class of voters worse than others or unduly burdening the right to vote for no good reason. Additionally, the state would have been prohibited from discriminating against a group of voters on the basis of race, ethnicity, or membership in a distinctive minority group.

If North Dakota wished to impose a strict identification requirement to confirm residency and that requirement were challenged in court, the state would have had the burden of demonstrating with actual evidence that it faced a real problem with nonresidents voting in North Dakota, and that its identification requirement was a reasonably necessary means of deterring that fraud. Among other things, the state would have had to show that this kind of system deterred appreciably more fraud than systems the state had previously used in which voters could sign affidavits under penalty of perjury identifying themselves and confirming their residency or rely upon election officials to vouch for their identity. The state also would have to show that the requirement would not have a racially discriminatory effect on protected Native American voters.

Under all these pro-voter rules contained in the constitutional right to vote amendment, North Dakota would have been hard-pressed to justify the law it enacted and unlikely to have had a court uphold it. Gone would have been the pass on providing evidence that the Supreme Court's *Crawford* opinion currently gives to states seeking to justify their restrictive voting rules. Likely the state would not have enacted the law it did without at least including a backup provision, such as an affidavit alternative assuring the ability to vote for voters lacking a residential address.

Any state truly concerned with deterring fraud would be able to take great comfort in the identification requirement imposed by the amendment. Mandating identification and coupling it with automatic voter registration would lead to a more secure system that would deter fraud. It could also bolster the confidence of anyone concerned about the security of the system. With the amendment in place, courts would have much less discretion to allow restrictive voting laws to remain in effect.

☑ ☑ ☑

More generally, the constitutional right-to-vote amendment would lower the amount of election-related litigation. Election litigation has grown steadily since the disputed 2000 election in Florida that culminated in the Supreme Court's decision in *Bush v. Gore*. Rates of litigation have nearly tripled in the

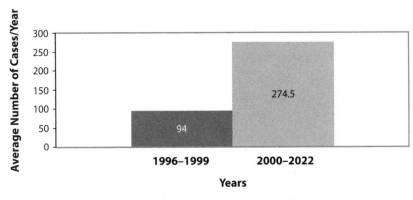

FIGURE 1. Sample of Election Litigation, Before and After Disputed 2000 Election. *Source*: Author research; underlying data posted at https://electionlawblog.org/wp-content/uploads/Election-Litigation -1996-2022.xlsx [https://perma.cc/RC6M-F5SY].

period since that decision compared to the period before it, averaging about ninety-four cases in my sample of cases in the period before the 2000 election and averaging 274.5 in the period after that election. There are reasons to believe the amount of election litigation will continue to rise, thanks in part to a provision of federal law giving political parties an incentive to raise funds primarily for litigation.[21]

Much of that litigation would disappear or become short and simple with the passage of a constitutional right-to-vote amendment. Disputes over voter registration, voter identification requirements, and the like make up a significant portion of the litigation each year in the sample of cases I regularly collect. With the new amendment, there would no longer be a basis for much of this current litigation.

Gone, too, would be significant litigation over bloated voter rolls and doubly registered voters, litigation that is now often brought by Republicans and conservatives. By assigning each voter a unique identification number, it will be much easier for states to reconcile numbers and assure the accuracy of voter registration records. And all of this can be accomplished without a federal "takeover" of election administration. States could continue to administer their elections within the parameters set by the amendment.[22]

As a whole, the constitutional right-to-vote amendment would deescalate the voting wars by mooting a great deal of litigation over certain types of election rules. It would increase voter access while making the election system more secure. It would also put a thumb on the scale favoring voters in such disputes. Overall litigation rates likely would decrease, and the skirmishes between "armies of lawyers" in the preelection period every four years would be less common and less consequential.

Now Americans are a litigious bunch, and the detail, length, and specificity of even the basic version of my constitutional amendment would leave room to litigate and for courts hostile to voting rights to try to read the rules narrowly. The risk is that judicialization will limit the amendment's scope, as courts have done with earlier voting amendments. As election law scholar Rick Pildes noted, in response to Alex Keyssar's calls after the 2000 election for a right-to-vote amendment, "Once you constitutionalize the issue, you're doing something other than nationalizing it; you're turning over control of that issue to the courts to a significant extent. And if you look at the history of judicial action with respect to the vote and democracy, it's a pretty mixed history."[23]

The specificity of the amendment should blunt many of these concerns by giving courts less discretion to be hostile to voting rights. If the amendment successfully constrains courts, then over time the amendment would render pointless many of the types of lawsuits that have been brought in the past over voting rules. In the event that postamendment courts, despite the clarity of the amendment, begin narrowly reading the undue burden standards and allowing more restrictive voting rules to remain in place, Congress could then exercise its broad enforcement powers under the amendment's final provision to legislate against such restrictive voting rules, without fear of the courts finding enforcement provisions exceeding the permissible scope of Congress's power.

States would learn that there would not be much to gain by further attempts to game election rules. One way or another, after a few years of litigation and potential legislation, there would be much less to litigate over and far more protection for voters across the board.

☑ ☑ ☑

Even with the passage of a constitutional right-to-vote amendment, there would be times when achieving the balance between voter access and election integrity would be difficult. Case in point: the third-party collection of absentee ballots (sometimes pejoratively referred to as "ballot harvesting"). On the one hand, laws against third-party collection of ballots do serve a valid antifraud purpose, given that we have seen, albeit rarely, recent provable instances of election crimes involving absentee ballots. On the other hand, for Native American voters in particular, bans on third-party collection of mail-in ballots can lead to provable instances of voter disenfranchisement. A constitutional amendment still provides a path through these difficult issues.

Fraud committed by illegally collecting, altering, or destroying mailed ballots is rare but has been documented. Most prominently, a ballot collecting scandal came to light in the 2018 elections in Bladen County, North Carolina. There was enough proof that political operatives collected, altered, and destroyed absentee ballots to help a Republican candidate win a U.S. congressional seat that the North Carolina Board of Elections had to order a new election.[24]

Although the activities in Bladen County may be the most prominent recent example of fraud committed with absentee ballots, it is not the only one. Paterson, New Jersey, conducted an all-mail election in 2020 during the COVID-19 pandemic, and there was enough evidence that nine hundred absentee ballots had been tampered with that a court threw out the election results. A Paterson councilman, a councilman-elect, and two others have been charged with election crimes.[25]

In 2021, in Rensselaer County, New York's Republican elections commissioner Jason Schofield pleaded guilty to election crimes premised on a pattern of illegal ballot harvesting over a two-year period. He obtained and filled out the absentee ballots of at least twelve voters without their permission.[26]

These proven cases of fraud could provide a reasonable predicate for states to ban or limit the collection of ballots—and some states, such as North Carolina, have done just that, often with an exception to allow collection by a relative or legal guardian. Other states limit the number of permissible collected ballots—to, for instance, ten in Colorado. Some, like California, allow unlimited collection of such ballots. The relative rarity of fraud unsurprisingly leaves states to take different views on balancing fraud against voter convenience.[27]

For some voters, however, an outright ban on collection of ballots might be less of a mere inconvenience and more of a substantial hardship. Consider a physically disabled person living in an assisted living facility who might need help mailing (and perhaps even filling out) a ballot. Of course, this could be just the sort of atmosphere where people would have their ballots tampered with, and for this reason election officials might provide extra security steps for dealing with ballots returned from such facilities.

The discussion earlier in this chapter shows that some Native American voters living on reservations face special difficulties receiving and returning mail ballots, given the distances that some must go to reach postal facilities and government offices. This issue arose in a major voting rights case the Supreme Court decided in 2021, *Brnovich v. Democratic National Committee*.[28]

The Democratic Party brought *Brnovich* in as a case under section 2 of the Voting Rights Act, challenging two provisions of Arizona law: one rejecting ballots that a voter casts in the wrong voting precinct and the other banning the third-party collection of ballots. ("Precincts" are just geographic areas to which voters are assigned to make sure they receive a ballot that properly reflects all the races in which they are eligible to vote based upon their residential address.) At the time of *Brnovich*, the Supreme Court had not yet weighed in on how section 2 of the Voting Rights Act, which requires states to offer minority voters the same opportunities as other voters "to participate in the political process and to elect representatives of their choice," applied to what have been termed "vote denial" claims.[29]

Vote denial claims are those aimed at state rules for registration or for voting. In contrast, "vote dilution" claims go after redistricting that draws lines that make it harder for minority voters to elect their preferred candidates. The Supreme Court developed standards for addressing vote dilution claims in a 1986 case, *Thornburg v. Gingles*.[30]

Lower courts had imposed a difficult-but-not-impossible standard for bringing a section 2 vote denial claim, and voting rights plaintiffs had some surprising success under it. Indeed, the U.S. Court of Appeals for the Fifth Circuit, arguably the most conservative federal appeals court in the country, had held that Texas violated section 2 when it passed its very strict voter identification law.[31]

Nonetheless, when plaintiffs brought *Brnovich*, I was quite critical. Both a ban on third-party collection of ballots and a refusal to count ballots cast in the wrong precinct were common state laws. Overall, they did not seem to have the kind of major negative effect on minority voting rights as something like Texas's very strict voter identification law.[32]

They say hard cases make bad law, but more to the point in this context, given the conservative Supreme Court's hostility to voting rights laws, it was important to avoid Supreme Court review when reasonably possible and to come to the court with only the best cases and the strongest records. *Brnovich* did not offer that, and Justice Samuel Alito, writing for the conservative court majority, used the court's opinion to reject the section 2 vote-denial claims and also to impose a standard that makes it much harder for minority plaintiffs to win such claims overall. He engaged in a state-friendly reading of section 2 that hurt minority plaintiffs and that was not in line with the Voting Rights Act's text, history, or precedent.[33]

For our purposes, the importance of *Brnovich* lay in how Justice Alito, for the majority, and Justice Elena Kagan, in dissent, differently balanced the burden of the ban on third-party ballot collection for Native American voters in Arizona against the state's interests in preventing fraud and other illegal activities.

Justice Alito began his analysis by stating that having to travel to drop off a ballot or to vote was nothing more than the "usual burdens of voting" for which a section 2 claim ordinarily would not arise, at least under the new hostile standard he created for the case. He noted that the Arizona law allowed certain family members to drop off ballots for others and that Arizona had special provisions for people like those confined by illness to drop off their ballots.

Justice Alito discounted the district court's holding that "minorities generally were more likely than nonminorities to return their early ballots with the assistance of third parties" because plaintiffs did not offer statistical evidence showing the disparity. Just as important, Justice Alito brushed by the finding that there had been no evidence of fraud in connection with the use of early voting in Arizona, pointing instead to general concerns around tampering with absentee ballots, as well as the risk of pressure and intimidation with ballots cast outside the polling place. Note how Justice Alito required minority voters to produce actual, systematic evidence of a burden while allowing the state to rest on allegations of fraud unsupported by any evidence from within the state. Noting the recent controversy in North Carolina, Alito concluded that Arizona need not wait for a similar problem in that state before acting.[34]

The burden on Native American voters in Arizona did not get sustained attention from Justice Alito until a lengthy footnote at the end of his analysis. He took the position that if not enough minority voters are affected by a voting burden, the Voting Rights Act does not forbid the state's conduct, even if some minority voters face great burdens. Responding to the dissent on the question of the lack of adequate postal service on reservations, he reiterated the lack of statistical evidence and called on the U.S. Postal Service to do a better job with mail service on reservations—as opposed to calling on the state to ensure the ease of voting access for vulnerable voters.[35]

Justice Kagan, for the three liberal dissenters, viewed the matter through a very different lens. Rather than relegating the plight of Native American voters to the end of her analysis of the ballot collection ban, she focused on the lack of reliable mail service on reservations and the large distances that some Native voters must travel to use mail service. "Most Arizonans vote by mail. But many rural Native American voters lack access to mail service, to a degree hard for most of us to fathom. Only 18% of Native voters in rural counties receive home mail delivery, compared to 86% of white voters living in those counties. And for many or most, there is no nearby post office. Native Americans in rural Arizona 'often must travel 45 minutes to 2 hours just to get to a mailbox.' And between a quarter to a half of households in these Native communities do not have a car. So getting ballots by mail and sending them back poses a serious challenge for Arizona's rural Native Americans."[36]

Justice Kagan noted the testimony offered from election officials and others in the case that the use of third-party ballot collection on reservations in Arizona was "standard practice" and a prediction by a tribal election official that stopping it "would be a huge devastation." As to the lack of statistical evidence on the use of ballot collection, Justice Kagan blamed the state for not collecting such data (although it is unclear why such data could not have been collected by plaintiffs during the litigation).[37]

As to the state's interest, Justice Kagan noted that tampering with absentee ballots was a crime in Arizona, which deterred fraud more directly than the ban on mere collection of ballots, and in any case there had been no reported cases of ballot tampering in the state. When Arizona first tried to enforce its ban, the Justice Department refused to preclear it under section 5 of the Voting Rights Act. After the Supreme Court killed off preclearance in *Shelby County*, the state revived it while knowing it would have a disparate impact on Native voters.

"The enacted law contains limited exceptions for family members and caregivers. But it includes no similar exceptions for clan members or others with Native kinship ties." She added, "What is an inconsequential burden for others is for these citizens a severe hardship. And the State has shown no need for the law to go so far." She further noted that given large distances and a lack of reliable transportation, in-person polling options were not a viable, easier alternative.[38]

Justice Kagan concluded by responding tartly to Justice Alito's decision to blame the postal service: "The majority's argument . . . is no better than if it condoned a literacy test on the ground that a State had long had a statutory obligation to teach all its citizens to read and write."[39]

How different would this disagreement look with a constitutional right-to-vote amendment in place? The shifting of the burden of proof to justify the state law, and the requirement to prevent unequal burdens on voters, especially minority voters, would make it much more likely that Arizona would write a ballot collection law to serve fraud prevention purposes but still accommodate Native voters. For example, the state could have allowed collection of ballots by those with tribal ties, as Justice Kagan suggested, or allowed a certain number of ballots to be collected per person, as Colorado does. Or the state might have proactively engaged in drives to have election officials collect the ballots or installed convenient drop boxes for the collection of ballots in areas without regular postal service.

A constitutional right-to-vote amendment would not disqualify all state laws aimed at deterring fraud. It certainly would not interfere with laws making tampering with such ballots a crime; there is no constitutionally protected right to mess with someone else's ballot.

Justice Alito was correct in his *Brnovich* majority opinion that for most voters a ban on third-party ballot collection is not a big deal. But for those voters for whom a ban on third-party ballot collection is a serious deterrent to voting, such as some Native American voters living on reservations, the amendment would require reasonable accommodations to deal with both the threat of fraud and the need for meaningfully equal voter access. It can—and should—be done: securing rights, deterring fraud, and promoting confidence in a fair election system, with less litigation all around.

Chapter 5

SAFEGUARDING AMERICAN DEMOCRACY

It was a remarkable day, and not only for the obvious reason that the first Black president of the United States was being sworn into office.

January 20, 2009, saw George W. Bush, a conservative Republican president who assumed the presidency in 2001 after a deeply contested presidential race in Florida, hand over power peacefully to Barack Obama, a liberal Democrat. Obama and his wife Michelle had coffee with Bush and his wife Laura at the White House. They rode over together to Capitol Hill for the inauguration ceremony. The *New York Times* reported that after the speech, "Obama escorted Mr. Bush to the East Front of the Capitol, where a helicopter was waiting to take the former president and his wife to Andrews Air Force Base outside Washington for a return trip to Texas."[1]

No one wondered whether a peaceful transition of power would happen or whether George W. Bush would seek to remain in the White House. The transition was simply assumed.

Over at the Election Law Blog, a website I have curated since 2003 covering election law issues, I wrote: "Regardless of your politics, today is a day to celebrate the remarkable peaceful transitions to power that occur in this country with each presidential transition. It is something we should not take for granted."[2]

When I wrote those words, I did not contemplate that the country would be facing a major crisis of election subversion and potential stolen elections a decade later. I would not have dreamed that I would be worrying about democracy at home, helping issue a report called "Fair Elections During a Crisis," or establishing the "Safeguarding Democracy Project" at UCLA.[3]

After all, the country had made it through the 2000 election dispute intact. Bush's 2000 opponent, Democrat Al Gore, conceded that presidential election after a bitter struggle between the parties, numerous lawsuits, and protests. It culminated with the Supreme Court ending the recount in Florida in the (in)famous *Bush v. Gore* case, in practice handing the election to Bush. "Let there be no doubt: While I strongly disagree with the court's decision, I accept it," Gore said in a speech the evening after the court released the *Bush* decision late the night before. "And tonight, for the sake of our unity as a people and the strength of our democracy, I offer my concession."[4]

But as Donald Trump joined the political scene, things quickly deteriorated.

In 2016, as Trump was running for office against Hillary Clinton, he hinted to Fox News that he would not accept the election results if he lost. "I'm telling you, Nov. 8, we'd better be careful, because that election is going to be rigged," Trump told Fox News. "And I hope the Republicans are watching closely or it's going to be taken away from us." President Obama, at a news conference, assured that he would do everything he could to assure a peaceful transition of power if Trump won, even though he viewed Trump as "unfit" for office. Trump was unrelenting. In a televised debate with Clinton, he twice refused to say he would accept the results, saying he would wait and see: "I will look at it at the time," Trump said. "I will keep you in suspense."[5]

It was not the first time that Donald Trump had made evidence-free claims about elections stolen from him. When he lost the Iowa caucuses to Ted Cruz while seeking (and ultimately winning) the 2016 Republican presidential nomination, Trump wrote on Twitter: "Ted Cruz didn't win Iowa, he stole it. That is why all of the polls were so wrong and why he got far more votes than anticipated. Bad!"[6]

The claims continued after Trump won the presidency in 2016 and began running for reelection in 2020, and escalated markedly as the COVID-19 pandemic began and states adjusted their voting rules to allow for safe and fair voting in the midst of an international health crisis. In July 2020, he told *Fox News Sunday* host Chris Wallace, "I think mail-in voting is—is going to rig the election. I really do." He again would not pledge to accept the election results as legitimate. When Wallace asked: "Can you give a direct answer, you will accept the election?" Trump replied: "I have to see. Look, you—I have to see. No, I'm not going to just say yes. I'm not going to say no. And I didn't last time either."[7]

Rather than the 2020 election being rigged against Trump, Trump tried to rig it in his favor. And although the country in response has just recently taken some basic steps to protect peaceful transitions of power in the future, a constitutional right-to-vote amendment can do much more to safeguard American democracy and to bolster the fight against election subversion.

☑   ☑   ☑

Republican claims of widespread voter fraud are not new, but they accelerated after the disputed 2000 election—despite all reliable evidence that voter fraud in the contemporary United States is rare and that when such fraud occurs it tends to happen on a small scale that does not tip the result of elections. The purported "evidence" of widespread voter fraud consists primarily of describing isolated instances of fraud as the "tip of the iceberg" or by taking administrative error or slack in election administration as conclusive proof of malfeasance.[8]

The primary purpose of such voter fraud claims, at least until the Trump presidency, was twofold: first, such claims served as the basis to pass laws, such as voter identification laws, aimed at making it harder for people likely to vote for Democrats to register and to vote. Second, such claims riled up the Republican base and helped with fundraising by convincing supporters that Democrats were cheating and did not legitimately deserve to serve in office. Never mind that the constant claims of fraud may have counterproductively deterred voting by Republicans. The claims fueled party tribalism and animus, convincing both sides that the other was trying to manipulate election outcomes. The Trump presidency moved the voting wars from a well-rehearsed debate over the relative threats of voter fraud compared to voter suppression to a new level of delegitimation of the election process itself, raising the danger of election subversion.

Trump's voter fraud claims were a hallmark of his presidency. He remarkably claimed that there was voter fraud in the 2016 election that he won against Democrat and former Secretary of State Hillary Clinton, falsely stating that at least three million noncitizens voted in the election, all for his opponent. Not coincidentally, the number of purported fraudulent votes matched the margin by which Clinton beat Trump in the national popular vote for president.[9]

Once in office, President Trump formed a presidential commission on voter fraud that was populated with commissioners, including former Kansas Secretary of State Kris Kobach (who served as vice-chair below Vice President Mike Pence), the Heritage Foundation's Hans von Spakovsky, and former Department of Justice (DOJ) lawyer and frequent Fox News contributor J. Christian Adams, each known for making false or exaggerated claims of voter fraud. The commission had only two meetings before it was disbanded, after numerous lawsuits over the commission's transparency and its work. Its purpose appears to have been to produce findings that widespread voter fraud was a real threat. Those findings would then serve as an excuse for Congress to pass a law allowing states to make it harder for people to register to vote.[10]

As the 2020 election neared with Trump's reelection chances uncertain and with the COVID-19 pandemic raging in the United States, Trump markedly increased his rhetoric, charging that the upcoming election would be "rigged" or "stolen," focusing primarily on vote-by-mail. The rate of voting by mail unsurprisingly exploded during the pandemic because many voters and election officials saw it as a safer way of balloting than voting in person at polling places, and President Trump himself voted by mail during the 2020 presidential primaries, even allowing his ballot to be "harvested" by someone else to deliver it to Florida election officials. Despite Trump's statements about fraud and the unprecedented nature of conducting a modern presidential election during a pandemic, no evidence emerged anywhere in the United States of significant fraud or other problems in the administration of the 2020 U.S. presidential election.[11]

Trump repeatedly used social media, including Twitter and Facebook, to spread false claims of fraud, going so far as to claim that the only way he could lose the election was if it was "rigged." The "cheap speech" revolution that lessened the news media's important intermediary role in helping voters receive truthful content facilitated the spread of Trump's false claims directly to tens of millions of followers. He disseminated over four hundred false claims of rigged or stolen elections to his supporters via Twitter in the weeks following the election in 2020.[12]

The turning point on electoral fraud claims came after President Trump lost the presidential election in November 2020 to his Democratic opponent, Joe Biden. Few people who closely followed Trump expected he would ever concede defeat; the question was whether he would merely grumble about voter fraud and acquiesce or double down on his false claims.

He did more than double down, pursuing a political and legal strategy with no precedent at any point in American history, aimed not just at sowing doubt but also at subverting the outcome of the presidential election.[13]

A key part of Trump's strategy was to activate his base by spreading false claims of a stolen election on social media and through friendly cable television and news outlets such as Fox, Newsmax, and the One America News Network. The claims included traditional false claims of ballot-box stuffing and fraudulent ballots, outlandish ones about Italian satellites being used to manipulate votes, and tired tropes of votes being stolen in Democratic cities in swing states with large populations of people of color. On November 27, 2020, for example, Trump tweeted: "Biden can only enter the White House as President if he can prove that his ridiculous '80,000,000 votes' were not fraudulently or illegally obtained. When you see what happened in Detroit, Atlanta, Philadelphia & Milwaukee, massive voter fraud, he's got a big unsolvable problem!"[14]

This drumbeating led to public protests over vote counting and threats of violence against election officials. It also helped to bring pressure from below on elected officials to consider taking steps to turn a Trump loss into a victory. Election offices where tabulating and recounting took place were subject to sometimes-violent protests, and election officials received death threats and intimidating messages.[15]

A report by the Brennan Center for Justice and Bipartisan Policy Center found that one in three election officials reported feeling unsafe because of their job. No doubt driven in part by this conduct, state and local governments are beginning to witness a mass exodus of election officials.[16]

By one count, Trump and his allies filed at least sixty-two lawsuits aimed at contesting the results of elections in states Biden had won. In none of the cases did Trump provide any evidence of pervasive fraud or problems that could have affected the outcome of the election. Among the most high-profile of these cases was an original action that the State of Texas filed directly in the U.S. Supreme Court against four other states, seeking to reverse the outcome of the election. The claims were based upon false evidence of voter fraud and unsupported legal theories, and the Supreme Court rejected them without a hearing. President Trump and his allies eventually lost all but one of the cases.[17]

Trump's behind-the-scenes activities were the most nefarious. He made over thirty contacts with governors, state election officials, state elected officials, and others to either stall or reverse official certification of presidential election results and to facilitate state legislative action on presidential election results. In one of the most notorious incidents captured on an audio recording, he pressured Georgia Secretary of State Brad Raffensperger to "find" at least 11,780 votes to reverse Biden's win in Georgia. The Republican Raffensperger refused.[18]

Trump's team also encouraged people to meet as electors in states that he lost, and these fake electors cast votes for Trump on the date for the casting of Electoral College votes even though there was no authorization to do so. Republican governors and legislators stood their ground against any official imprimatur. But Trump allies submitted the false votes to Congress to be counted on January 6, 2021.[19]

In addition to reaching out to state officials, Trump was working with an assistant attorney general in in the DOJ, Jeffrey Clark—whose day job involved environmental matters, not elections—to get the DOJ to weigh in on election disputes by falsely claiming fraud cost President Trump the election. Clark prepared a letter that would have had the DOJ falsely claim that there were serious irregularities in the conduct of the election in Georgia, and he pushed for the DOJ to file federal litigation in the Supreme Court mirroring the defeated Texas lawsuit. Acting Attorney General Jeffrey Rosen rejected Clark's attempts, and Trump considered firing Rosen and replacing him with Clark, an attempt that apparently failed only because several high-profile DOJ officials threatened to resign in protest.[20]

Trump, along with at least one Republican member of Congress and members of his own legal team, including his attorney John Eastman, unsuccessfully attempted to pressure Vice President Pence to help Trump steal the election. Pence presided over the joint congressional session counting Electoral College votes on January 6, 2021. Trump wanted him either to delay the proceedings to give state legislatures a chance to send in alternative slates of electors or simply to declare Trump the election winner.[21]

Putting together all of these actions, the endgame was: to get state legislatures to rely on purported evidence of fraud or other irregularities to declare alternative slates of presidential electors, despite a lack of legal authority to do so; to argue that the Electoral Count Act, which governed the counting of Electoral College votes, permitted Congress to consider these alternative slates of electors because the irregularities constituted a "failed" election under the act, or that portions of the act limiting the discretion of Congress to count legislatively submitted alternative slates of electors were unconstitutional; and either to get Vice President Pence to delay the counting of Electoral College votes until enough states could declare alternative slates of electors (or simply declare President Trump the winner), or to prevent Biden from obtaining a majority of Electoral College votes, triggering a procedure for choosing the president via votes by each state's House of Representatives delegation, which would have favored Trump.[22]

Pence refused to participate in the scheme, and the counting on January 6, 2021, confirmed Biden's victory, even as it was interrupted by a violent invasion of the U.S. Capitol. Even after the insurrection, 138 Republican members of the House and seven Republican senators voted to object to the counting of Pennsylvania's Electoral College votes based upon spurious grounds.[23]

The bravery of Republican and other election officials prevented Trump's gambit from succeeding. It was not just Pence, Raffensperger, and Rosen who stood up to President Trump, but also Republican governors, Republican-appointed election officials, and others, many of whom faced pressure and condemnation from both Trump and the base of the Republican Party.

Trump riled up his supporters to attend "wild" protests in Washington, D.C., and thousands of his supporters obliged. And at his January 6 rally, he directed his supporters to the Capitol after he and other speakers once again claimed a rigged and stolen election and demanded that Vice President Pence and others do something about it.[24]

The January 6, 2021, riot left over 140 law enforcement officers injured, four Trump supporters dead, and four Capitol police officers who died by suicide by August 2021. Some officers' injuries were serious, including a lost eye, broken ribs and spinal disks, and concussions; insurrectionists tased one officer so many times he had a heart attack.[25]

It was the first successful violent attack on the Capitol since the British attacked during the War of 1812. Had things gone even slightly differently, the vice president and congressional leadership could have been captured or killed; the events could have provoked a military response and left the counting of election results incomplete. Thanks to the bravery of law enforcement officials and members of Congress, the counting resumed after the violence, and Biden was declared the winner by Pence early on the morning of January 7.[26]

Trump reluctantly left office at his constitutionally prescribed time on January 20, 2021, but he refused to participate in the custom of attending his successor's inauguration and affirming the peaceful transition of power that has been a hallmark of U.S. elections. He instead continues to falsely insist that the 2020 election was stolen, even as many of his comments on the subject reach fewer readers thanks to the decisions of Facebook and Twitter to remove his accounts from their websites. (In 2022, Elon Musk restored Trump to Twitter, and in 2023 Meta restored Trump to Facebook and Instagram.)[27]

Deplatforming Trump did little to dampen the enthusiasm among some conservatives and Republicans to relitigate November 2020 and insist on a Trump victory. Arizona's Republican-led Senate ordered an "audit" of the state's presidential election results months after President Biden took office.

The senators employed a firm, "Cyber Ninjas," that had no experience conducting election audits and that was headed by someone who had parroted Trump's false claims of a stolen election; the sham audit revealed no evidence of a stolen election. Pressure fell on Republicans in other states to emulate the "audit," and similar bogus investigations began in states including Wisconsin and Pennsylvania. Some Wisconsin Republicans advocated eliminating the state's bipartisan election agency to replace it with party loyalists.[28]

Some Republican election officials and elected officials who stood up to Trump in 2020 have faced censure, removal from office, and other consequences. Party organizations condemned secretaries of state and governors who vouched for the fairness of the 2020 election; a Republican on Michigan's Board of State Canvassers, who served in a ceremonial role in certifying the state's presidential election results, was replaced by Republicans unhappy that he did his ministerial duty. Only two of the ten Republicans in the House of Representatives who voted for Trump's second impeachment for his role in fomenting the January 6 insurrection returned to Congress after the 2022 elections; the rest lost or chose not to run again.[29]

The State of Georgia passed a law removing Raffensperger from his position as chair of the State Election Board, replacing him with someone chosen by the state legislature. That same legislation gave the board authority to suspend county election officials, including in heavily Democratic counties such as Fulton County.[30]

The Georgia law was one of 216 bills across forty-one states that gave or would give partisan state legislators greater control of the election process over state and local election officials, according to a report by the States United Democracy Center, Protect Democracy, and Law Forward. In Iowa, local election officials could face criminal penalties for sending an absentee ballot application to a voter unless first requested by the voter; in Texas, poll workers could face criminal sanctions for interfering with the activities of "poll watchers," who can now engage in intimidation and interference at polling places. While many of these laws have provisions that might be seen as aimed at voter suppression, at least some of them appear geared to providing a path for overturning election results. Perhaps the most troubling bills introduced so far (but not passed) are those in Arizona, which would have given the state legislature authority to ignore the vote of Arizonans and appoint its own slate of presidential electors upon flimsy allegations of election irregularities or for any reason at all.[31]

The changed laws and continued threats and harassment aimed at election officials caused an unprecedented exodus of election officials, who already faced harsh conditions and budget shortfalls. The loss of these officials creates two simultaneous risks to election integrity. First, lack of professionalization increases the risk of election-administrator error, which, in the current hyperpolarized atmosphere in the United States, can further undermine confidence in the election process. Second, these vacancies could be filled by those who believe the 2020 election was stolen and who may be more willing to break the rules out of a mistaken desire to "level the playing field."[32]

The risk of election officials undermining the security of election systems was on full display in August 2021, when the election administrator of Mesa County, Colorado, Tina Peters, spoke at a conference organized by MyPillow chief executive Mike Lindell that perpetuated false statements that the 2020 election was stolen. Peters has been accused of releasing the source code used on Dominion Voting Systems voting machines. She admitted copying it, and at the Lindell conference she made the code publicly available, raising serious questions about whether those machines would now be more vulnerable to hacking. Peters has since been indicted on charges related to her election security breach.[33]

And among the Republican base, beliefs have hardened that the 2020 election was stolen. In a September 2021 CNN poll, 59 percent of Republican and Republican-leaning independents said that "[b]elieving that Donald Trump won the 2020 election" was "very" or "somewhat" important to what it means to be a Republican today. Overall, 36 percent of Americans polled in the summer of 2021 did not believe that Biden was the legitimate president. Seventy-eight percent of Republicans "say that Biden did not win," and 54 percent "believe there is solid evidence of that, despite the fact that no such evidence exists. That view is also deeply connected to support for Trump."[34]

Indeed, what's most amazing about the continued Republican belief that the election was stolen from Trump is the utter lack of reliable evidence supporting the claim. A pandemic-laden election raised the risk of serious errors in election administration, certainly—but this was perhaps the best administered presidential election in American history. Turnout was high, and reported instances of fraud and machine malfunction were very low.[35]

☑   ☑   ☑

Donald Trump's attempted election subversion was a wake-up call for the United States about the dangers posed to the integrity of our election system—especially for the presidential election, which had many convoluted steps between the time voters vote and the time that Congress counts certified state Electoral College results. It was a system ripe for manipulation by bad actors at many steps of the process.

Fortunately, the country responded to the threat, and in the two years after the attempt to steal the 2020 election, political actors have taken steps that should lower the risk of election subversion in the future. But a constitutional right-to-vote amendment can do much more to protect American democracy for the near future and beyond.

Let's begin with the steps that have taken place to help secure American democracy since 2020. A deep, bipartisan investigation by a special committee in the House of Representatives led to the issuance of an 845-page comprehensive report, along with accompanying transcripts and documentation. It created a substantial, persuasive record about exactly how Trump and people allied with him tried to manipulate the 2020 election outcome to turn Trump's loss into in illegitimate bid to stay in power.[36]

As of March 2023, over a thousand individuals who were involved in the invasion of the U.S. Capitol have been charged or convicted of crimes or taken plea deals. Some of the most serious actors involved in planning or taking part in the physical invasion have pleaded guilty to the serious crime of seditious conspiracy.[37]

In August 2023, the United States Department of Justice charged Trump with three conspiracies related to his attempt to subvert the 2020 election results through schemes including the fake electors plan and the pressure on Pence to throw out Electoral College votes or delay Congress's count. Trump and eighteen others also were charged under state law in Georgia with forty-one crimes related to attempting to steal the 2020 election.[38]

Congress included a set of fixes to the Electoral Count Act within the 4,155-page, $1.7 trillion omnibus spending bill that was the last piece of legislation passed by the 117th Congress in December 2022. The Electoral Count Act is the arcane and poorly written 1887 law that Trump and his allies tried to exploit following the 2020 election. The new Electoral Count Reform Act confirmed that the vice president had no authority, unilateral or otherwise, to throw out a state's Electoral College votes; removed language allowing states to send in a slate of electors following a "failed" election; raised the threshold for members of Congress to a state's Electoral College votes from one in each chamber to 20 percent of the membership of each House of Congress; and provided expedited judicial review procedures in the event a rogue governor sought to send in a rogue slate of presidential electors.[39]

Politically, election deniers—people running for office who publicly embraced the false claim that Trump won the 2020 election—lost in key races in swing states. Republican gubernatorial candidates Kari Lake in Arizona and Doug Mastriano in Pennsylvania, for example, both lost their races. Each had said they would not have certified Biden's presidential win in their states in 2020. Lake refused to concede her own loss as Arizona governor. Candidates for secretary of state in Arizona, Michigan, and Nevada lost similar races. Although many other election deniers, including members of Congress, did win their elections, when the issue was salient and discussed in the races, voters were turned off by the extreme claims, suggesting a ceiling of support for dangerous denialism.[40]

☑   ☑   ☑

Despite these advances, there are still risks of election subversion in the political system, and these risks can be mitigated by the passage of a constitutional right-to-vote amendment.

First, even with the passage of new congressional legislation fixing and clarifying the rules for Congress to count the Electoral College votes, some would-be election subverters could well argue that such legislation is unconstitutional, much as they argued that the Electoral Count Act was unconstitutional. The claim was that Article II of the constitution gives state legislatures plenary power to choose electors, even after the people in a state have voted for their choice for president, and nothing Congress can do by statute can limit that power.

Trump lawyer Cleta Mitchell—who was involved in Trump's attempt to convince Georgia's Secretary of State Brad Raffensperger to "find" enough votes to flip the state from Biden to Trump—espoused this position in a remarkable deposition before the House committee investigating the January 6 insurrection and the attempt to subvert the 2020 election. Speaking about the 1887 Electoral Count Act, Mitchell said: "The Constitution of the United States grants plenary power to state legislatures to choose electors of the State. Congress has enacted a statute which is an enabling law, which I happen to think is unconstitutional, because the power granted in the Constitution to state legislatures . . . is complete and total. There's nothing in the Constitution about allowing people, citizens to vote on electors." She added: "Now that is something that legislatures have over time decided they want to do. But in my view, according to the Constitution that's an advisory role that happens because the legislature has created a mechanism to conduct the election . . . [T]he legislature can use—can choose to use what the people have decided, but that's not in the Constitution."[41]

In short, Mitchell was arguing that even if a state legislature allows voters to vote for president, that vote is just "advisory," and a legislature can ignore those votes and submit its own slate of electors based on its own preferences.

Mitchell's claim is wrong under the constitution. Once a state has made the choice under Article II to allow voters to vote, the right to vote in that election becomes "fundamental."

And it would violate due process, as well as Congress's power to set a uniform date for choosing presidential electors under Article II, for a state to change the results of the election after it has granted voters the right to vote for president. Further, in the 2023 *Moore v. Harper* case, the Supreme Court rejected the extreme version of the "independent state legislature" theory embraced by Mitchell and others. *Moore* held that state legislatures do not have plenary power over federal elections, unconstrained by state constitutions or state law.[42]

But a constitutional right-to-vote amendment would provide many additional protections. First, it would confirm that within each state voters have the right to vote for president in an election; the choice would no longer be up to the state legislature. And a state cannot put an undue burden on that vote or discriminate against voters on the basis of race, ethnicity, or language preference. There would simply be no room for arguments such as Mitchell's that state legislatures can usurp the powers of the voters or discriminate either against voters or among voters.

Second, a constitutional right-to-vote amendment can deal with the insider threat to elections from election officials. Under the amendment, voters would have the right to vote in a fair system that assures votes are accurately counted. This means that voters would have the right to sue to assure transparency in voting processes by election officials. An election official who deliberately manipulates election results also would be open to liability for violating the constitutional rights of voters. Manipulation could be in the form of altering vote totals, preventing groups of voters from being able to fairly cast a ballot, or releasing voting technology software code or other information that assures that the voting system is safe and secure.

The constitutional right to vote amendment also would be useful in determining whether laws such as Georgia's, which

allow a takeover of local election offices upon findings of incompetence or misfeasance, are actually aimed at subverting
the will of the voters or suppressing turnout in large, Democratic counties. It would not be unconstitutional for states to
take over counties that are failing to conduct elections compe-
tently; indeed, it would be the responsibility of states to do so
under the new amendment to assure that votes are being fairly
and accurately counted. But using purported incompetence of
local election officials as subterfuge for subversion or suppression would not be permissible, and the amendment would provide the predicate for courts to ascertain both the purposes of
the law and whether invocation of the law for a takeover is war-
ranted or instead pretextual and unconstitutional.

Finally, because election results may also be undermined by
violence and intimidation of voters, an amendment would be a
new tool for voters to assure protection from law enforcement
for free and fair voting. Under current law, the government has
no affirmative responsibility to provide any amount of police
protection and cannot be sued under the U.S. Constitution for
failing to do so. Under the amendment, states and the federal
government would have an affirmative obligation to ensure free
and fair elections, and assure that voters can participate equally
in the electoral process without undue burdens upon them.
States that fail to prevent violence or threats of violence against
voters may face liability as well as orders from courts requiring
the provision of adequate protection.[43]

To combat all of these threats of election subversion, the
constitutional right-to-vote amendment would give Congress
key enforcement powers. This means that Congress would have
authority to act not just to protect federal elections (as it already has the power to do under Article I's Elections Clause)
but state elections as well. For example, Congress could pass a

law requiring that in all elections states must use voting technology that produces a piece of paper that could be counted in the event of an election dispute.[44]

Congress could also act by requiring certain transparency requirements for election officials in state and local elections, or create federal crimes for tampering with voting equipment, releasing proprietary information that could be used to hack voting technology, or engaging in activities to intimidate voters or subvert legitimate election outcomes. Although Congress has the power to do many of these things already in connection with federal elections, an amendment would make that power unquestionably clear and would bolster its power to do so for state and local elections as well.[45]

A constitutional right-to-vote amendment that also abolished the Electoral College would do even more to thwart election subversion. It would be quite surprising to see as little as a one-million-vote margin between two candidates out of at least 150 million votes cast. Messing with how votes are tallied within states would have to be on a tremendous scale to have the chance of altering a presidential election result. That change, perhaps more than any other, would help secure the integrity of a presidential vote count.

☑   ☑   ☑

A constitutional right-to-vote amendment makes sense on the grounds that it will promote political equality and create an election system that both protects voter access and election integrity, lowering the amount of overall election litigation. But election subversion is a threat so serious that it provides an independent compelling reason to support such an amendment. We now know that peaceful transitions of power, and even democracy itself, cannot be taken for granted in the United States. A morning with coffee between the outgoing and incoming presidents and a ride together over to the Capitol matter a lot for democracy. The amendment helps assure those continued rides, and it would be a major step toward preserving free and fair elections.

Chapter 6

HOW TO GET A REAL RIGHT TO VOTE

The original U.S. Constitution did not guarantee anyone's right to vote, and it explicitly gave states the power to set the rules for choosing U.S. senators and assigning Electoral College votes for president. If you were not a white, property-owning male in 1789, when the constitution was ratified, your chances of being able to vote in any election in the United States were small. The tension between the ideals of political equality contained in the Declaration of Independence and the constitution on the one hand, and the reality of limited suffrage in the early United States on the other, is jarring to contemporary egalitarian sensibilities.

Change happened incrementally; the expansion of voting rights to cover most citizen, adult, resident, nonfelons did not emerge quickly or smoothly. Nor did the expansion fully protect voters' rights. Adding an affirmative right to vote as an amendment to the constitution will not effortlessly happen either, and the amendment's passage and ratification is not guaranteed, even if most Americans would support it.

But history shows that expansion of voting rights can happen when enough people band together and work long enough at it. For some amendments, the struggles paid dividends along the way, as state-by-state action led to greater enfranchisement and inclusion in state and local government. The same would likely be true of an effort to add an affirmative right to vote to the constitution.

Amending the constitution, the most difficult path toward making changes in voting rules, is probably the means of election reform with the greatest chance of securing real and lasting change. But even passing an amendment protecting the right to vote does not guarantee immediate or full transformation. It took the Civil War to spur passage of the Fifteenth Amendment barring racial discrimination in voting; some defeated southern states had to ratify the amendment as a condition to their readmission into the Union after the war. Southern states resisted the amendment for nearly a century after its 1870 ratification, regularly depriving African American voters and others of the chance to register and vote until the 1965 passage of the Voting Rights Act led to federal enforcement of the amendment. And it took the Supreme Court upholding the power of Congress to impose strong remedies on resistant states, as the court first did in 1966, and as it did consistently until the 2013 *Shelby County* ruling.[1]

As we saw in chapter 1, other election reforms passed via constitutional amendment had somewhat easier, but generally not easy, paths. Each depended upon specific political circumstances that normally stymie election reform through this arduous route.

The conditions that allowed passage of the seventeenth, nineteenth, twenty-third, twenty-fourth, and twenty-sixth amendments seem unlikely to replicate themselves for other election reforms in the near-to-medium term in the United States. In the 1960s and early 1970s, for example, when the most recent voting amendments passed, Congress was far less polarized by party. Cross-partisan coalitions could support the expansion of voting rights, even given resistance, primarily from Democrats in the south.

Today, close and intense partisan competition have spilled over into disputes on voting and enfranchisement itself, all but eliminating room for the kind of bipartisan approval necessary to run through the supermajority requirements for constitutional amendment. Given strong support for Democrats among residents of Washington, D.C., it is hard to imagine the Twenty-Third Amendment giving Electoral College representation to Washington, D.C., gaining any significant Republican support if it came up for a vote today, much less sailing through ratification in the states as this amendment did.

☑   ☑   ☑

The idea of including an affirmative right to vote in the U.S. Constitution is not a new one. As we saw in chapter 1, some of the early supporters of the Fifteenth Amendment favored a much broader amendment than one aimed only at barring discrimination in voting on the basis of race. The broader measure failed for lack of centrist support, but the idea never died.

In 1959, for example, the U.S. Commission on Civil Rights, seeing the persistence of discrimination against African Americans in the Jim Crow South, issued an extensive report on voting conditions in the United States and recommendations for reform. Among the recommendations of the northerners sitting on the commission was a proposal for a constitutional amendment reading: "The right of citizens of the United States to vote shall not be denied or abridged by the United States or by any State or by any person for any cause except inability to meet State age or length-of-residence requirements uniformly applied to all persons within the State, or legal confinement at the time of registration or election. This right to vote shall include the right to register or otherwise qualify to vote, and to have one's vote counted."[2]

Over the next half-decade, various members of Congress spoke in support of the proposal. In 1959, Representative John Bademas of Indiana proposed a joint resolution in Congress supporting the commission's proposal for a constitutional amendment. He said that "only those who do not believe in America can possibly object to this amendment. Only those who are opposed to the American principles of freedom and democracy can range themselves against this proposal."[3]

Bademas began a trend: between 1959 and 1963, representatives and senators introduced seven resolutions in Congress to establish a constitutional right to vote. None of the measures appears to have been put up for a vote or even gotten a committee hearing, however, and the movement for voting rights shifted toward more pinpointed voting rights laws. Congress passed the Twenty-Third Amendment regarding presidential voting rights for Washington, D.C., residents in 1961, the Twenty-Fourth Amendment repealing poll taxes in federal elections in 1962, the Voting Rights Act in 1965, and the Twenty-Sixth Amendment lowering the voting age to eighteen in 1971. Before Congress passed the Voting Rights Act in 1965, Attorney General Nicholas Katzenbach sent President Lyndon Johnson a memo outlining a more ambitious proposed constitutional amendment guaranteeing a right to vote to most Americans, but Johnson never brought it forward.[4]

Movement toward a constitutional right to vote reemerged after the disputed presidential election of 2000 and the start of the modern voting wars. In 2001, Jesse Jackson Jr., a member of

Congress from Illinois, introduced a proposal to amend the constitution to protect the right to vote: "All citizens of the United States who are eighteen years of age or older shall have the right to vote in any public election held in the jurisdiction in which the citizen resides. The right to vote shall not be denied or abridged by the United States, any state, or any other public or private person or entity, except that the United States or any State may establish regulations narrowly tailored to produced efficient and honest elections."[5]

The measure was supported not just by Jackson, but by other scholars and leaders including then-election law professor (and now member of Congress) Jamin Raskin and historian Alexander Keyssar. In 2004, the Democratic Party declined to endorse the proposed amendment as part of its platform. A 2007 version of the measure had fifty-one Democratic co-sponsors in the House but no Senate co-sponsors and no Republican support, and the measure never got a hearing in the House.[6]

In his 2003 book, *Overruling Democracy*, Raskin put forward his own version of a constitutional amendment that would guarantee the right of all citizens to vote for offices, including the president and vice president; give residents of Washington, D.C., voting rights; and prevent discrimination in voting on the basis of "political party affiliation, wealth, or prior condition of incarceration." He wrote that the "campaign for this amendment will galvanize Americans for the basic right we wrongly assume is protected already and give national coherence to the scattered, lonely and woefully incomplete efforts that sprang up across the country after 2000 to reform anachronistic and manipulable electoral structures in literally thousands of self-regulating jurisdictions." Raskin wrote those words as a scholar and continued to push for expanded voting rights when he became a member of Congress.[7]

More recently, in 2017, Representative Mark Pocan, a Wisconsin Democrat, introduced a simple proposed constitutional amendment reading: "Every citizen of the United States, who is of legal voting age, shall have the fundamental right to vote in any public election held in the jurisdiction in which the citizen resides." The measure had numerous Democratic co-sponsors and the support of the voting rights organization FairVote, but so far it has not gotten a hearing.[8]

FairVote convened a serious conference on a right-to-vote amendment in 2003, and since then, two major reports by civil rights organizations also have pushed the idea of an affirmative right to vote. Much like the work of this book, the Advancement Project's 2008 report considered both the question of whether to go broad or narrow in the crafting of a constitutional amendment, and also the political value of organizing a political movement around a voting rights amendment. "A proposal to enshrine an affirmative right to vote could be an inspiring vehicle for collective, purposeful organizing. Introducing the proposal in every congressional session while engaging in grassroots voting rights activities could keep the issue alive in the media and on the national policy agenda. The effort could become a successful social movement with political roots and implications, especially when combined with aggressive communications strategies."[9]

Even as it considered questions of the amendment's scope, such as whether to include Electoral College reform in a proposed constitutional amendment, the Advancement Project's report did not offer specific proposed amendment language. In contrast, a 2020 report from Demos offers specific constitutional language and a capacious proposed amendment. Demos's constitutional amendment would tackle not just voting rights and an end to felon disenfranchisement but also make partisan gerrymandering unconstitutional and give the government the ability to limit campaign spending, overturning Supreme Court decisions that held that such limits violate the First Amendment.[10]

☑   ☑   ☑

It is heartening that a constitutional amendment recognizing an affirmative right to vote remains a topic of interest among those thinking and writing about voting rights. The recent efforts are no surprise, given the emergence of the voting wars since the 2000s and the increasingly acerbic nature of political competition in the years since Donald Trump emerged on the political scene.

Yet these efforts have been almost exclusively discussed on the left side of the political spectrum. None of them appears to have garnered any Republican support, and it is easy to imagine that some people also will view my argument for a constitutional amendment as just another progressive calling for an expansion of voting rights and excoriating Republicans for efforts to make it harder to register and vote. It is not enough to say—as Representative Bandemas did in 1959—that opposing a constitutional right to vote is un-American in order to get everyone on board, especially in these polarized times.

One-sided support is not the path toward likely approval of a constitutional amendment that needs the support of two-thirds of members of Congress and ratification by three-quarters of state legislatures.

Given how important wide support across the political spectrum is to constitutional ratification, it is worth considering whether there would be any way to write an amendment that could garner significant Republican buy-in in the current polarized political era. That calculation in turn may dictate the scope of the constitutional amendment that should be pursued.

Why would Republicans support an amendment to the constitution guaranteeing voting rights when some Republican legislators and officeholders in recent years have been the primary culprits in making it harder for some people to register and vote? Indeed, some in the Republican Party, including former Texas Governor Rick Perry and late Supreme Court Justice Antonin Scalia, supported repealing the Seventeenth Amendment and allowing state legislatures to directly pick U.S. senators, moving enfranchisement efforts in the wrong direction. Those conservatives like Senator Mike Lee of Utah, who say that the United States is a republic and "not a democracy," are surely not those who will support the expansion of voting rights. (The claim nonetheless proves far less than those who embrace it think that it does: in a republic, the people still rule through fair election of their representatives.) And, as Yale Law School Dean Heather Gerken argues, to the extent conservatives would only support a weak constitutional amendment that contains little but platitudes, such an amendment would not be worth the candle.[11]

To begin with, Republicans have proceeded along the incorrect premise that lower turnout necessarily hurts their electoral chances. That was not true in Texas in 2020, for example, when despite Texas's refusal to make voting easier during the pandemic, turnout went up and Republican candidates did quite well statewide. (The Texas legislature nonetheless made voting harder after 2020, perhaps because Democrats did well in some parts of the state like Houston, where voting was made easier during the pandemic with creations like 24-hour drive-thru early voting.)[12]

More generally, in the most comprehensive study of the question of the relationship between voter turnout and partisan outcomes, Daron Shaw and John Petrocik debunk the claim that low turnout necessarily helps Democrats and hurts Republicans: "The presidential elections of 2012 and 2016, both with high turnout, did nothing to help the Democrats; Republican majorities in Congress and the states actually increased. If we look at election outcomes before 1990—specifically, the years since 1950—Republican presidential candidates have won in relatively high turnout elections (1952), lost in other high-turnout years (1960), and lost in low-turnout years (1976)."[13]

Although political scientists continue to debate whether measures easing voting and registration restrictions generally boost turnout or not, the past few elections demonstrate that discouraging Republican voters from voting early or by mail can hurt their electoral chances. In 2020, Donald Trump railed against mail-in voting in the midst of the pandemic, even though Republicans in many states had extensive get-out-the-vote efforts tied to mail-in balloting. Following Trump's lead, but wishing to avoid Election Day crowds during the pandemic, Republicans shifted more toward early in-person voting rather than mail-in balloting. There is no way to know for sure, but Trump might have pulled out a narrow Electoral College victory in the 2020 presidential election had he not discouraged vote-by-mail.[14]

Self-defeating conduct by some Republicans persisted in 2022. False claims of fraud led candidates such as Trump acolyte Kari Lake, the Republican Arizona gubernatorial candidate, to argue against early voting. Lake lost the governor's race by only about 17,000 votes, and she without evidence blamed her loss in part on delays and confusion in Election Day voting in the state's most populous county, Maricopa. Those delays were caused by malfunctions with machines used to tabulate completed ballots. It is possible the election could have been closer, or Lake even could have won, if she and her party had pursued a broader get-out-the-vote strategy relying in part on early mail-in voting, a form of voting long used by Arizona Republicans and others.[15]

There is recognition among at least some Republicans that making voting harder can be self-defeating. Kentucky's Republican legislature, for example, has made early voting easier, and the result has neither increased cases of election fraud nor benefitted Democrats. Further, given the failure of election denial as a motivator for Republicans in general elections, we may see a pendulum swing away from the language of voter fraud and calls for new restrictive voting rules, at least in some Republican states.[16]

Moreover, the Republican Party is in transition, and it has been making new appeals to poorer, working class voters. These voters are more likely to be disenfranchised by certain impediments to voting, making some Republican-sponsored voting restrictions especially self-defeating. If enough Republicans could be convinced that increasing turnout is in their interest, or at least that increased turnout is not necessarily harmful, it might be easier to get some Republican support for an amendment guaranteeing the right to vote, depending on what else the amendment could offer Republicans.

And there is much more in the constitutional right-to-vote amendment that Republicans should like. The amendment would make elections more secure. Automatic voter registration and national voter identification would end most fights over whether voting rolls are clean, and there would be less concern about whether people are voting more than once in multiple states. A decrease in litigation and a rationalization of the rules for elections means Republicans, like Democrats, could put more effort into getting out the vote and persuasion of swing voters than in fighting the voting wars.

Of course, these arguments will not be persuasive to the extent that concerns about election integrity and security are just a pretext for voter suppression, and opposition to automatic voter registration being more about keeping those who might vote for Democrats from registering to vote.

Republican support for a constitutional right to vote also could help Republicans make greater political inroads with minority voters. Think less of the party's Trumpist wing and more of the approach of the George W. Bush wing and its building of a big tent party. The Bush wing is not ascendant right now, but winds do shift in politics; consider how much politics shifted from the colonial period, when the women's suffrage movement began, through the post–Civil War passage of the Reconstruction Amendments in the 1860s, to 1920, when the Nineteenth Amendment was finally ratified.

Republicans also have an interest in preventing election subversion. Recall that many Republican leaders in power, such as Georgia's Secretary of State Brad Raffensperger, rejected Trump's attempts to steal the 2020 election, and a bipartisan group of senators supported the 2022 Electoral Count Reform Act that closed off some avenues of potential election subversion. Republicans may worry not only about members of their own party trying to steal a future election; not knowing who the demagogue might be in the future means that it is in both parties' rational interest to assure there are safeguards for voting and the ballot-counting process.

The basic constitutional right-to-vote amendment that appears in the appendix accomplishes all of this—enfranchising eligible voters, deescalating the voting wars through new election integrity measures, and safeguarding American democracy—

without "federalizing" or nationalizing election administration. States would be able to run their own election systems, subject to complying with the constitution and with any additional procedures Congress could put in place under its power to enforce this amendment and other voting-related amendments.

This decentralized approach is personally not my first choice. Since my 2012 book, *The Voting Wars*, I have supported national nonpartisan administration of elections as the most sensible way to run elections (and in line with how just about every other advanced democratic country runs their elections). But national, nonpartisan election administration is such a political nonstarter that I have not included it in my proposal for a constitutional amendment, as its inclusion would only harden the opposition of both Republican states and state and local election administrators of both parties, which have long fought to keep elections in the United States decentralized.[17]

The constitutional right-to-vote amendment, particularly the basic version, is a much more modest reform. It does not federalize elections, remake the Electoral College or the Senate, expand voting rights for those living in U.S. territories, or mandate the reenfranchisement of former felons. If there is the realistic possibility that in the next decade enough Republicans could unite with Democrats behind the basic amendment, then that basic version would be worth pursuing, with these other issues of political equality pursued separately. Perhaps it might be possible to add felon reenfranchisement into the proposed amendment, given that felon reenfranchisement, even in Republican states such as Florida, has gained bipartisan support.

Pursuing the basic amendment has a cost, however, in that it might generate less enthusiasm on the left and center than if advocates pursued the broader amendment. When I speak to groups of voters about election reform, reforming the Electoral

College is often at the top of the list of desired reforms, along with concerns about the Senate. The basic amendment might seem too modest to those willing to work the hardest for passage.

This tradeoff is a difficult one. It is hard to see a broader constitutional amendment, such as one that would eliminate the Electoral College, gaining Republican support to achieve supermajority status in Congress and in state legislatures. On the other hand, getting Republican support even for the basic amendment will be difficult, and therefore giving up the ideal version of the amendment out of hope of garnering such support could be foolish and naïve.

The odds may seem daunting, but they are not nearly as daunting as the odds facing those who eventually secured passage of the fifteenth or nineteenth amendments barring racial and gender discrimination in voting. It is never easy to get leaders to support election rules that might lessen their own power. Activists behind the movement for the Seventeenth Amendment establishing direct election of U.S. senators no doubt knew that getting state legislatures to give up their own power to choose senators would be difficult.

A key point is the time horizon. Although a few voting amendments, such as the twenty-third (on D.C. Electoral College votes) and twenty-sixth (on voting for eighteen- to twenty-one-year-olds) passed and were ratified quickly, most took decades or more of struggle. Those who commit to improving U.S. elections over time can help to build a movement toward greater enfranchisement by organizing around a constitutional amendment.

☑ ☑ ☑

Even if a constitutional right-to-vote amendment is unlikely to pass in the near term, it can still pay political dividends in the interim. It could create momentum for important statutory reform. In particular, potential Republican resistance to the proposed amendment could galvanize support for Democrats' taking more radical steps to expand voting rights through legislation. The general idea is what professors Joey Fishkin and David Pozen call "constitutional anti-hardball."[18]

Constitutional hardball is using norm-breaking, but not strictly illegal, tactics to maximize political power, such as when a state legislature engages in extreme partisan gerrymandering during a period when courts are unwilling to find such tactics unconstitutional. "Anti-hardball" is the idea of using the same tough norm-breaking tactics not forbidden by the constitution in order to lock in changes that benefit democracy.

As Fishkin and Pozen explain, "A second possible response [to constitutional hardball on the Republican side] is not to play constitutional hardball whenever the opportunity arises, but instead to use temporary points of leverage to press for procedural changes that amount to *anti-hardball*. For instance, independent redistricting commissions, professionalized nonpartisan election bureaucracies, and the like, while far from optimal in terms of maximizing political advantage, have the effect of taking certain types of constitutional hardball off the table (and also, in the case of the redistricting commissions, of altering the constituencies of Republican and Democratic representatives alike so that elected officials would have somewhat less to fear from ideological primary challengers and thus from being seen as moderate, an effect that would likely be more transformative on the Republican side)."[19]

It is easy to imagine anti-hardball tactics that Democrats could pursue to further voting rights should they be fortunate enough to get the same constellation of power as they had in 2021 and 2022: control of the presidency, the U.S. House of

Representatives, and majority (but not supermajority) control of the Senate.

Under existing Senate rules, ordinarily it requires a supermajority of sixty senators to get things done. Without sixty votes, a measure can be "filibustered," and it takes sixty votes to "invoke cloture" and proceed to a final vote. Cloture is a subconstitutional rule that is the product of the Senate's own procedures, not something that Article I requires. Indeed, over time the Senate has changed the threshold for invoking cloture and it has created exceptions to the cloture rule.[20]

Certain budget-related bills are not subject to cloture, and so a party with a majority in the Senate but not a filibuster-proof majority will try to put as much into such "reconciliation" bills as possible to maximize advantage under the rules. When Democrats faced Republican resistance to confirming President Obama's judicial and executive branch nominees in 2013, Democrats changed the filibuster rule to allow such nominations (except for Supreme Court nominees) to be subject only to a majority vote, exempt from the filibuster rules. When Republicans took back control of the Senate and Democrats opposed Trump's Supreme Court nominees, Republicans changed the rules to allow those nominees to be subject to a majority vote as well.[21]

In both of these instances, the rule changes did not proceed along the normal path of requiring a two-thirds vote (or sixty-seven of one hundred senators); instead, the rules were changed through a bare majority vote and a ruling from the president of the Senate. This is the so-called nuclear option that some opponents have argued would change the deliberative nature of the Senate.[22]

These changes in Senate rules were examples of constitutional hardball; the parties changed the rules within that which was allowed by the constitution to secure political advantage. The issue was especially contentious when it came to Supreme Court nominations. When President Obama nominated Judge Merrick Garland for the Supreme Court in March 2016 to take the seat of Antonin Scalia, the ultra-conservative Supreme Court justice who died in office, Republican Senate Majority Leader Mitch McConnell refused to even give Garland a hearing, much less a vote, claiming that then-Senator Biden created a precedent of no Supreme Court confirmations close to a presidential election. Republicans controlled the majority and would not budge. When Donald Trump came into office, his nominees got quick hearings and confirmations: Neil Gorsuch, Brett Kavanaugh, and Amy Coney Barrett. McConnell pushed Barrett's nomination through very quickly, with her confirmation vote along party lines coming just about a week before Election Day in 2020; so much for the so-called Biden rule that Supreme Court confirmations should not come in the last months of a presidency.[23]

Democrats had a chance to use the same "nuclear option" to blow up the filibuster to pass voting rights legislation, including the John R. Lewis Voting Rights Advancement Act and the For the People Act. These two pieces of legislation, which were later combined into something called the Freedom to Vote Act, got majority support in the House and Senate, but did not become law because of the filibuster. At least two Democratic senators— Joe Manchin of West Virginia and Kyrsten Sinema of Arizona— were unwilling to eliminate the filibuster for voting rights legislation. The measures therefore failed, and Democrats lost control of the House in 2022, taking the possibility of significant voting rights legislation passing off the table until at least 2025.[24]

Passing this kind of voting legislation in the future would be a strong form of anti-hardball. The argument in favor of doing so is that democracy is at least as important as nominations or budgets and that if there is continued Republican opposition to a voting rights amendment that protects all voters, this change in rules is defensible and necessary. The unequal nature of the Senate, which privileges small states and does not comply with the one-person, one-vote principle, provides a strong normative argument to make an exception to the filibuster rule for voting rights legislation.[25]

In addition to restoring preclearance that the Supreme Court killed in the *Shelby County* case, the combined legislation would have limited partisan gerrymandering, ended some felon disenfranchisement, and provided other voting rights protections. Democrats could also consider other legislation as well, such as statehood for Washington, D.C., and Puerto Rico.

Much good on voting rights could be accomplished through statutory reform, but such reform would not be nearly as good as a constitutional amendment. As we have seen in earlier chapters, there is a good chance that the current Supreme Court would strike key parts of this legislation, such as those restoring preclearance or requiring states to reenfranchise felons who have completed their sentences. It is also uncertain if the court would allow Congress to require the use of redistricting commissions, either for Congress or for state legislatures. It would depend on how the court would view Congress's powers to legislate voting rights legislation under the Elections Clause in Article I and under its powers to enforce the voting rights amendments already in the constitution. So far, the signs from the current Supreme Court are not encouraging.

But if Democrats played anti-hardball and passed these voting measures only to see the Supreme Court strike them down, there would be additional pressure, as is already growing, for Democrats to add more justices to the Supreme Court to change the court's partisan balance. That additional anti-hardball threat of "court packing" in turn could potentially lead the court to moderate its rulings on democracy issues and avoid pushes to change the composition of the court itself.[26]

In sum, a serious push for a constitutional amendment could help to create the conditions for using democracy-enhancing anti-hardball tactics if necessary. These tactics could improve voting rights, and the reaction of other political actors, including the Supreme Court, could spur further action and even the passage of the amendment itself.

☑   ☑   ☑

The United States has lost its muscle memory when it comes to passing constitutional amendments. Given the extreme polarization in the contemporary United States, pursuing an amendment may appear quixotic and naïve. But that view misses the historical perspective: most amendments to the constitution that have expanded voting rights took decades or more of struggle. Further, organization to pass such an amendment can pay dividends along the way in the form of local, state, and federal legislation expanding voting rights. It is time to think of the push for a constitutional amendment less as an all-or-nothing proposition and more as a means to achieve a series of worthy ends.

The status quo is an unpalatable alternative in which people who are pro-voter and believe in fair elections and enfranchisement are constantly fighting new voting hurdles. Every election cycle features new restrictions on the right to vote—whether those are targeted at students, minority voters, former felons whose voting rights should have been restored, or others. The air on the right is filled with talk of voter fraud. Those on the left have a hard time calibrating their alarm, treating everything as a five-alarm fire and making it harder to tell when we have a real election emergency that requires urgent action.

Every election season features stories about the "armies of lawyers" that are being positioned for the latest skirmishes in the ongoing voting wars. The voter fraud/voter suppression frame continues, election after election. And now we have a new problem: election subversion. No longer can we have complete confidence that our elections are going to be run in a way that ensures that election winners can always take office.

We depend on courts to protect voting rights, but they only do a partial job and only some of the time. Courts successfully fought back election subversion in the 2020 presidential election, but there is no guarantee that this trend will continue. The courts' record on protecting voting rights is decidedly more mixed, and the Supreme Court's record in particular has been abysmal on voting protections over the last few years. Even worse, there is reason to believe that some of the earlier voter-protective precedents of the Warren Court that provide the basis for many voter-protective decisions of the courts could be in danger in front of the current Supreme Court.

Part of the lack of voter protection from the judiciary is thanks to the composition of the court itself and the deep conservative ideology of a majority of its members. Their natural inclination is protecting states' rights over both voting rights and congressional power to protect voters. But another part of the problem is the U.S. Constitution, which has never adequately protected voting rights.

To be sure, things are better now than at the time of the ratification of the constitution. Discrimination against women, African Americans, poor people, and others was allowed under the original constitution, as interpreted by the Supreme Court, up through a good part of the twentieth century. And even after amendments passed, courts have hardly been the leaders in protecting voting rights. A stronger voting amendment will both make judicial resistance much harder and congressional protection of voting rights more effective.

The piecemeal approach toward enfranchisement, and the reliance upon the preferences of a majority of life-tenured lawyers sitting on the Supreme Court who have not shown pro-voter proclivities, is untenable.

The promise of equality contained in the Declaration of Independence and the constitution has not been enough. This country needs to live up to its ideals and join other modern democratic countries in affirmatively protecting the right to vote. We need to roll up our sleeves and get to work. Our democracy is not going to protect itself.[27]

Appendix

DRAFT VERSIONS OF A CONSTITUTIONAL AMENDMENT AFFIRMATIVELY PROTECTING THE RIGHT TO VOTE

The Basic Version

(1) Notwithstanding Article II or any other provision of this Constitution, all citizen, adult, resident, nonfelons of the United States shall have the right to vote in all elections for federal, state, and local offices within their residential areas, including for President and Vice President, and to have each ballot fairly and accurately counted. Provided, however, that the right to vote for President and Vice President shall apply only to residents of the states and the District of Columbia, and the right to vote for Members of the House and Senate shall apply only to residents of the states. Votes for President and Vice President shall count equally toward allocating each state's electors.

(2) All votes conducted for federal, state, or local office shall be substantially equally weighted, except for the weighting of electors across states mandated under Article II in choosing the President and Vice President.

(3) States shall create and maintain a system to automatically register all eligible individuals to vote and shall provide each eligible voter with a unique voter identification number that may be used for voter registration purposes across states. States have the authority by statute to delegate to a federal government agency determined by Congress the responsibility to create and maintain the system of automatic voter registration and voter identification. The agency shall create and maintain the system for all states so delegating. The agency shall create and maintain a system for providing each eligible voter with a unique voter identification number. Voter identification numbers shall be different from a voter's social security number. Automatic voter registration requires the states or agency to take all steps and pay all costs associated with establishing the identity and eligibility of each individual within a state and to register all eligible individuals to vote.

(4) States must provide equal and not unduly burdensome voting opportunities for all voters to vote in every election for federal, state, and local office, as measured by ease of voting. The burdens of voting shall be substantially equal among the voters of each state. A state must have valid and substantial reasons, backed by real and significant evidence, for imposing restrictions on or impediments to casting a ballot and the means must go no further than reasonably necessary to satisfy those valid and substantial reasons. Voters shall have standing to enforce all aspects of this Amendment through a lawsuit filed in federal court.

(5) Voters shall have a fair opportunity to participate in the political process and to elect representatives of their choice regardless of race, ethnicity, or membership in a language minority group. In measuring such opportunities, courts shall examine the effect of laws regulating registration and voting on voters and not require proof of discriminatory intent. Voting

rules with a disparate impact on minority voters are presumptively unconstitutional unless justified by overriding state interests in election integrity and sound election administration.

(6) Congress shall have broad power to protect voting rights under this Amendment and previous Amendments to this Constitution by appropriate legislation. This power is not subject to narrow judicial interpretation and shall be interpreted by courts to broadly favor enfranchisement and equality of voters. Nothing in this Amendment shall be read to lessen the powers given to Congress elsewhere in this Constitution to protect voting rights.

Addition 1: The Inclusion of a Ban on Felon Disenfranchisement

Revise Section (1) of the Proposed Amendment as follows (additions in bold; deletions in strike-out):

(1) Notwithstanding Article II or any other provision of this Constitution, all citizen, adult, residents, non felons of the United States shall have the right to vote in all elections for federal, state, and local offices within their residential areas, including for President and Vice President, and to have each ballot fairly and accurately counted. Provided, however, that the right to vote for President and Vice President shall apply only to residents of the states and the District of Columbia, and the right to vote for Members of the House and Senate shall apply only to residents of the states. Votes for President and Vice President shall count equally toward allocating each state's electors.

A state may not deny the right to vote to any otherwise eligible person convicted of a felony who has completed a sentence of incarceration or parole. Failure to pay any fines or fees shall not be grounds for withholding the franchise.

Addition 2: The Inclusion of Voters in United States Territories to Vote for President

Revise Section (1) of the Proposed Amendment as follows (additions in bold; deletions in strike-out):

(1) Notwithstanding Article II or any other provision of this Constitution, all citizen, adult, resident, nonfelons of the United States shall have the right to vote in all elections for federal, state, and local offices within their residential areas, including for President and Vice President, and to have each ballot fairly and accurately counted. Provided, however, that ~~the right to vote for President and Vice President shall apply only to residents of the states and the District of Columbia, and~~ the right to vote for Members of the House and Senate shall apply only to residents of the states. ~~Votes for President and Vice President shall count equally toward allocating each state's electors.~~ **Votes cast by residents of United States territories for President and Vice President shall be tallied with votes cast by residents of the District constituting the seat of Government of the United States for determining the electors assigned to the District of Columbia under Amendment XXIII.**[*]

Addition 3: Elimination of the Electoral College

Revise Sections (1) and (2) of the Proposed Amendment as follows (additions in bold; deletions in strike-out):

(1) ~~Notwithstanding Article II or any other provision of this Constitution, a~~ **All** citizen, adult, resident, nonfelons of the United States shall have the right to vote in all elections for

---

[*] In the event that the amendment also will eliminate the Electoral College under Addition 3, then the bolded language should not be added.

federal, state, and local offices within their residential areas, including for President and Vice President, and to have each ballot fairly and accurately counted. **Those portions of Article II regarding the choosing of electors are hereby abolished. States and territories shall submit to Congress the vote totals for each candidate for President and Vice President as a pair at the time and in the manner that Congress shall direct. The winner of the election for President and Vice President as a pair shall be the candidate for President and candidate for Vice President who have received the most votes nationally among the candidates as determined by Congress.** Provided, however, that ~~the right to vote for President and Vice President shall apply only to residents of the states and the District of Columbia, and~~ the right to vote for Members of the House and Senate shall apply only to residents of the states. ~~Votes for President and Vice President shall count equally toward allocating each state's electors.~~

(2) All votes conducted for federal, state, or local office shall be substantially equally weighted ~~except for the weighting of Electoral College votes across states mandated under Article II in choosing the President and Vice President~~.

Addition 4: Changing the Composition of the United States Senate

Add the following after Section (1) of the Proposed Amendment, and renumber the remaining Sections of the Proposed Amendment to begin with Section 4:

(2) **The final phrase of Article V is hereby repealed.**[*]

---

[*] It may be necessary for this Article V repeal to be acted upon first before the rest of the amendment may pass. See chapter 3, note 49.

(3) Notwithstanding Article I, section 3(1), Article V, and Amendment XVII, Senators shall be apportioned among the several states in the same manner as Representatives in the House of Representatives, as directed in Amendment XIV, Section 2. In conducting the apportionment, each state shall have at least two Senators. This amendment shall not be construed as to affect the election or term of any Senator chosen before it becomes valid as part of the Constitution. Terms of Senators shall be staggered in accordance with Article I, section 3, clause 2.

NOTES

Introduction. Why We Need a Real Right to Vote

1. Minor v. Happersett, 88 U.S. 162, 163–64 (1874).

2. *Id.* at 175, 178.

3. Ellen Carol DuBois, *Suffrage: Women's Long Battle for the Vote* (New York: Simon and Schuster, 2020), 104–5.

4. U.S. Const., amend XIX; Breedlove v. Suttles, 302 U.S. 277, 282 (1937); Harper v. Virginia State Board of Elections, 383 U.S. 663 (1966); *id.* at 673 (Black, J., dissenting) ("The *Breedlove* case upheld a poll tax which was imposed on men but was not equally imposed on women and minors, and the Court today does not overrule that part of *Breedlove* which approved those discriminatory provisions."); see also *id.* at 669 (majority opinion) (overruling *Breedlove* only to "that extent" that it upheld a poll tax against equal protection challenge); Richard L. Hasen and Leah M. Litman, *Thin and Thick Conceptions of the Nineteenth Amendment Right to Vote and Congress's Power to Enforce It,* 108 Geo. L. J. 27, 32 (19th Amendment Edition 2020).

5. Steve Kolbert, *The Nineteenth Amendment Enforcement Power (but First, Which Is the Nineteenth Amendment, Again?),* 43 Fla. St. U. L. Rev. 507, 511–16 (2016).

6. Jo Yurcuba, "Over 200,000 Trans People Could Face Voting Restrictions Because of State Voter ID Laws," NBC News, November 1, 2022, https://www.nbcnews.com/nbc-out/out-politics-and-policy/200000-trans-people-face-voting-restrictions-state-id-laws-rcna52853 [https://perma.cc/UDU8-K6UD].

7. Kathryn K. O'Neill et al., *The Potential Impact of Voter Identification Laws on Transgender Voters in the 2022 General Election,* UCLA Williams Inst. (September 2022), https://williamsinstitute.law.ucla.edu/wp-content/uploads/Trans-Voter-ID-Sep-2022.pdf [https://perma.cc/6HXY-9MKF].

8. Tex. Democratic Party v. Abbott, 978 F.3d 168, 174 (5th Cir. 2020); see generally Vikram Amar, *Taking (Equal Voting) Rights Seriously: The Fifteenth Amendment as a Constitutional Foundation, and the Need for Judges to Remodel Their Approach to Age Discrimination in Political Rights,* 97 Notre Dame L. Rev. 1619 (2022).

9. Richard L. Hasen, *Election Meltdown: Dirty Tricks, Distrust, and the Threat to American Democracy* (New Haven: Yale University Press, 2020), 15–24.

10. I first wrote about a constitutional right to vote in Richard L. Hasen, "Bring on the 28th Amendment," *New York Times,* June 29, 2020, https://www.nytimes.com/2020/06/29/opinion/sunday/voting-rights.html. Few other scholars have explored the question in any depth. The most developed argument is Jamin B. Raskin, *What's Wrong with* Bush v. Gore *and Why We Need to Amend the Constitution to Ensure It Never Happens Again*, 61 Md. L. Rev. 652, 682–86 (2002). Raskin expanded on these ideas in his book, *Overruling Democracy: The Supreme Court vs. the American People* (New York: Routledge, 2003), 43–44. I discuss these ideas more fully in chapter 6. Chapter 6 also explores political attempts beginning in 1959 and again after the 2000 election to pass a constitutional amendment guaranteeing a right to vote.

11. See generally Richard L. Hasen, *The Voting Wars: From Florida 2000 to the Next Election Meltdown* (New Haven: Yale University Press, 2012), ch. 1; Hasen, *Election Meltdown, supra* note 9.

12. Hasen, *Voting Wars, supra* note 11; Hasen, *Election Meltdown, supra* note 9. See also *infra* chapter 4.

13. Richard L. Hasen, *Cheap Speech: How Disinformation Poisons Our Politics—and How to Cure It* (New Haven: Yale University Press, 2022), 1–19. See also *infra* chapter 5.

14. See *infra* chapter 5.

15. Hasen, *Voting Wars, supra* note 11; see also *infra* chapter 1.

16. U.S. Const., art. I; *id.,* amend XVII.

17. See *infra* chapter 1.

18. See *id.* (discussing Shelby County v. Holder, 570 U.S. 529 (2013)).

19. On the financial incentives for political parties to raise funds for litigation, see Derek T. Muller, *Reducing Election Litigation*, 90 Fordham L. Rev. 561, 563–67 (2021).

20. On those pathologies, see Richard L. Hasen, *Three Pathologies of American Voting Rights Illuminated by the COVID-19 Pandemic, and How to Treat and Cure Them*, 19 Election L. J. 263 (2020).

21. Clare Foran, Ali Zaslav, and Ted Barrett, "Senate Democrats Suffer Defeat on Voting Rights after Vote to Change Rules Fails," CNN, January 19, 2022, https://www.cnn.com/2022/01/19/politics/senate-voting-legislation-filibuster/index.html [https://perma.cc/XC43-XM9Q]. For a statement of the difficulties of getting from "here to there" on a constitutional amendment in the face of polarization between the parties over election rules, see Heather K. Gerken, *The Right to Vote: Is the Amendment Game Worth the Candle?*, 23 Wm. & Mary Bill Rts. J. 11, 12–13 (2014).

22. Mike Schneider and John Russell, "Majority of Population Now under Age 40," Voice of America, August 13, 2020, https://learningenglish.voanews.com/a

/study-majority-of-us-population-now-under-age-40-/5532061.html [https://perma.cc/DBS3-H696]; U.S. Const., amend XXVI. See National Archives, *The Constitution: Amendments 11–27*, https://www.archives.gov/founding-docs/amendments-11-27 [https://perma.cc/9RZR-PZZD] (noting that the Twenty-Sixth Amendment was passed by Congress and ratified by the states in 1971).

The only constitutional amendment ratified since then was the Twenty-Seventh Amendment, related to pay for members of Congress. That amendment was passed by Congress in 1789 but astonishingly was not ratified until 1992. See *id.*

The Equal Rights Amendment was passed in 1972, and it provided that it had to be ratified by 1979 to be effective. It was not ratified by then, but enough states signed on later to allow it to be ratified if one ignored the ratification deadline. A federal court has held that the amendment is not in effect because not enough states ratified by the deadline. Illinois v. Ferriero, 60 F.4th 704 (D.C. Cir. 2023).

An alternative path to passing a constitutional amendment is a constitutional convention convened under Article V of the constitution, followed by ratification by three-quarters of the state legislatures. See U.S. Const., art. V. I see no reason to believe that convening such a convention would provide an easier path to the passage of a constitutional right-to-vote amendment, and so I do not discuss this alternative possibility further in this book. On constitutional reform generally, see Sanford Levinson, *Our Undemocratic Constitution: Where the Constitution Goes Wrong (and How the People Can Correct It)* (Oxford: Oxford University Press, 2008).

23. Corrine M. McConnaughy, *The Woman Suffrage Movement in America: A Reassessment* (Cambridge: Cambridge University Press, 2013), 251.

Chapter 1. Courts Are Not Enough

1. Carrington v. Rash, 378 S.W.2d 304, 305–06 (Texas 1964), *rev'd*, 380 U.S. 89 (1965); Carrington v. Rash, 380 U.S. 89, 90–91, 94 n.4. The state constitution allowed military members to register to vote once they had completed their military service. *Carrington*, 378 S.W.2d at 305 ("Any member of the Armed Forces of the United States or component branches thereof, or in the military services of the United States, may vote only in the county in which he or she resided at the time of entering such service so long as he or she is a member of the Armed Forces.") (quoting Suffrage Article VI of the Texas Constitution). Before 1954, the Texas Constitution prohibited "all soldiers, marines and seamen employed in the service of the Army or Navy of the United States" from voting in Texas elections. In 1954, the state amended its constitution to allow those who were Texas residents before joining the military to vote. But under the amendment the state continued to disenfranchise those military members such as Carrington who moved to Texas from another state in the course of military duty.

2. U.S. Const., amend XIV; *Carrington*, 378 S.W.2d at 306–07 (rejecting Carrington's equal protection argument).

3. *Id.* at 307; Lassiter v. Northampton Cnty. Bd of Elections, 360 U.S. 45, 51 (1959).

4. *Carrington*, 378 S.W.2d at 306. The dissenters saw it differently:

> With present day mobility and industrialization, large groups, other than servicemen, move into the various communities of this state for limited stays, and establish voting residence. One need only look to the large shifts of civilian population to major construction areas as an illustration of this fact.
>
> Wherein lies the reasonable basis for distinguishing between these groups?

Id. at 310 (Smith, J., dissenting).

5. *Carrington*, 380 U.S. at 93.

6. *Id.* at 94, 97. The court briefly cited *Lassiter* for the proposition that states have broad powers to determine the conditions of suffrage. Justice Harlan, the lone dissenter in *Carrington*, also argued that neither *Lassiter* nor any of the other cases cited by the majority supported *Carrington's* holding striking down the provision in the Texas Constitution and enfranchising military voters. *Id.* at 98 n.1 (Harlan, J., dissenting).

7. For a brief introduction to the Warren Court, see Bernard Schwartz, ed., *The Warren Court: A Retrospective* (New York: Oxford University Press, 1996). For a look at the Warren Court's approach to political equality in election law cases and a comparison to post-Warren Court decisions, see Richard L. Hasen, *The Supreme Court and Election Law: Judging Equality from* Baker v. Carr *to* Bush v. Gore (New York: New York University Press, 2003).

8. Kramer v. Union Free School Dist. No. 15, 395 U.S. 621, 622–23 (1969). For good background on the case and litigation, see Eugene D. Mazo, "The Right to Vote in Local Elections: The Story of *Kramer v. Union Free School District No. 15*," in *Election Law Stories*, eds. Joshua A. Douglas and Eugene D. Mazo (St. Paul, MN: Foundation Press, 2016), 87.

9. *Kramer*, 395 U.S. at 630, 633. As Richard Briffault has noted, the court's discussion of the government's interest in *Kramer* contained a kind of sleight of hand. It conflated Kramer's subjective interest in voting in the school board elections with his objective interest in voting in such elections. Richard Briffault, *Who Rules at Home? One Person/One Vote and Local Governments*, 60 U. Chi. L. Rev. 339, 355–56 (1993).

10. On Carrington being white, see his military record originally posted at Ancestry.com [https://perma.cc/H5WQ-DEKP]. On Kramer's Jewish heritage, see Mazo, *supra* note 8, at 91–92.

11. Scott v. Sandford, 60 U.S. 393 (1857).

12. U.S. Const., amends XIII, XIV, XV. On the history of the Reconstruction Amendments and their aftermath, see Eric Foner, *The Second Founding: How the Civil War and Reconstruction Remade the Constitution* (New York: W. W. Norton, 2019); Eric Foner, *Reconstruction: America's Unfinished Revolution 1863–1877* (New York: Harper, updated ed. 2014); Alexander Keyssar, *The Right to Vote: The Contested History of Democracy in the United States* (New York: Basic Books, rev'd ed. 2009), 71–93. For an excellent compilation of key documents related to the passage, see the two-volume set, *The Reconstruction Amendments: The Essential Documents* (Kurt T. Lash, ed., Chicago and London: University of Chicago Press, 2021).

13. Giles v. Harris, 189 U.S. 475 (1903). For a critical examination of the failure to teach *Giles* as part of the constitutional canon of cases taught in American law schools, see Richard H. Pildes, *Democracy, Anti-Democracy, and the Canon*, 17 Const. Comment. 295 (2000). For an in-depth look at Jackson Giles's life and his case, see Bryan Lyman, "The Journey of Jackson Giles," *Montgomery Advertiser*, February 7, 2022, https://www.montgomeryadvertiser.com/in-depth/news/2022/01/27/jim-crow-alabama-jackson-giles-supreme-court/7995760002/ [https://perma.cc/3YFP-ZE3S].

14. On the brief history of enfranchisement of African Americans in the period right after the Civil War before the rise of Jim Crow, see J. Morgan Kousser, *The Shaping of Southern Politics: Suffrage Restriction and the Establishment of the One-Party South, 1880–1910* (New Haven: Yale University Press, 1974).

15. Voting Rights Act of 1965, § 5, now codified at 52 U.S.C. § 10304. Section 4 of the act, now codified at 52 U.S.C. § 10303, set forth the formula for determining which jurisdictions were covered by Section 5 preclearance. On the history of the passage of the Voting Rights Act, see Gary May, *Bending Toward Justice: The Voting Rights Act and the Transformation of American Democracy* (Durham, NC: Duke University Press, 2014). Before *Shelby County*, 570 U.S. 529 (2013), which struck down the coverage formula for the preclearance provision of the Voting Rights Act on the grounds that it violated a principle of "equal sovereignty" between states, the court had repeatedly upheld the provisions against constitutional challenge. Lopez v. Monterey County, 525 U.S. 266, 287 (1999); City of Rome v. United States, 446 U.S. 156, 187 (1980); South Carolina v. Katzenbach, 383 U.S. 301, 337 (1966). The court early read the scope of the preclearance provision broadly as well. Allen v. State Bd. Of Elections, 393 U.S. 544 (1969).

After the Supreme Court in *City of Mobile v. Bolden*, 446 U.S. 55 (1980), required proof of intentional racial vote dilution to make out a Fifteenth Amendment vote dilution claim, Congress amended Section 2 of the Voting Rights Act in 1982 to require only proof of discriminatory effect for a statutory vote dilution claim. See 52 U.S.C. § 10301(b) (violation of statute when "the political processes leading to nomination or election in the State or political subdivision are not equally open to participation" by members of a protected class "in that its members have less opportunity than other members of the electorate to participate in the political process and to elect representatives of their choice."); Thornburg v. Gingles, 478 U.S. 30 (1986) (construing the 1982 amendments to Section 2). *Gingles* read Section 2 broadly to allow for many successful vote dilution claims.

In more recent years, the court has cut back on its reading of Section 2, making proof of a violation much more difficult. See, e.g., Abbott v. Perez, 138 S. Ct. 2305 (2018); Brnovich v. Democratic Nat'l Comm., 141 S. Ct. 2321 (2021). For an analysis of how *Brnovich* significantly weakened Section 2 outside the context of redistricting, see Hearing on *"Restoring the Voting Rights Act After* Brnovich *and* Shelby County*"* Before the Subcomm. On the Const. of the S. Comm. On the Judiciary, 117th Cong. 4–5 (2021) (statement of Richard L. Hasen, Chancellor's Professor of L. and Pol. Sci., UC Irvine School of Law) (hereafter, Hasen Testimony). However, in *Allen v. Milligan*, 143 S. Ct. 1487 (2023), the Supreme Court surprisingly reaffirmed the constitutionality of Section 2 and upheld the general, somewhat difficult, framework it applies to such claims in the redistricting context. See Richard L. Hasen, "John Roberts Throws a Curveball," *New York Times*, June 8, 2023, https://www.nytimes.com/2023/06/08/opinion/milligan-roberts-court-voting-right-act.html.

For an examination of the success of Section 2 plaintiffs over time, see Ellen Katz et al., *Documenting Discrimination in Voting: Judicial Findings Under Section 2 of the Voting Rights Act Since 1982*, 39 U. Mich. J. L. Reform 643 (2006).

16. Richardson v. Ramirez, 418 U.S. 24 (1974) (rejecting equal protection challenge to felon disenfranchisement); Adams v. Clinton, 90 F. Supp. 2d 35 (D.D.C.), aff'd, 531 U.S. 941 (2000) (rejecting argument that D.C. residents have the right to vote for members of Congress); Igartúa v. United States, 626 F.3d 592, 597–98 (1st Cir. 2010) ("There has been no amendment that would permit the residents of Puerto Rico to vote for Representatives to the U.S. House of Representatives. . . . Voting rights for the House of Representatives are limited to the citizens of the states absent constitutional amendment to the contrary."); Brnovich v. Democratic Nat'l Comm., 141 S. Ct. 2321 (upholding Arizona ban on third-party collection of mailed ballots). For a critique of *Adams*, see Jamin B. Raskin, *What's Wrong with* Bush v. Gore *and Why We Need to Amend the Constitution to Ensure It Never Happens Again*, 61 Md. L. Rev. 652, 682–86 (2002). The statutory provision barring literacy tests in the Voting Rights Act is codified at 52 U.S.C. § 10501.

17. On the emergence of the strict scrutiny standard in the voting cases, see Daniel H. Lowenstein et al., *Election Law—Cases and Materials* (Durham, NC: Carolina Academic Press, 7th ed. 2022), 59–60. On student voting rights, see *infra* chapter 2.

18. Bush v. Gore, 531 U.S. 98, 104 (2000).

19. Crawford v. Marion Cnty. Election Bd., 553 U.S. 181 (2008). For a critique of the burdens imposed on voters seeking to prove the unconstitutionality of strict voting requirements compared to the burdens imposed on the state to defend their requirements, see Richard L. Hasen, *Softening Voter ID Laws Through Litigation: Is It Enough?*, 2016 Wis. L. Rev. Forward, 100.

20. Canadian Charter of Rights & Freedoms § 3; Basic Law of the Federal Republic of Germany art. 38, cl. 2 (official English translation).

21. U.S. Const., art. I, § 2; art. II; Alex Keyssar, "Constitutional Amendments and the Right to Vote: Some Reflections on History 1," a manuscript prepared for the Claiming Democracy conference, Washington, D.C., November 2003, and posted at https://archive.fairvote.org/media/rtv/keyssar.pdf [https://perma.cc/8L8Y-J8FT].

22. Keyssar, *supra* note 12, at 74–81. For a more in-depth look at the fight over how broadly to write the Fifteenth Amendment, see Travis Crum, *The Unabridged Fifteenth Amendment*, 133 Yale L. J. (forthcoming 2023), *draft available*, https://papers.ssrn.com/abstract_id=4390108. One version of Senator Wilson's proposed universalist amendment that passed the Senate, quoted in Appendix B to the Crum article, reads: "There shall be no discrimination in any State among the citizens of the United States in the exercise of the elective franchise in any election therein, or in the qualifications of office in any State, on account of race, color, nativity, property, education, or religious belief." Meanwhile, Senator Warner's proposed amendment, which did not pass the Senate, contained more of an affirmative right to vote: "The right of citizens of the United States to hold office shall not be denied or abridged by the United States or any State on account of property, race, color, or previous condition of servitude; and every male citizen of the United States of the age of twenty-one years or over, and who is of sound mind, shall have an equal vote at all elections in the State in which he shall have actually resided for a period of one year next preceding such election, except such as may hereafter engage in insurrection or rebellion against the United States, and such as shall be duly convicted of treason, felony, or other infamous crime." *Id.* at 45 n.282 (citation omitted).

23. For a general look at election reform efforts through American history, as summarized below, see Richard L. Hasen, "Election Reform: Past, Present, and Future," in *Oxford Handbook of American Election Law* (Eugene Mazo, ed., Oxford: Oxford University Press, forthcoming 2024). Some of the discussion in the next few paragraphs draws from this discussion. On the passage of the Voting Rights Act, see May, *supra* note 15.

24. Minor v. Happersett, 88 U.S. 162 (1874). For a summary of the literature on the path to passage of the Nineteenth Amendment, see Richard L. Hasen and Leah M. Litman, *Thin and Thick Conceptions of the Nineteenth Amendment Right to Vote and Congress's Power to Enforce It*, 108 Geo. L. J. 2 (19th Amendment Edition 2020). Among the most important historical accounts are Ellen Carol DuBois, *Suffrage:*

Women's Long Battle for the Vote (New York: Simon and Schuster, 2020); Reva B. Siegel, Essay, *The Nineteenth Amendment and the Democratization of the Family*, 129 Yale L. J. F. 450, 456–62 (2020); Steve Kolbert, *The Nineteenth Amendment Enforcement Power (But First, Which One is the Nineteenth Amendment, Again?)*, 43 Fla. St. U. L. Rev. 507 (2016); Zornitsa Keremidchieva, *The Congressional Debates on the 19th Amendment: Jurisdictional Rhetoric and the Assemblage of the US Body Politic*, 99 Q. J. Speech 51 (2013); Corrine M. McConnaughy, *The Woman Suffrage Movement in America: A Reassessment* (Cambridge: Cambridge University Press, 2013); Rosalyn Terborg-Penn, *African American Women in the Struggle for the Vote, 1850–1920* (Bloomington: Indiana University Press, 1998); Aileen S. Kraditor, *The Ideas of the Woman Suffrage Movement: 1890–1920* (New York: W. W. Norton, 1981, 1965).

25. David Schleicher, *The Seventeenth Amendment and Federalism in an Age of National Political Parties*, 65 Hastings L. J. 1043, 1058 (2014). The Seventeenth Amendment changed the Senate selection mechanism contained in Article I, section 3 of the constitution, reading: "The Senate of the United States shall be composed of two Senators from each State, chosen by the Legislature thereof, for six Years; and each Senator shall have one Vote."

Schleicher suggests a reason why state legislators would give up their own power to choose U.S. senators: united national political parties had started emerging, and voters began viewing their votes for state legislators as proxies for choosing senators. This nationalization of state legislative elections meant that state legislators had less control of their own destinies. Legislator self-interest ironically supported divesting state legislatures of their power to choose U.S. senators. Business interests seeking to influence state legislators and legislative elections also had an incentive to decouple state legislative races from national races over which they had less leverage. Schleicher, *supra*, at 1062–81; see also Daniel Wirls, *Regionalism, Rotten Boroughs, Race, and Realignment: The Seventeenth Amendment and the Politics of Representation*, 13 Stud. Am. Pol. Dev. 1 (1999) (positing that regional divisions rather than partisan politics helps explain support for passage of the Seventeenth Amendment); Todd J. Zywicki, *Beyond the Shell and Husk of History: The History of the Seventeenth Amendment and Its Implications for Current Reform Proposals*, 45 Clev. St. L. Rev. 165 (1997) (offering a public choice theory based upon interest and business group pressure for passage of the amendment).

There were other factors as well. In states such as Oregon, legislative candidates were required to state on the ballot whether they would abide by the results of a nonbinding popular vote for U.S. senator. Further, urban political machines, normal adversaries to Progressivists, had their own reasons for supporting ratification of the Seventeenth Amendment. Rural interests were overrepresented in state legislatures, and urban areas had a greater chance of influencing the choice of senator through direct election than through indirectly electing the state legislature. Schleicher, *supra*, at 1056; John D. Buenker, *The Urban Political Machine and the Seventeenth Amendment*, 56 J. Am. Hist. 305 (1969).

26. See John F. Kowal and Wilfred U. Codrington III, *The People's Constitution: 200 Years, 27 Amendments, and the Promise of a More Perfect Union* (New York: The New Press, 2021), 181–215. See also *id.* at 185–87 (on passage of the Twenty-Third Amendment).

27. See *id.* at 192 ("By 1942, due to demographic changes, for every *three* African Americans the poll tax kept from the ballot, *five* white Americans were also disenfranchised.") (original emphasis and citation omitted); *id.* at 192–97 (recounting history of Twenty-Fourth Amendment).

28. Bruce Ackerman and Jennifer Nou, *Canonizing the Civil Rights Revolution: The People and the Poll Tax*, 103 Nw. U. L. Rev. 63, 67 (2009) (original emphasis and footnote omitted); see also Michael Waldman, *The Fight to Vote* (New York: Simon & Schuster, 2016), 160–63; Kowal and Codrington, *supra* note 26, at 195.

29. Kowal and Codrington, *supra* note 26, at 195; Harper v. Virginia St. Bd. of Elections, 383 U.S. 663 (1966).

30. Kowal and Codrington, *supra* note 26, at 207–12.

31. *Oregon v. Mitchell*, 400 U.S. 112 (1970), was the case in which the Supreme Court upheld the lowering of the voting age to eighteen in federal but not state elections. On the passage of the Twenty-Sixth Amendment, see Kowal and Codrington, *supra* note 26, at 207–15.

32. On the overturning of *Roe v. Wade*, 410 U.S. 113 (1973), see *Dobbs v. Jackson Women's Health Org.*, 142 S. Ct. 2228 (2022). On the whittling away of Voting Rights Act protections through chary statutory interpretation, see Hasen Testimony, *supra* note 15.

33. Baker v. Carr, 369 U.S. 186 (1962); Reynolds v. Sims, 377 U.S. 533 (1964); Wesberry v. Sanders, 376 U.S. 1 (1964); Miranda v. Arizona, 384 U.S. 436 (1966). On *Baker* being the most important case in his tenure on the court, see Earl Warren, *The Memoirs of Chief Justice Earl Warren* (Chicago: University of Chicago Press, 1977), 306.

34. Evenwel v. Abbott, 578 U.S. 54 (2016). On the open question following *Evenwel* about whether equal numbers of people are constitutionally required, see Daniel P. Tokaji, *Evenwel and the Next Case*, ACS Expert Forum, December 3, 2015, https://www.acslaw.org/?post_type=acsblog&p=11242 [https://perma.cc/YZG2 -M89L].

35. *Evenwel*, 578 U.S. at 74–75; *id.* at 75–76 (Thomas, J., concurring in the judgment) ("In my view, the majority has failed to provide a sound basis for the one-person, one-vote principle because no such basis exists. The Constitution does not prescribe any one basis for apportionment within States."); *id.* at 103 (Alito J., joined by Thomas, J., concurring in the judgment) ("In light of the history of Article I, § 2, of the original Constitution and § 2 of the Fourteenth Amendment, it is clear that

the apportionment of seats in the House of Representatives was based in substantial part on the distribution of political power among the States and not merely on some theory regarding the proper nature of representation. It is impossible to draw any clear constitutional command from this complex history.").

For a critique of originalist methodology applied to constitutional interpretation, see Erwin Chemerinsky, *Worse than Nothing: The Dangerous Fallacy of Originalism* (New Haven: Yale University Press, 2022). For a look at the inconsistent originalism of one of the theory's main proponents, Justice Antonin Scalia, See Richard L. Hasen, *The Justice of Contradictions: Antonin Scalia and the Politics of Disruption* (New Haven: Yale University Press, 2018), 40–63.

36. U.S. Const., art. I, § 8; *id.*, amend X.

37. Shelby County v. Holder, 570 U.S. 529, 567 n.2 (2013) (Ginsburg, J., dissenting).

38. For a detailed examination of the preclearance process and the cases interpreting it, see Lowenstein et al., *supra* note 17, at 221–66.

39. On the history of preclearance and renewals of section 5, see *Shelby County*, 570 U.S. at 537–39; U.S. Department of Justice, "Jurisdictions Previously Covered by Section 5," https://www.justice.gov/crt/jurisdictions-previously-covered-section-5 [https://perma.cc/TXQ8-G8AE?type=standard] (listing when jurisdictions became covered by the preclearance provision of the Voting Rights Act). On section 5 as "strong medicine," see Voting Rights Act: Hearings on H.R. 6400 Before Subcomm. No. 5 of the House Comm. on the Judiciary, 89th Cong. 110 (1965) (statement of Rep. Chelf). In *South Carolina v. Katzenbach*, 383 U.S. at 315, 334 (1966) the Supreme Court called the Voting Rights Act a "complex scheme of stringent remedies" and it called preclearance an "uncommon exercise of congressional power" that was justified by the extreme circumstances.

The effects of *Shelby County* killing off preclearance were immediate and bad for minority voters, as Justice Kagan explained in a recent dissent:

> Once Section 5's strictures came off, States and localities put in place new restrictive voting laws, with foreseeably adverse effects on minority voters. On the very day *Shelby County* issued, Texas announced that it would implement a strict voter-identification requirement that had failed to clear Section 5. Other States—Alabama, Virginia, Mississippi—fell like dominoes, adopting measures similarly vulnerable to preclearance review. The North Carolina Legislature, starting work the day after *Shelby County*, enacted a sweeping election bill eliminating same-day registration, forbidding out-of-precinct voting, and reducing early voting, including souls-to-the-polls Sundays. (That law went too far even without Section 5: A court struck it down because the State's legislators had a racially discriminatory purpose.) States and localities

redistricted—drawing new boundary lines or replacing neighborhood-based seats with at-large seats—in ways guaranteed to reduce minority representation. And jurisdictions closed polling places in mostly minority areas, enhancing an already pronounced problem. Pettigrew, The Racial Gap in Wait Times, 132 Pol. Sci. Q 527, 527 (2017) (finding that lines in minority precincts are twice as long as in white ones, and that a minority voter is six times more likely to wait more than an hour).

Brnovich v. Democratic National Committee, 141 S. Ct. 2321, 2355 (2021) (Kagan, J., dissenting) (some citations omitted).

40. U.S. Department of Justice, *supra* note 39.

41. For background on Congress's failure to change the preclearance formula during the debate over the 2006 Voting Rights Act amendments, see Nathaniel Persily, *The Promises and Pitfalls of the New Voting Rights Act*, 117 Yale L. J. 174 (2007); Richard H. Pildes, *Political Avoidance, Constitutional Theory, and the VRA*, 117 Yale L. J. Pocket Part 148 (2007). On the history and demise of section 5, see J. Morgan Kousser, *The Strange, Ironic Career of Section 5 of the Voting Rights Act, 1965–2007*, 86 Texas L. Rev. 667 (2008).

42. The court held in a series of cases that to regulate the states, Congress needed to create a legislative record, subject to review by the courts, demonstrating that states were engaged in unconstitutional conduct, and that the means that Congress chose to address the states' unconstitutional conduct were "congruent" and "proportional" to the nature of that conduct. On these federalism cases generally, see Ruth Colker and James J. Brudney, *Dissing Congress*, 100 Mich. L. Rev. 80 (2001). On the potential application to these federalism cases to the Voting Rights Act before the Supreme Court decided *Shelby County*, see Richard L. Hasen, *Congressional Power to Renew the Preclearance Provisions of the Voting Rights Act after* Tennessee v. Lane, 66 Ohio St. L. J. 177 (2005); Hasen, "Congressional Power to Renew the Preclearance Provisions," in *The Future of the Voting Rights Act*, eds. David Epstein, Rodolfo O. de la Garza, Sharyn O'Halloran, and Richard Pildes (New York: Russell Sage Foundation, 2006), 81–106.

43. Professor Persily, in Persily, *supra* note 41, at 183 n. 32 described the debate in the Senate:

The debate in the Senate hearings revealed a bit of a rift between legal academics and voting rights advocates. See generally Rick Hasen, Why Bother Trying To Fix Section 5, Election Law Blog, May 13, 2006, http://electionlawblog.org /archives/005607.html (describing the testimony of law professors). Loyola Law School Professor Richard Hasen alerted the committee to the potential constitutional difficulties with the bill and provided suggestions on how to save it. An Introduction to the Expiring Provisions of the Voting Rights Act and Legal Issues Relating to Reauthorization: Hearing Before the S. Comm. on the Judiciary, 109th Cong. 214–19 (2006) [hereinafter Introductory Senate Hearings] (statement of Richard Hasen). NYU Law School Professor Samuel Issacharoff suggested a dramatically different enforcement regime for section 5. Id. at 220–25 (statement of Samuel Issacharoff). NYU Law School Professor Richard Pildes raised concerns about the new retrogression standard that overruled Georgia v. Ashcroft, 539 U.S. 461 (2003), the constitutional deficiencies in the record supporting reauthorization, and the inability of the section 5 architecture to deal with contemporary voting rights problems. The Continuing Need for Section 5 Pre-Clearance: Hearing Before the S. Comm. on the Judiciary, 109th Cong. 198–207 (2006) [hereinafter Need for Section 5 Pre-Clearance Senate Hearing] (statement of Richard Pildes). Stanford Law School Professor Pamela Karlan defended the constitutionality of the bill. Id. at 174–95 (statement of Pamela S. Karlan). I focused my remarks . . . on what the retrogression standard should mean in practice. Understanding the Benefits and Costs of Preclearance: Hearing Before the S. Comm. on the Judiciary, 109th Cong. 11–13, 105–37 (2006) (statement of Nathaniel Persily). Professor Drew Days of Yale Law School detailed his experiences as Solicitor General and Assistant Attorney General for Civil Rights, suggesting that the VRA was still necessary and constitutional, and reinforced the findings of the National Commission on the VRA. Id. at 5–7, 31–70 (statement of Drew Days). Professor Sherrilyn Ifill of the University of Maryland attempted to explain why the Supreme Court's decision in League of United Latin American Citizens v. Perry, 126 S. Ct. 2594 (2006), reinforced the need for a strong VRA. Renewing the Temporary Provisions of the Voting Rights Act: Legislative Options After LULAC v. Perry: Hearing Before the Subcomm. on the Constitution, Civil Rights and Property Rights of the S. Comm. on the Judiciary, 109th Cong. 6–8, 50–60 (2006) [hereinafter Section 5 Renewal Senate Hearing] (statement of Sherrilyn Ifill). Seattle University Law School's Joaquin Avila attested to the persistence of racially polarized voting in California. Id. at 11–13, 27–44 (statement of Joaquin G. Avila).

44. Northwest Austin Mun. Util. Dist. No. One v. Holder, 557 U.S. 193 (2009); *id.* at 212. On how the court was disingenuous in refusing to reach the constitutional question, see Richard L. Hasen, *Constitutional Avoidance and Anti-Avoidance by the Roberts Court*, 2009 Sup. Ct. Rev. 181 (2010).

45. *Shelby County*, 570 U.S. at 544 ("Not only do States retain sovereignty under the Constitution, there is also a 'fundamental principle of equal sovereignty' among the States. The Voting Rights Act sharply departs from these basic principles." (quoting *NAMUDNO*)). For a trenchant critique of the equal sovereignty principle, see Leah M. Litman, *Inventing Equal Sovereignty*, 114 Mich. L. Rev. 1207 (2016).

46. On the faux minimalism of the decision, see Richard L. Hasen, *Shelby County and the Illusion of Minimalism*, 22 Wm. & Mary Bill Rts. J. 713 (2014).

47. *Shelby County*, 570 U.S. at 590 (Ginsburg, J., dissenting).

48. Colker and Brudney, *supra* note 42.

49. For some examples of recent bold voting rights legislation that passed the House but did not survive in the Senate, see, H.R. 1, 117th Cong. (2021) (For the People Act); H.R. 5746, 117th Cong. (2022) (combining the Freedom to Vote Act and the John R. Lewis Voting Rights Advancement Act).

50. Franita Tolson, *In Congress We Trust?: Enforcing Voting Rights from the Founding to the Jim Crow Era* (Cambridge: Cambridge University Press, forthcoming 2024).

51. Keyssar, *supra* note 12, at 292 ("Many Democrats were also wary [of a 2001 proposal to amend the constitution to include an affirmative right to vote.] Some argued that an amendment was unnecessary, that there was already an implicit right to vote in the Constitution . . ."); email from Pamela S. Karlan to author (May 14, 2020) ("the problem with proposing [a constitutional right to vote] amendment might be that it would have the negative implication that the current Fourteenth Amendment substantive equal protection doctrine can't be read to do so and that it wasn't clear what laws would become unconstitutional that weren't so already").

Chapter 2. An Amendment for Political Equals

1. Carrington v. Rash, 380 U.S. 89, 93 (1965).

2. Residency is a generally accepted criterion for voting around the world. See ACE, The Electoral Knowledge Network, Legal Framework, Voter Registration, Requirements, https://aceproject.org/ace-en/topics/lf/lfb/lfb04/default#_edn2 [https://perma.cc/W6SL-6B8H] (listing "residence," along with citizenship, age, and other restrictions such as mental competence as "reasonable limits on the right to vote" that have been established under international law). See also Human Rights Comm., General Comment 25 (57), General Comments under article 40, paragraph 4, of the International Covenant on Civil and Political Rights, U.N. Doc. CCPR/C/21/Rev.1/Add.7 (1996), available at: http://hrlibrary.umn.edu/gencomm /hrcom25.htm#:~:text=Article%2025%20of%20the%20Covenant,have%20 access%20to%20public%20service; International Covenant on Civil & Political Rights, art. 25, December 16, 1966 (setting forth universal voting conditions for the franchise); Alexander Kirschner, *The International Status of the Right to Vote* (undated manuscript) (posted on FairVote website, https://fairvote.app.box.com/v/kirshner -international-rtv [https://perma.cc/Z4XM-37AA]).

3. Analogizing to residency requirements for voting, some have defended campaign finance limits on contributions from out-of-state residents in state elections.

These laws have faced mixed reception in the courts when challenged on First Amendment grounds. See Daniel H. Lowenstein et al., *Election Law—Cases and Materials* (Durham, NC: Carolina Academic Press, 7th ed. 2022), 1072–73:

> Oregon voters amended their constitution to penalize state and local candidates who accepted more than ten percent of their funds from out-of-district contributors. The Ninth Circuit struck down the ban as unconstitutional. *VanNatta v. Keisling*, 151 F.3d 1215 (9th Cir. 1998), cert. denied *sub nom. Miller v. VanNatta*, 525 U.S.1104 (1999). It held that the ban was not narrowly tailored to prevent corruption because the measure "bans all out-of-district donations, regardless of size or any other factor that would tend to indicate corruption." In *State v. Alaska Civil Liberties Union*, 978 P.2d 597, 616 (Alaska 1999), the Alaska Supreme Court distinguished *VanNatta* in upholding Alaska's ban on campaign contributions by non-residents. "Oregon's out-of-district restrictions applied to both nonresidents and residents of Oregon. But Alaska's challenged provisions apply only to nonresidents of Alaska, and do not limit speech of those most likely to be directly affected by the outcome of a campaign for state office—Alaska residents regardless of what district they live in." . . .

In *Thompson v. Hebdon*, 7 F.4th 811 (9th Cir. 2021) . . . , the Ninth Circuit held unconstitutional a provision of Alaska law limiting candidates from accepting more than $3,000 per year from out-of-state residents. The dissenting judge would have accepted as compelling Alaska's stated interest in "self-governance" to justify the limitation on accepting contributions from out-of-state residents . . .

4. Mills v. Bartlett, 377 S.W.2d 636, 637 (Tex. 1964).

5. *Carrington*, 380 U.S. at 91.

6. The Texas Supreme Court wrote that military personnel "in the nature of their sojourn at a particular place [they] are not, and cannot be, a part of the local community in the same sense as its permanent residents." Carrington v. Rash, 378 S.W.2d 304, 306 (Tex. 1964), *rev'd*, 380 U.S. 89 (1965).

The Supreme Court's decision in *Evans v. Cornman*, 398 U.S. 419 (1970), is in line with its *Carrington* decision. In *Evans*, Maryland residents who lived in a federal enclave in Maryland for the National Institutes of Health were denied the right to vote in Maryland elections. The Supreme Court affirmed a district court decision holding the disenfranchisement violated the Fourteenth Amendment's Equal Protection Clause: "In their day-to-day affairs, residents of the NIH grounds are just as interested in and connected with electoral decisions as they were prior to 1953 when the area came under federal jurisdiction and as are their neighbors who live off the enclave. In nearly every election, federal, state, and local, for offices from the Presidency to the school board, and on the entire variety of other ballot propositions, appellees have a stake equal to that of other Maryland residents. As the District Court concluded, they are entitled under the Fourteenth Amendment to protect that stake by exercising the equal right to vote." *Id.* at 426.

In a series of Warren Court cases, the Supreme Court had held that while states could require residency of a few months before someone could be allowed to vote, a greater period of time would violate the Equal Protection Clause of the Fourteenth Amendment. See, e.g., Dunn v. Blumstein, 405 U.S. 330 (1972) (striking down Tennessee three-month residency requirement for voting). In *Dunn*, the court explained the importance of *Carrington* to the question of the constitutionality of residency requirements:

> *Carrington* sufficiently disposes of this defense of durational residence requirements. The State's legitimate purpose is to determine whether certain persons in the community are bona fide residents. A durational residence requirement creates a classification that may, in a crude way, exclude nonresidents from that group. But it also excludes many residents. Given the State's legitimate purpose and the individual interests that are affected, the classification is all too imprecise.

Dunn, 405 U.S. at 351.

7. *Carrington*, 380 U.S. at 93.

8. *Id.* at 94.

9. United States v. Texas, 445 F. Supp. 1245 (S. D. Tex. 1978), *aff'd in memorandum op. sub nom.* Symm v. United States, 439 U.S. 1105 (1979).

10. *Id.* at 1252.

11. *Id.* at 1257. Given the emphasis on equal protection, it is odd that the court held the restriction violated the Twenty-Sixth Amendment, about which the court offered little analysis.

Justice William Rehnquist, joined by Chief Justice Warren Berger dissented from the summary affirmance in *Symm*, stating the view that the three-judge court lacked subject matter jurisdiction over the case. *Symm*, 439 U.S. at 1105 (Rehnquist, J., dissenting).

12. Geoffrey S. Connor, Secretary of State, State of Texas, Election Law Opinion GSC-1, January 22, 2004, https://www.sos.state.tx.us/elections/elo/gsc1.pdf [https://perma.cc/H85L-NKKK].

13. Alex Nguyen, "College Voters Held Back by Texas Election Law, Lack of On-Campus Polling Sites," *Texas Tribune*, October 28, 2022, https://www.texastribune .org/2022/10/28/texas-young-voter-turnout-access/ [https://perma.cc/2MNP -WBY3] ("Texas also remains one of the few states to not accept student ID cards as a form of voter ID"); Jen Rice, "Why Texas Doesn't Have Online Voter Registration," *Houston Chronicle*, December 13, 2022, https://www.houstonchronicle.com

/politics/texas/article/texas-online-voter-registration-17632872.php. ("For the vast majority of Americans, registering to vote is easier than ordering food delivery from a phone app. Not so in Texas, where, unlike 42 states and Washington, D.C., not all residents are offered the convenience. Instead, Texans must obtain a paper copy of the application and mail it in, happen across voter registrars who get them signed up, or are lucky enough to be registered by volunteers with the League of Women Voters at a naturalization ceremony when they become new U.S. citizens. There is one exception: a federal judge in 2020 forced Texas to allow online voter registration when residents renew or update their driver licenses using the Texas Department of Public Safety website, after ruling the state was violating federal law. In the first year and a half of the program, 1.5 million residents used that option, according to state data.")

14. Andrew Eversden and Emma Platoff, "Campaign for Congressional Candidate Mike Siegel Disputes Account of Worker's Arrest," *Texas Tribune*, October 11, 2018, https://www.texastribune.org/2018/10/11/campaign-congressional-candidate-mike-siegel-disputes-account-workers-/ [https://perma.cc/FS4N-5X2H]; Matt Zdun, "Prairie View A&M University's Voter Registration Issues Are Resolved, But Voting Barriers Remain," *Texas Tribune*, October 16, 2018, https://www.texastribune.org/2018/10/16/Prairie-View-voter-registration/ [https://perma.cc/4E9P-CC8K].

The county apparently had told the students who lived in dorms that they had to register to vote using one of two general addresses for campus mail because the dorms did not have individual addresses. One of those two general addresses, however, was outside the district, and those students were told they would not be allowed to vote in the congressional election unless they filled out a change-of-address form. The secretary of state intervened and said that students did not need to fill out the form in order to be able to vote. *Id.*

15. Interview with Jacob Aronowitz, December 22, 2022 (on file with the author).

16. Alexa Ura, "Texas' Oldest Black University Was Built on a Former Plantation. Its Students Still Fight a Legacy of Voter Suppression," *Texas Tribune*, February 25, 2021, https://www.texastribune.org/2021/02/25/waller-county-texas-voter-suppression/ [https://perma.cc/5SZN-QQ4G].

17. Johnson v. Waller County, 593 F.Supp.3d 540, 548 (S.D. Texas 2022).

18. Press Release, "Texas Court Fails to Recognize Waller County's Denial of Black Students and Voters' Access to Equitable Early Voting," LDF Media, March 31, 2022, https://www.naacpldf.org/wp-content/uploads/Statement-Waller-Outcome-Negative-FINAL.pdf [https://perma.cc/BU4N-XPD9].

19. "Sandra Bland: Timeline of Her Arrest and Death," ABC 13, May 24, 2019, https://abc13.com/sandra-bland-arrest-death-jailhouse/2211158/ [https://perma

.cc/9FB9-GS3C]; David Montgomery, "Sandra Bland, It Turns Out, Filmed Traffic Stop Confrontation Herself," *New York Times*, May 7, 2019, https://www.nytimes .com/2019/05/07/us/sandra-bland-video-brian-encinia.html [https://perma.cc /JDN6-8PDU].

20. Pew Research Center, "Religious Landscape Study, Party Affiliation Among Adults in Texas by Race/Ethnicity," (n.d.), https://www.pewresearch.org/religion /religious-landscape-study/compare/party-affiliation/by/racial-and-ethnic -composition/among/state/texas/ [https://perma.cc/XBR7-QKC8].

21. Lassiter v. Northampton Cnty. Bd. of Elections, 360 U.S. 45, 51 (1959); 52 U.S.C. § 10501 (2023) (portion of Voting Rights Act banning literacy tests by statute). On the analogous argument in *Shelby County*, see chapter 1.

22. Reynolds v. Sims, 377 U.S. 533 (1964). On the arguments in *Evenwel v. Abbott*, 578 U.S. 54 (2016), see chapter 1. There is another set of cases involving special purpose district elections that is not subject to the one-person, one-vote rule. See *infra* note 35.

23. For a summary and citations to the relevant literature, see Jonas Hultin Rosenberg and Johan Wejryd, *Attitudes Toward Competing Voting-Right Requirements: Evidence from a Conjoint Experiment*, 77 Electoral Studies 102470, 1–2 (2022), https://www.sciencedirect.com/science/article/pii/S0261379422000300?via%3Dihub.

24. Richard L. Hasen, *Cheap Speech: How Disinformation Poisons Our Politics—and How to Cure It* (New Haven: Yale University Press, 2022).

25. Alexander Keyssar, *The Right to Vote: The Contested History of Democracy in the United States* (New York: Basic Books, rev'd ed. 2009), 3–22 (describing voting restrictions in the early United States). On international law and comparative norms, see *supra* note 2. See also Article 21 of the Universal Declaration of Human Rights, stating in pertinent part that the "will of the people shall be the basis of the authority of government; this will shall be expressed in periodic and genuine election which shall be by universal and equal suffrage and shall be held by secret vote or by equivalent free voting procedures." G. A. Res. 217 (III) A, Universal Declaration of Human Rights, art. 21 (December 10, 1948).

26. This statement is subject, of course, to protection of rights in the constitution that cannot be infringed through legislation, such as religious liberty, freedom of speech, and criminal procedure protections.

27. Richard Briffault, *Three Questions for the "Right to Vote" Amendment*, 23 Wm. & Mary Bill Rts. J. 27, 30 (2014); Rosenberg and Wejryd, *supra* note 23, at 7. There was also support in the survey for disenfranchising citizens who had not resided in the United States for some time. See *id.* ("Summing up, the right to vote for all adult, law-abiding U.S. citizens is supported in a firm majority of the cases while, at the same time, considerable minorities support disenfranchising citizens who do not pay income taxes or are not residents in the U.S.")

28. Jonah Goldberg, "The Cellblock Voting Bloc," *Los Angeles Times*, March 8, 2005, at B11. Along similar lines, see Jonah Goldberg, "Column: Why Lena Dunham Shouldn't Be Allowed to Vote," *Los Angeles Times*, November 3, 2014, https://www.latimes.com/opinion/op-ed/la-oe-goldberg-voting-citizenship-20141104-column.html. For a sharp response, see Jon Healey, "Opinion: Jonah Goldberg and the Elitist Argument Against High Turnout Elections," *Los Angeles Times*, November 4, 2014, https://www.latimes.com/opinion/opinion-la/la-ol-jonah-goldberg-low-information-voters-elitism-20141104-story.html.

29. I focus here on the election of representatives and leave open whether these rules should apply to ballot measures in states and localities that use direct democracy.

30. This provision could be tweaked to exclude voting rights for those who have been found to be mentally incompetent. I discuss this issue further in chapter 3. One study found that 58 democratic countries limited voting on the basis of mental incompetence while only four did not. Louis Massicotte, André Blais and Antoine Yoshinaka, *Establishing the Rules of the Game: Election Laws in Democracies* (Toronto: University of Toronto Press, 2004), 27.

31. Although not phrased as a matter of due process, the Supreme Court in *United States v. Classic*, 313 U.S. 299, 315 (1941) held that "[o]bviously included within the right to choose, secured by the Constitution, is the right of qualified voters within a state to cast their ballots and have them counted at Congressional elections."

As I argued in a recent amicus brief filed in the Supreme Court, "It would violate the Due Process Clause of the Fourteenth Amendment for a state legislature to seek to retroactively disenfranchise its own voters. See *Roe v. State of Ala.*, 43 F.3d 574, 580–81 (11th Cir. 1995); see also Justin Levitt, *Failed Elections and the Legislative Selection of Presidential Electors*, 96 N.Y.U. L. Rev. 1052, 1071 (2021) ('[T]he Due Process Clause would be implicated in any attempt to replace, after the election had begun, the popular election processes currently authorized by statute with another means of elector selection.'); Edward B. Foley, *Due Process, Fair Play, and Excessive Partisanship: A New Principle for Judicial Review of Election Laws*, 84 U. Chi. L. Rev. 655, 731 (2017); Richard H. Pildes, *Judging 'New Law' in Election Disputes*, 29 Fla. St. U. L. Rev. 691, 706–07 (2001)." Brief of Professor Richard L. Hasen as Amicus Curiae Supporting Respondents, Moore v. Harper, No. 21–1271, https://www.supremecourt.gov/DocketPDF/21/21-1271/243888/20221025153857936_42915%20Hubbard%20BR.pdf.

32. Bush v. Gore, 531 U.S. 98, 104 (2000). For an argument following the disputed 2000 presidential election in favor of letting voters vote directly for president, see Demetrios James Caraley, *Editor's Opinion: Why Americans Need a Constitutional Right to Vote for Presidential Electors*, 116 Pol. Sci. Q. 1 (2001).

33. Meilan Solly, "Why Do Maine and Nebraska Split Their Electoral College Votes?," *Smithsonian Magazine*, November 5, 2020, https://www.smithsonianmag .com/smart-news/why-do-maine-and-nebraska-split-their-electoral-votes-180976219 / [https://perma.cc/N337-7RDQ].

This discussion does highlight the fact that my proposed constitutional right to vote amendment does not tackle the issue of partisan gerrymandering. That issue is further from the core of the concerns of a constitutional right to vote, although it is easy to see the extension of a constitutional right to vote to cover cases of extreme partisan gerrymanders.

34. Reynolds v. Sims, 377 U.S. 533 (1964) (holding one-person, one-vote principle stems from the Equal Protection Clause of the Fourteenth Amendment as to state elections); Wesberry v. Sanders, 376 U.S. 1 (1964) (holding one-person, one-vote principle stems from Article I, section 2 as to congressional elections); Avery v. Midland County, 390 U.S. 474 (1968) (extending *Reynolds* holding to local elections).

35. The Supreme Court, in cases such as *Salyer Land Co. v. Tulare Lake Basin Water Storage District*, 410 U.S. 719 (1973) and *Ball v. James*, 451 U.S. 355 (1981), held that neither the one-person, one-vote principle nor the recognition of voting as a fundamental right for citizen, adult, resident, nonfelons applies to "special purpose" district elections that impose special burdens on some classes of voters more than others and that involve elections for entities that do not exercise traditional governmental functions. The amendment would overrule this line of cases. For criticism of these cases as inconsistent with ordinary democratic principles and about the unworkability of the tests used to determine which districts are entitled to this exemption, see the sources cited in Lowenstein et. al, *supra* note 3, at 131–37.

Alternative voting systems such as ranked-choice voting, in which voters rank their top few choices among the list of candidates, and the "counting process then operates as a series of runoff elections, narrowing the field until candidates reach a designated threshold of votes," *id.* at 123, have been found to not violate the one-person, one-vote principle. Minnesota Voters Alliance v. City of Minneapolis, 766 N.W.2d 683 (Minn. 2009), and Dudum v. Arntz, 640 F.3d 1098 (9th Cir. 2011).

36. On how such standards work in practice, see Lowenstein et al., *supra* note 3, at 105–7. The proposed amendment as written does not weigh in on the question the Supreme Court left open in *Evenwel*, as described in the last chapter: whether states may choose equality of voters rather than total population as their denominator when creating roughly equal districts. At first blush, equality of voters seems more in line with the one-person, one-vote principle by treating voters as equals. But some have argued that equality of total population better satisfies political equality, because population equality gives some virtual representation to those members of the population (such as children) who do not have the right to vote. See Justin

Levitt, *Citizenship and the Census*, 119 Colum. L. Rev. 1355, 1391–97 (2019); Joseph Fishkin, *Weightless Votes*, 121 Yale L. J. 1888 (2012).

37. U.S. Const., art. II.

38. *Id.*, art. I.

39. I first proposed coupling automatic voter registration with a national voter identification program run by the federal government in Richard L. Hasen, *The Voting Wars: From Florida 2000 to the Next Election Meltdown* (New Haven: Yale University Press, 2012), 131–58.

40. I explain the workings of this uniformity of voters principle in Richard L. Hasen, *When Is Uniformity of People, Not Counties, Appropriate in Election Administration? The Cases of Early and Sunday Voting*, 2015 U. Chi. Legal F. 193 (2015).

41. The thirty-minute standard for waiting in line to vote on election day, and other sensible voting standards, appear in the report put together by a presidential commission on fixing election problems created by President Barack Obama and chaired by Democratic election lawyer Bob Bauer and Republican election lawyer Ben Ginsberg. See *The American Voting Experience: Report and Recommendations of the Presidential Commission on Election Administration*, January 2014, https://www.eac.gov/sites/default/files/eac_assets/1/6/Amer-Voting-Exper-final-draft-01-09-14-508.pdf [https://perma.cc/38QU-3UUE].

42. Crawford v. Marion Cnty. Election Bd., 553 U.S. 181 (2008). One way to think of the instruction to the courts is that it shifts burden to the states, rather than keeping it on the voters, to come forward with evidence related to a state restriction on voting. Current law, in contrast, puts a thumb on the scale favoring the state by allowing it to merely posit, and not actually prove, that such laws are reasonably necessary to promote compelling state interests.

43. For an extended critique of the argument that states should get a free pass on providing evidence to show that their laws actually serve compelling state interests, see Richard L. Hasen, *Bad Legislative Intent*, 2006 Wis. L. Rev. 843.

For a parallel argument that a broad reading of section 2 of the Voting Rights Act would call virtually all voting decisions into legal question, see Farrakhan v. Washington, 359 F.3d 1116, 1125–26 (9th Cir. 2004) (Kozinski, C. J., dissenting from denial of reh'g en banc) ("The panel's decision also has widespread implications for other legitimate state electoral practices. All sorts of state and local decisions about the time, place and manner of elections will be subject to attack by anyone who can show a disparate impact in an area external to voting that translates into a disparate impact on voting.").

44. Language to ensure a proper interpretation of section 2 could draw from the John R. Lewis Voting Rights Advancement Act, H.R. 4, 117th Cong. (1st. Sess. 2021), https://www.congress.gov/bill/117th-congress/house-bill/4/text, which seeks to

reverse some of the incorrect statutory interpretation of section 2 in recent Supreme Court cases. For a quick discussion of how the court recently deviated from section 2 in "vote denial" cases, see my testimony before a subcommittee of the Senate Judiciary Committee: *Hearing on "Restoring the Voting Rights Act After* Brnovich *and* Shelby County" *Before the Subcomm. on the Const. of the S. Comm. on the Judiciary*, 117th Cong. 4–5 (2021) (statement of Richard L. Hasen, Chancellor's Professor of Law and Political Science, UC Irvine School of Law).

45. On the application of section 2 of the Voting Rights Act following *Thornburg v. Gingles*, 478 U.S. 30 (1986), see Lowenstein et al., *supra* note 3, at 275–303.

46. On this line of cases, see the analyses in the sources cited in chapter 1, note 43.

47. *See supra* chapter 1.

Chapter 3. Expanding the Right to Vote?

1. For philosophical discussions over whether citizenship properly defines the community of those who should be enfranchised, see Lowenstein et. al, *Election Law—Cases and Materials* (Durham, NC: Carolina Academic Press, 7th ed. 2022), 65–67; Frank I. Michelman, *Conceptions of Democracy in American Constitutional Argument: Voting Rights*, 41 Fla. L. Rev. 443 (1989). Sanford Levinson, Suffrage and Community: *Who Should Vote?*, 41 Fla. L. Rev. 545, 557 (1989), is particularly skeptical about citizenship as a reasonable means of dividing the enfranchised from the disenfranchised. See also Jamin B. Raskin, *Legal Aliens, Local Citizens: The Historical, Constitutional and Theoretical Meanings of Alien Suffrage*, 141 U. Pa. L. Rev. 1391, 1431–32 (1993). ("None of the principal excluded national groups who gained access to the ballot in American history did so by way of judicial action through the Equal Protection Clause. Rather, they fought their way in through political agitation. This history encloses an important democratic logic: it is the standing citizenry, after hearing and debating appeals from the voteless, that must extend rights of political membership to disenfranchised outsiders seeking entry and equality.")

2. On the ease of establishing residency, see chapter 2, footnote 6 (discussing *Dunn v. Blumstein* and durational residency).

3. There is currently litigation around the country over whether permitting noncitizens to vote in school board elections violates provisions of state constitutions. See Lisa Moreno, "San Francisco Superior Court Revokes Non-Citizen Parents' Right to Vote in School Board Elections," *San Francisco Standard*, July 29, 2022, https://sfstandard.com/community/san-francisco-superior-court-revokes -non-citizen-parents-right-to-vote-in-school-board-elections/ [https://perma.cc /7TL7-Q9VQ]. On nonresident landowners: "Permitting nonresident landowners to vote in Town elections was upheld in *May v. Town of Mountain Village*, 132 F.3d 576

(10th Cir. 1997), cert. denied 524 U.S. 938 (1998). This is the majority position; courts typically reason that rational basis review applies to a jurisdiction's decision to allow nonresidents to vote, and that the decision is rational because the nonresidents permitted to vote have a substantial interest in the election. See, e.g., *Duncan v. Coffee Cty.*, 69 F.3d 88 (6th Cir. 1995); *Collins v. Town of Goshen*, 635 F.2d 954 (2d Cir. 1980); *Cantwell v. Hudnut*, 566 F.2d 30 (7th Cir. 1977). However, extraterritorial voting was struck down as an unconstitutional dilution of residents' votes in *Board of County Commissioners of Shelby County v. Burson*, 121 F.3d 244 (6th Cir. 1997), cert. denied sub nom. *Walkup v. Board of Commissioners of Shelby County*, 522 U.S. 1113 (1998)." Lowenstein et al., *supra* note 1, at 81.

4. Robert W. Bennett, *Should Parents Be Given Extra Votes on Account of Their Children?: Toward a Conversational Understanding of American Democracy*, 94 Nw. U. L. Rev. 503 (1999–2000).

5. For an argument in favor of lowering the voting age to sixteen, see Joshua Douglas, "The Case for the 16-Year-Old Vote," *Washington Monthly*, August 25, 2022, https://washingtonmonthly.com/2022/08/25/the-case-for-the-16-year-old-vote/ [https://perma.cc/Y279-BSTM].

6. For a survey of American laws on mental capacity and voting, see Courtney Schiffler, *Voting Rights for People with Diminished Mental Capacity*, 48 Mitchell Hamline L. Rev. 657 (2022); for an international and comparative perspective, see Dinesh Bhugra, *Mental Illness and the Right to Vote: A Review of Legislation Across the World*, 28 Int'l Rev. Psy. 395 (2016), https://www.tandfonline.com/doi/abs/10.1080/09540261.2016.1211096. See chapter 2, footnote 30, for a discussion of international norms regarding the question of excluding voters based on mental incompetency.

7. The video of the press conference, posted by *The Independent*, which took place on August 18, 2022 (although the video is dated August 19) appears at: https://www.youtube.com/watch?v=qtl0fyeLIlQ.

8. Steve Contorno and Fredreka Schouten, "DeSantis' Proposed Election Police Force Alarms Voting Rights Advocates," CNN, January 19, 2022, https://www.cnn.com/2022/01/19/politics/ron-desantis-pushes-election-police-force/index.html [https://perma.cc/6HB6-9XP4]. On the generally low rates of voter fraud in the contemporary United States, see Richard L. Hasen, *Election Meltdown: Dirty Tricks, Distrust, and the Threat to American Democracy* (New Haven: Yale University Press, 2020), 15–46 (2020); Richard L. Hasen, *The Voting Wars: From Florida 2000 to the Next Election Meltdown* (New Haven: Yale University Press, 2012), 41–74.

9. Patricia Mazzei, "Florida's Election Police Have a Million-Dollar Budget and Just a Few Cases," *New York Times*, November 8, 2022, https://www.nytimes.com/2022/11/08/us/politics/florida-election-police-budget.html; Ashley Lopez, "Florida's Effort to Charge 20 People with Voter Fraud Has Hit Some Roadblocks,"

NPR, December 21, 2022, https://www.npr.org/2022/12/21/1144265521/florida
-voter-fraud-cases-prosecution-update [https://perma.cc/4RUA-63PW]; "3rd Case
Brought by DeSantis' Election Police Dismissed," AP, December 24, 2022, https://
apnews.com/article/2022-midterm-elections-ron-desantis-crime-florida-4038f0cf
039628981f72009ecd866924 [https://perma.cc/F6Y3-Q7SZ]. These early cases
were dismissed on grounds that state (as opposed to county) prosecutors had
jurisdiction only to bring charges for crimes committed in two or more Florida counties, and these crimes involved only a single county.

    10. Lawrence Mower, "Police Cameras Show Confusion, Anger Over DeSantis'
Voter Fraud Arrests," *Tampa Bay Times*, October 18, 2022, https://www.tampabay.com
/news/florida-politics/2022/10/18/body-camera-video-police-voter-fraud-desantis
-arrests/ [https://perma.cc/QP6F-N987] ("Mower I"); Lawrence Mower, "Prosecutors Drop Charges against DeSantis' Voter Fraud Suspect," *Tampa Bay Times*, November 21, 2022, https://www.tampabay.com/news/florida-politics/2022/11/21/tampa
-illegal-vote-desantis-voter-fraud-arrest-charges-dropped-hillsborough/ [https://
perma.cc/88XR-S5F4] ("Mower II").

    11. Mower I, *supra* note 10; "Trumper Arrested in Voter Fraud Case Wants Crimi-
nal History Erased," *Villages-News*, December 17, 2022, https://www.villages-news
.com/2022/12/17/trumper-caught-up-in-voter-fraud-case-wants-criminal-history
-erased/ [https://perma.cc/3BYN-A65A].

    12. A. G. Gancarski, "Felon Rights Restoration a Winner with Voters, Survey
Says," *Florida Politics*, September 24, 2018, https://floridapolitics.com/archives
/275520-felon-rights-restoration-a-winner-with-voters-survey-says/ [https://perma
.cc/6EDG-RJDP]; Florida Division of Elections, Voter Restoration Amendment
14–01, https://dos.elections.myflorida.com/initiatives/initdetail.asp?account
=64388&seqnum=1 [https://perma.cc/5P8J-245M].

    13. Brennan Center for Justice, Litigation to Protect Amendment 4 in Florida
(last updated September 11, 2020), https://www.brennancenter.org/our-work/court
-cases/litigation-protect-amendment-4-florida [https://perma.cc/FBN3-6J6N];
Nicole Lewis and Alexandra Arriaga, "Florida's Voter Fraud Arrests Are Scaring
Away Formerly Incarcerated Voters," The Marshall Project, November 4, 2022,
https://www.themarshallproject.org/2022/11/04/florida-s-voter-fraud-arrests-are
-scaring-away-formerly-incarcerated-voters [https://perma.cc/CE46-5WJA]. For a
list of the status of felon disenfranchisement laws in each state, see National Conference Legislatures, Felon Voting Rights, Restoration of Voting Rights for Felons,
https://www.ncsl.org/research/elections-and-campaigns/felon-voting-rights.aspx
[https://perma.cc/BMK4-9CXF].

    14. Advisory Opinion to the Governor re: Implementation of Amendment 4, the
Voter Restoration Amendment, 288 So.3d 1070 (Fla.2020); In re Advisory Op. to
the AG, 215 So. 3d 1202 (Fla. 2017).

15. Jones v. DeSantis, 462 F.Supp.3d 1196 (N.D. Fla. 2020), *rev'd*, Jones v. Governor of Florida, 975 F.3d 1016 (11th Cir. 2020) (en banc).

16. Jones v. Governor of Florida, 975 F.3d 1016, 1049 (11th Cir. 2020) (en banc) (original emphasis). For the party affiliation of the judges on the panel deciding the case, see this entry at Ballotpedia: https://ballotpedia.org/United_States_Court_of _Appeals_for_the_Eleventh_Circuit#:~:text=Justice%20Clarence%20 Thomas%20is%20the,Northern%20District%20of%20Alabama [https://perma.cc /8HHB-2K3Q]. Judge Martin, who retired, was appointed by Democratic President Obama. Press Release, "President Obama Nominates Judge Joseph A. Greenaway, Jr. for the Third Circuit, and Judge Beverly B. Martin for United States Court of Appeals for the Eleventh Circuit," June 19, 2009, https://obamawhitehouse.archives.gov/the -press-office/president-obama-nominates-judge-joseph-a-greenaway-jr-third -circuit-and-judge-bever [https://perma.cc/L8EV-GR53]. Two judges, one Democrat-appointed and one Republican-appointed, did not participate in decid- ing the case.

Before the Eleventh Circuit's final ruling, the plaintiffs sought an emergency order reinstating the district court's stay of the Florida legislature's law that had been lifted without explanation by the Eleventh Circuit just before the 2020 primary elec- tion. Justice Sotomayor, for three justices, dissented from the court's refusal to grant a stay: "This Court's order prevents thousands of otherwise eligible voters from par- ticipating in Florida's primary election simply because they are poor." Raysor v. De- Santis, 140 S. Ct. 2600 (2020) (Sotomayor, J., dissenting from denial of application to vacate stay).

17. *Jones*, 975 F.3d at 1111 (Pryor, (Jill) J., dissenting).

18. Gary Fineout, "Final Tally: Group Says 67,000 Felons Registered in Florida after Amendment 4," *Politico*, October 19, 2020, https://www.politico.com/states /florida/story/2020/10/19/final-tally-group-says-67-000-felons-registered-in -florida-after-amendment-4-1327176 [https://perma.cc/P5DT-BNP5]; Patricia Mazzei and Michael Wines, "How Republicans Undermined Ex-Felon Voting Rights in Florida," *New York Times*, September 17, 2020 (Updated April 30, 2021), https:// www.nytimes.com/2020/09/17/us/florida-felons-voting.html.

19. See Fla. Const., Art. VI, § 4(b), added by Amendment 4, as shown in Voting Restoration Amendment, Constitutional Amendment Petition Form, https://dos .elections.myflorida.com/initiatives/fulltext/pdf/64388-1.pdf [https://perma.cc /P6A6-7RN2]. ("No person convicted of murder or a felony sexual offense shall be qualified to vote until restoration of civil rights.")

20. Dan Sullivan, "2 DeSantis Election Fraud Cases End with Guilty Pleas in Hillsborough," *Tampa Bay Times*, March 29, 2023, https://www.tampabay.com/news /florida-politics/elections/2023/03/29/ron-desantis-voter-fraud-in-florida/ [https://perma.cc/K6YD-SB4T].

Mower II, *supra* note 10. Patterson headed back to jail for a year and a day in a separate case under a no contest deal for breaking another Florida law, which required registered sex offenders to report ownership of a new vehicle to the sheriff within 48 hours of the change. *Id.*

21. Lewis and Arriaga, *supra* note 13.

22. Mazzei and Wines, *supra* note 18; Lawrence Mower and Langston Taylor, "In Florida, the Gutting of a Landmark Law Leaves Few Felons Likely to Vote," Electionland from ProPublica, October 7, 2020, https://www.propublica.org/article/in -florida-the-gutting-of-a-landmark-law-leaves-few-felons-likely-to-vote [https://perma .cc/WAX3-C8F9].

23. Richardson v. Ramirez, 418 U.S. 24 (1974); Hunter v. Underwood, 471 U.S. 222 (1985).

24. The cases holding that section 2 of the Voting Right Act does not apply to ban felon disenfranchisement (with some suggesting that if it did, it would be unconstitutional) are: Simmons v. Galvin, 575 F.3d 24 (1st Cir. 2009); Farrakhan v. Gregoire, 623 F.3d 990 (9th Cir. 2010) (en banc); Hayden v. Pataki, 449 F.3d 305 (2d Cir. 2006) (en banc); Johnson v. Governor of Florida, 405 F.3d 1214 (11th Cir. 2005) (en banc). The federal legislation is H.R. 1, § 1403 117th Cong. (1st Sess. 2021). ("The right of an individual who is a citizen of the United States to vote in any election for Federal office shall not be denied or abridged because that individual has been convicted of a criminal offense unless such individual is serving a felony sentence in a correctional institution or facility at the time of the election.")

For an early look at the constitutional problems, see Richard L. Hasen, *The Uncertain Congressional Power to Ban State Felon Disenfranchisement Law*, 49 Howard L. J. 767 (2006).

25. National Conference of State Legislatures, *supra* note 13.

26. Donald Trump (@realdonaldtrump), Twitter, August 28, 2019, https://twitter .com/realDonaldTrump/status/1166723477879087104 [https://perma.cc/N8EW -FHJN]; *id.*, https://twitter.com/realDonaldTrump/status/1166723478776684544 [https://perma.cc/QZP3-36D7].

27. Tucker Higgins, "Trump Unloads on 'Corrupt' Puerto Rico as Tropical Storm Dorian Threatens Island—San Juan Mayor Tells Him to 'Calm Down,'" CNBC, August 28, 2019, https://www.cnbc.com/2019/08/28/trump-unloads-on-puerto-rico -as-tropical-storm-dorian-threatens-island.html [https://perma.cc/5BM7-LR8K]. I say a "so-called" unincorporated territory so as not to legitimate the Supreme Court's determination of this second-class status.

28. Adam Edelman, "Trump Says 3,000 Did Not Die in Puerto Rico Hurricane, Claims Democrats Manipulated Numbers," NBC News, September 13, 2018, https:// www.nbcnews.com/politics/donald-trump/trump-claims-3-000-did-not-die -puerto-rico-hurricane-n909221 [https://perma.cc/3HJB-KVDP].

29. Michael D. Shear, "Leading Homeland Security under a President Who Embraces 'Hate-Filled' Talk," *New York Times*, July 10, 2020 (updated July 28, 2020), https://www.nytimes.com/2020/07/10/us/politics/elaine-duke-homeland -security-trump.html; Hallie Jackson, "Ex-DHS Official: Trump Wanted to Trade Puerto Rico for Greenland," MSNBC, August 19, 2020, https://www.msnbc.com /hallie-jackson/watch/ex-dhs-official-trump-wanted-to-trade-puerto-rico-for -greenland-90306117878 (video at 5:50 mark) [https://perma.cc/6PTP-ZB2A].

30. For an account of the passage of the Twenty-Third Amendment, see John F. Kowal and Wilfred U. Codrington III, *The People's Constitution: 200 Years, 27 Amendments, and the Promise of a More Perfect Union* (New York: The New Press, 2021), 185–87; Richard L. Hasen, "Election Reform: Past, Present, and Future," in *Oxford Handbook of American Election Law* (Eugene Mazo, ed., Oxford: Oxford University Press, forthcoming 2024).

31. Karl A. Racine and Leevin T. Camacho, "Opinion: Dear Supreme Court: 3.5 Million Americans in Territories Deserve Same Federal Benefits," *USA Today*, November 9, 2021, https://www.usatoday.com/story/opinion/2021/11/09/social-security -puerto-rico-supreme-court-justice/6307011001/ [https://perma.cc/LD9X-3C39].

32. United States v. Vaello Madero, 142 S. Ct. 1539 (2022).

33. *Id.* at 1561 (Sotomayor, J., dissenting); Ariane de Vogue, "Supreme Court Declines to Take Up Effort to Secure Birthright Citizenship for American Samoans," CNN, October 17, 2022, https://www.cnn.com/2022/10/17/politics/american -samoans-birthright-case-supreme-court/index.html [https://perma.cc/RS3Q -EBJL] (noting that parents of Justice Sotomayor were born in Puerto Rico).

34. *Id.* at 1552 (Gorsuch, J., concurring). Justice Gorsuch's opinion explains the origin of the cases in detail and links to both the historical legal scholarship justifying the cases as well as modern originalist scholarship rejecting the cases.

35. *Id.* at 1557 (Gorsuch, J., concurring), see also *id.* at 1560 n.4 (Sotomayor, J., dissenting). For additional background on the Insular Cases, see Kal Raustiala, *Does the Constitution Follow the Flag?* 83–91 (2009).

36. Petition for Writ of Certiorari, Fitisemanu v. United States, No. 21–1394, at i, https://www.supremecourt.gov/DocketPDF/21/21-1394/222022/202204 27125759871_Fitisemanu%20v.%20United%20States%20-%20Cert%20Petition%20 -%20TO%20FILE.pdf; Brief in Opposition for Respondents American Samoa Government and the Honorable Aumua Amata, Fitisemanu v. United States, No. 21–1394, at i, https://www.supremecourt.gov/DocketPDF/21/21-1394/236566/2022082912 5923506_2022-08-29%209am%20FINAL%20Fitisemanu%20BIO.pdf.

37. De Vogue, *supra* note 33; *Fitisemanu v. United States*, 1 F.4th 862 (10th Cir. 2022), cert. denied, 143 S. Ct. 362 (2022).

38. De Vogue, *supra* note 33 ("Notably, the government of American Samoa as well as the American Samoa's non-voting delegate in the US House of Representa-

tives believed the Supreme Court should not take up the case because 'establishing birthright citizenship by judicial fiat could have unintended and potentially harmful impact upon American Samoa society.'"); Gene Demby, "How Birthright Citizenship for American Samoans Could Threaten 'the Samoan Way,'" Code Switch, NPR, February 24, 2015, https://www.npr.org/sections/codeswitch/2015/02/24/388716342/how-birthright-citizenship-for-american-samoans-could-destroy-the-samoan-way [https://perma.cc/LD6P-9ALN]. ("But not all residents of this 55,000-person cluster of Pacific islands are behind the push for birthright citizenship, which has been hotly contested since well before the current case. Many American Samoans worry that it might unravel *fa'asamoa*, or the Samoan way. *Fa'asamoa* rests on an extended familial system called *aiga* and communally held land controlled by a chief, called a *matai*.")

39. Emily Cochrane and Patricia Mazzei, "House Passes Bill That Could Pave the Way for Puerto Rican Statehood," *New York Times*, December 15, 2022 https://www.nytimes.com/2022/12/15/us/politics/house-puerto-rican-statehood.html. ("Puerto Rico has held six plebiscites on whether it should become a state, most recently in 2020, when 52 percent of voters on the island endorsed the move. None of the plebiscites has been binding, however, and turnout has often been low, amid boycotts by critics who support the status quo or independence.") On criticism of the Puerto Rico vote on statehood, see Julio Ricardo Varela, "Is Puerto Rico Having a Defining Vote on Statehood? No, It's Just a Political Stunt," *Washington Post*, May 21, 2020, https://www.washingtonpost.com/opinions/2020/05/21/is-puerto-rico-having-defining-vote-statehood-no-its-just-political-stunt/ [https://perma.cc/7HCD-L6YS]. On the basic steps for Congress to admit new states into the Union, see Congressional Research Service, *Statehood Process and Political Status of U.S. Territories: Brief Policy Background*, Report IF11972, Version 4 (updated July 29, 2022), https://crsreports.congress.gov/product/pdf/IF/IF11792.

40. Olivia Reingold, "Is Puerto Rico the Next Senate Battleground?" *Politico*, September 9, 2020, https://www.politico.com/news/magazine/2020/09/09/puerto-rico-statehood-politics-democrats-republicans-senate-409191 [https://perma.cc/Y8G4-ZFFZ]; Cochrane and Mazzei, *supra* note 39; see also *id*. ("Puerto Ricans have sought greater self-determination for decades, with the island's territorial status deeply dividing its people. The three main political parties, which do not neatly align with Democrats and Republicans, are also divided over the question of status: The Puerto Rican Independence Party favors separating from the United States; the New Progressive Party favors statehood, and the Popular Democratic Party favors remaining a U.S. commonwealth."); the current governor, Pedro Pierluisi, is a Democrat. National Governor's Association, https://www.nga.org/governor/pedro-pierluisi/ [https://perma.cc/26LL-974L]. The current nonvoting representative in the U.S. House of Representatives from Puerto Rico, Jenniffer A.

González Colón, is a Republican. U.S. Congresswoman Jenniffer A. González Colón, *What Is A Resident Commissioner,* https://gonzalez-colon.house.gov/about/what-resident-commissioner [https://perma.cc/BT95-935S].

41. For an argument to extend voting rights to Americans living in U.S. territories, see Neil Weare, *Equally American: Amending the Constitution to Provide Voting Rights in U.S. Territories and the District of Columbia,* 46 Stetson L. Rev. 259 (2017).

42. Mark Sherman, "Electoral College Makes It Official: Biden Won, Trump Lost," AP, December 14, 2020, https://apnews.com/article/joe-biden-270-electoral-college-vote-d429ef97af2bf574d16463384dc7cc1e [https://perma.cc/BS7K-VAVU]. The calculations of the popular vote totals in this paragraph and the next are taken from David Wasserman, Sophie Andrews, Leo Saenger, Lev Cohen, Ally Flinn, and Griff Tatarsky, *2020 National Popular Vote Tracker,* The Cook Political Report, https://www.cookpolitical.com/2020-national-popular-vote-tracker [https://perma.cc/L68Z-C3XZ].

43. Drew DeSilver, *It's Not Just 2020: U.S. Presidential Elections Have Long Featured Close State Races,* Pew Research Center, December 4, 2020, https://www.pewresearch.org/fact-tank/2020/12/04/its-not-just-2020-u-s-presidential-elections-have-long-featured-close-state-races/ [https://perma.cc/TEW7-7G44]; "2016 Election Results," *New York Times,* August 9, 2017, https://www.nytimes.com/elections/2016/results/president.

44. Alexander Keyssar, *Why Do We Still Have the Electoral College?* 1 (Cambridge & London: Harvard University Press, 2020).

45. *Id.;* Jesse Wegman, *Let the People Pick the President: The Case for Abolishing the Electoral College* (New York: St. Martin's Press, 2020).

46. Wegman, *supra* note 45 at 14–15.

47. Rand Paul, "Rand Paul: If We Believe in Limited Government, We Must Save the Electoral College," *Louisville Courier-Journal,* December 19, 2022, https://www.courier-journal.com/story/opinion/2022/12/19/rand-paul-we-must-save-the-electoral-college-for-limited-government/69734204007/ [https://perma.cc/LNA7-TT5F].

48. Wegman, *supra* note 45, chapter 9 (supporting National Popular Vote Interstate Compact); Sarah Fortinsky and Shawna Mizelle, "January 6 Panelist Points to Electoral College Reform as Next Priority to Safeguard Democracy," CNN, December 25, 2022, https://www.cnn.com/2022/12/25/politics/jamie-raskin-electoral-college-reform-january-6/index.html [https://perma.cc/JWU5-JQWJ]. ("'The truth is that we need to be continually renovating and improving our institutions,' Raskin said, later noting that he supports the National Popular Vote Interstate Compact, which represents a pledge made by certain states and the District of Columbia to award their electoral votes to whichever candidate wins the popular vote

nationwide.") For details on the workings of the Compact, see John R. Koza et al., *Every Vote Equal: A State-Based Plan for Electing the President by National Popular Vote* (2013). The full text of the book is freely available at: https://www.every-vote-equal.com/sites/default/files/everyvoteequal-4th-ed-2013-02-21.pdf.

The National Popular Vote Interstate Compact has been offered as a solution short of amending the constitution to deal with the Electoral College. A number of opponents of the Electoral College, including Wegman and Representative Jamie Raskin, have lined up behind it. Some of the details are complex, but the basic idea is this: a state signs on to pledge to vote its Electoral College votes not for the popular winner in the state, but to the winner of the national popular vote. The measure only takes effect when enough states making up a majority of the Electoral College sign on. So far only states with Democratic legislatures have opted into the compact.

There are a number of important legal questions about this potential arrangement, including whether such a "compact" would require congressional approval under the constitution. My main concern about the measure is that it could fall apart at the last minute and trigger a constitutional crisis.

Suppose there is a state within the compact where the voters of the state strongly support one candidate but the national popular vote winner is another candidate. There could be great pressure for that state to withdraw from the compact at the last minute. Although the compact itself says that a withdrawal less than six months before the election would not be effective until the following election, it is not clear that the Supreme Court would enforce such a provision given Article II of the constitution that lets the state legislature direct the means of assigning Electoral College votes before the election. That worry about a potential crisis under this scenario leads me to oppose the compact even while I support a standalone constitutional amendment abolishing the Electoral College.

The provision making a withdrawal ineffective for the next election if it is within six months of that election appears in Article IV.2 of the compact. See Koza et al., *supra*, at 276. In section 9.11.1, the book discusses the potential withdrawal of a state from the compact after voters have voted but before electors have met. See *id.* at 517. My concern is about withdrawal in the months before the people vote, with the legislature passing new legislation, signed by the governor, withdrawing from the compact.

49. Jonathan M. Ladd, "The Senate Is a Much Bigger Problem than the Electoral College," *Vox*, April 19, 2019, https://www.vox.com/mischiefs-of-faction/2019/4/9/18300749/senate-problem-electoral-college [https://perma.cc/CEP6-PLQB]. On whether one would need a double amendment to abolish the Senate, see Note, *Pack the Union: A Proposal to Admit New States for the Purpose of Amending the Constitution to Ensure Equal Representation*, 133 Harv. L. Rev. 1049, 1061 (2020) (suggesting transfer of Senate's power to get around Senate Entrenchment Clause); Richard Albert,

Amending Constitutional Amendment Rules, 13 Int'l J. Const. L. 655, 662–63 (2015) (arguing that the Equal Suffrage Clause is susceptible to "double amendment"). On congressional power to set the terms for Article V amendments, see David E. Pozen and Thomas P. Schmidt, *The Puzzles and Possibilities of Article V*, 121 Colum. L. Rev. 2317 (2021).

50. Ladd, *supra* note 49.

Chapter 4. Deescalating the Voting Wars

1. For retrospectives on voting during the pandemic, see Nathaniel Persily and Charles Stewart III, *The Miracle and Tragedy of the 2020 U.S. Election*, 32 J. Democracy 159, 159 (April 2021). For a look back at the election-related litigation, see Richard L. Hasen, *Three Pathologies of American Voting Rights Illuminated by the COVID-19 Pandemic, and How to Treat and Cure Them*, 19 Elect. L. J. 263 (2020). For recommendations for conducting fair and safe elections during the twin crises of the pandemic and Donald Trump's undermining of confidence in the election process, see UCI Law, Ad Hoc Comm. for 2020 Election Fairness and Legitimacy, *Fair Elections During a Crisis: Urgent Recommendations in Law, Media, Politics, and Tech to Advance the Legitimacy of, and the Public's Confidence in, the 2020 U.S. Elections*, April 2020, https://www.law.uci.edu/news/press-releases/2020/2020ElectionReport.pdf [https://perma.cc/C3X5-URGJ].

2. On these points generally, see Hasen, *supra* note 1. During the 2020 election, the Supreme Court of Texas held that a Texas statute allowing voters with a "disability" to vote by mail did not apply to voters who feared contracting COVID-19 but were not infected by the disease. In re State, 602 S.W.3d 549 (Tex. 2020); see also Mo. State Conference of the NAACP v. State, 607 S.W.3d 728 (Mo. 2020) (en banc) (construing statute allowing absentee voting for person "confine[d] due to illness" as not applying to person not sick but who feared contracting COVID-19).

3. Ellie Kaufman and Marshall Cohen, "Nevada Approves Plan to Mail Ballots to All Registered Voters," CNN, August 5, 2020, https://www.cnn.com/2020/08/03/politics/nevada-mail-ballots-registered-voters/index.html [https://perma.cc/E9RB-M9SF] ("President Donald Trump quickly slammed the move on Monday. He falsely accused Nevada Democrats of orchestrating an 'illegal . . . coup' and threatened to bring a lawsuit to stop the state from expanding mail-in voting, which he says will weaken his chances of winning reelection."). For Trump's general claims of fraud during the 2020 election tied to mail-in voting, and his use of social media to amplify such claims, see Richard L. Hasen, *Cheap Speech: How Disinformation Poisons Our Politics—and How to Cure It* (New Haven: Yale University Press, 2022), ch. 1.

4. Native Americans Rights Fund, *Obstacles at Every Turn: Barriers to Political Participation Faced by Native American Voters* 33 (2020), https://vote.narf.org/wp

-content/uploads/2020/06/obstacles_at_every_turn.pdf [https://perma.cc/3BFB -MF6J] (hereafter, "NARF Report").

5. For the circumstances under which it was necessary to provide a copy of an identification when voting after registering by mail, see *Mail Ballot Voting*, Nevada Secretary of State, https://www.nvsos.gov/sos/elections/voters/mail-ballot-voting [https://perma.cc/XGZ4-LUK5]. On the lack of close and reliable mail service, see NARF Report, *supra* note 4, at 40–41:

> Throughout Indian Country, many Native voters can only receive election mail through post office boxes. There is an insufficient supply of post office boxes on or near tribal lands to meet the high demand, requiring many tribal members to obtain post office boxes in communities that can be located more than 100 miles away. That causes multiple families to share a single post office box, including unrelated adults living in different households.
>
> When a family is kicked off a shared mailbox, they are effectively disenfranchised because there is no way for them to receive early ballots they have requested by mail. The same result could occur when county officials do not accept tribal post office box addresses, such as on the Gila River Indian Community in Pinal County, Arizona. . . .
>
> Another complicating factor is when Native voters receive their mail from a post office across state or county lines because it is the closest location to their home. Many Navajo voters have difficulty getting mail "because of the state line" between Arizona and Utah. Navajos who live in Kayenta and Navajo Mountain in San Juan County, Utah have post office boxes with Arizona zip codes.
>
> In Navajo Mountain, Utah, there is a small post office in the chapter house that is located in Utah. However, it uses a Tonalea, Arizona zip code because it is a sub-branch of the post office on the Arizona side of the border. The county clerk disqualifies Utah residents there claiming they live in Arizona because of their post office address. San Juan County uses "all sorts of methods like that to reduce the number of voters" and purge them from the voting list.

Id. (footnotes omitted).

6. Candice Norwood, "How the Pandemic Has Complicated Voting Access for Millions of Native Americans," PBS News Hour, October 6, 2020, https://www.pbs .org/newshour/politics/how-the-pandemic-has-complicated-voting-access-for -millions-of-native-americans [https://perma.cc/X4P6-KEGF].

7. Jessica Douglas, "Tribal Nations Face Continued Voter Suppression," *High Country News*, September 14, 2020, https://www.hcn.org/issues/52.10/ideas -election2020-tribal-nations-face-continued-voter-suppression [https://perma.cc /3C72-DPN5].

8. Jean Reith Schroedel, *Voting in Indian Country: The View from the Trenches* ix, xi (Philadelphia: University of Pennsylvania Press, 2020); written Statement of Jacqueline De León, Staff Attorney for the Native American Rights Foundation, for a Hearing on Restoring the Voting Rights Act: Protecting the Native American and Alaska Native Vote, Submitted to the Senate Judiciary Committee on the Constitution, United States Senate 18–21, October 20, 2021, https://www.judiciary.senate.gov/imo/media/doc/De%20Leon%20Testimony1.pdf [https://perma.cc/D2J7-QJ5G] (footnote omitted). For more relevant background on Native American voting rights in the contemporary United States, see White House, *Report of the Interagency Steering Group on Native American Voting Rights* (March 2022), https://www.whitehouse.gov/wp-content/uploads/2022/03/Tribal-Voting-Report-FINAL.pdf [https://perma.cc/R8Y8-3DQ7]. On the passage of the Snyder Act conferring citizenship on Native Americans, see *id.* at 10. The Supreme Court case denying Native Americans rights under the fourteenth and fifteenth amendments is Elk v. Wilkins, 112 U.S. 94 (1884).

For more on voting in Indian country during pandemics, see Matthew M. L. Fletcher, *Pandemics in Indian Country: The Making of the Tribal State*, 18 U. St. Thomas L. J. 295 (2022).

9. Blake Nicholson, "Thousands of Native Voters in North Dakota Getting Free IDs," AP, October 31, 2018, https://apnews.com/article/16c11874f3cb4ac6b4ffca30ff5fdb3e [https://perma.cc/HF4J-YZ6P] ("Changes to North Dakota's voter ID laws came just months after Heitkamp's win by fewer than 3,000 votes with the help of Native Americans in 2012, though Republicans say that had nothing to do with updates aimed at guarding against voter fraud. American Indians make up about 5 percent of North Dakota's population."); Written Statement of Matthew Campbell, Staff Attorney for the Native American Rights Fund for a Hearing on Voting in America: The Potential for Voter ID Laws, Proof-of-Citizenship Laws, and Lack of Multi-Lingual Support to Interfere with Free and Fair Access to the Ballot, Submitted to the Committee on House Administration, Subcommittee on Elections United States House of Representatives, May 24, 2021, at 12 https://docs.house.gov/meetings/HA/HA08/20210524/112670/HHRG-117-HA08-Wstate-CampbellM-20210524.pdf [https://perma.cc/CU2X-QNV9] (hereafter, "Campbell Testimony") ("In 2012, North Dakotans elected Democrat Heidi Heitkamp to the U.S. Senate. She won by less than 3,000 votes. Most Native Americans in North Dakota are Democrats and their votes were instrumental to Senator Heitkamp's success" [footnotes omitted]).

10. Much of this account of North Dakota's dispute over its voter identification laws draws from Campbell Testimony, *supra* note 9, at 10–19; see *id.* at 13 (describing "hoghouse amendment" process). For more on the hoghouse amendment process, see North Dakota Legislative Drafting Manual 65 (2023), https://ndlegis.gov/files

/documents/legislativedraftingmanual.pdf [https://perma.cc/85QG-H7S7]. ("In some cases it is acceptable to propose the removal of all the text of a bill through use of a 'hoghouse' amendment. Use of 'hoghouse' amendments is discouraged, but if clarity is enhanced, a 'hoghouse' amendment may be used.") (Emphasis omitted.)

Among the FAQs on North Dakota secretary of state's website, answering the question, "When do eligible voters register for an election?" is the answer: "North Dakota does not require voter registration. Therefore, an eligible voter may vote in an election if the voter provides acceptable identification." See North Dakota Secretary of State, *North Dakota Voices Count, nd.gov,* https://vip.sos.nd.gov /PortalListDetails.aspx?ptlhPKID=79&ptlPKID=7 [https://perma.cc/X9MR -NKYH].

11. Campbell Testimony, *supra* note 9, at 10; *id.* at 13 (footnote omitted).

12. Brakebill v. Jaeger, No. 1:16-CV-008, 2016 WL 7118548, at *2 (D.N.D. August 1, 2016).

13. Campbell Testimony, *supra* note 9, at 14 (quoting Brakebill, 2016 WL 7118548, at *4). According to the court, "Obtaining any one of the approved forms of ID al- most always involves a fee or charge, and in nearly all cases requires travel. It also helps to have a computer with Internet access, a credit card, a car, the ability to take time off work, and familiarity with the government and its bureaucracy. Thus, obtain- ing a qualifying voter ID is much easier to accomplish for people who live in urban areas, have a good income, are computer-literate, have a computer and printer, have a good car and gas money, have a flexible schedule, and understand how to navigate the state's administrative procedures. The declarations from the Plaintiffs' expert witnesses show that the typical Native American voter living in North Dakota who lacks qualifying ID simply does not have these assets." *Brakebill,* 2016 WL 7118548, at *5 (citation omitted).

14. *Id.* at *10, *12-*13; Campbell Testimony, *supra* note 9, at 16.

15. *Id.* at 17–18; Brakebill v. Jaeger, No. 1:16-CV-008, 2018 WL 1612190, at *4 (D.N.D. April 3, 2018) (citations omitted and original emphasis). The law did not include any alternative ways of verifying identity for voting as the district court had required in 2016. In holding that the new law was still partially unconstitutional, the court in a 2018 ruling noted that "the State has acknowledged that Native American communities often lack residential street addresses or do not have clear residential addresses. Nevertheless, *under current State law an individual who does not have a 'current residential street address' will never be qualified to vote.* This is a clear 'legal obstacle' inhibiting the opportunity to vote. The State can easily remedy this prob- lem by simply eliminating the absolute need for a 'current residential street address' and allowing for either a residential address, a mailing address (P.O. Box), or simply an address." *Id.* at 7 (original emphasis).

16. Brakebill v. Jaeger, 905 F.3d 553, 557–60, 561 (8th Cir. 2018) (footnote omitted). Judges Colloton and Beneton in the majority were appointed by Republican President George W. Bush. Judge Kelly, the sole Democrat-appointed judge on the Eighth Circuit, was appointed by President Obama.

The appeals court held that the district court improperly granted relief statewide. It held that there had not been a showing that the current residential street address requirement would severely burden people across the state. "Here, the district court thought the statutory requirement to produce an identification with a current residential street address posed a legal obstacle to the right to vote for Native Americans, because Native American communities often lack residential street addresses . . . But even assuming that some communities lack residential street addresses, that fact does not justify a statewide injunction that prevents the Secretary from requiring a form of identification with a residential street address from the vast majority of residents who have residential street addresses." The appeals court left open the possibility of narrower relief for a class of Native American voters who were burdened by the law, but there was not time to get a new injunction helping those voters for the 2018 elections, which by then were only weeks away. And the appeals court refused to reinstate the alternative means of establishing identity in time for the 2018 elections.

In justifying these burdens on Native voters in North Dakota, the Eighth Circuit relied upon the potential for fraud, despite the lack of evidence of this kind of fraud actually ever occurring in North Dakota: "The inability to require proof of a residential street address in North Dakota also opens the possibility of fraud by voters who have obtained a North Dakota form of identification but reside in another State while maintaining a mailing address in North Dakota to vote. The dissent deems this impossible, because only a resident of the State is supposed to receive a form of identification, but the injunction prevents election officials from verifying that a voter with such an identification has a current residential street address in the State. Even if the State can prosecute fraudulent voters after the fact, it would be irreparably harmed by allowing them to vote in the election." *Id.* At 560.

17. *Id.* At 563 (Kelly, J., dissenting) (citation omitted).

18. Brakebill v. Jaeger, 139 S. Ct. 10, 11 (2018).

19. Standing Lake Tribe v. Jaeger, 2018 WL 5722665 (D.N.D. November 1, 2018). Nicholson, *supra* note 9.

20. Brakebill v. Jaeger, 932 F.3d 671 (8th Cir. 2019); Brakkton Booker, "North Dakota and Native American Tribes Settle Voter ID Lawsuits," NPR, February 14, 2020, https://www.npr.org/2020/02/14/806083852/north-dakota-and-native-american -tribes-settle-voter-id-lawsuits [https://perma.cc/R6NT-LUHA]; Joint Statement by North Dakota Secretary of State Al Jaeger, Spirit Lake Nation, and Standing Rock Sioux Tribe, https://campaignlegal.org/press-releases/secretary-state-and-north -dakota-tribes-agree-settle-voter-id-lawsuit [https://perma.cc/4TNG-9H8K].

21. I have posted the data and list of my sample "election challenge" litigation cases from 1996–2022 at https://electionlawblog.org/wp-content/uploads/Election -Litigation-1996-2022.xlsx [https://perma.cc/RC6M-F5SY]. For an explanation of the relevant methodology and analysis of statistics on election litigation through 2020, see Richard L. Hasen, *Research Note: Record Election Litigation Rates in the 2020 Election: An Aberration or a Sign of Things to Come?*, 21 Elect. L. J. 150, 150 n.1 (2022).

On the new fundraising opportunities for political parties that may be spurring litigation, see Derek T. Muller, *Reducing Election Litigation*, 90 Fordham L. Rev. 561 (2021).

22. Among the groups on the right that have brought such claims under the National Voter Registration Act are the Public Interest Legal Foundation, the Honest Elections Project, and Judicial Watch. See, e.g., Press Release, *Win for Election Integrity: PILF Forces to More Minnesota Counties to Remove over 300 Duplicate Voter Registrations*, Public Int. Legal Found., December 16, 2022, https://publicinterestlegal.org /press/win-for-election-integrity-pilf-forces-two-more-minnesota-counties-to -remove-over-300-duplicate-voter-registrations/ [https://perma.cc/W46M-RPBV]; Jason Snead, Release, *Honest Elections Project on NVRA Lawsuit by North Carolina Voters Against Executive Director of NC Board of Elections*, Honest Elections Project, September 17, 2021, https://www.honestelections.org/honest-elections-project-on -nvra-lawsuit-by-north-carolina-voters-against-executive-director-of-nc-board-of -elections/ [https://perma.cc/2HVA-53HF]; Katie Meyer, "The Partisan Conflict Behind a Quest to Purge 800,000 from Pa's Rolls," WHYY, August 6, 2020, https:// whyy.org/articles/the-partisan-conflict-behind-a-quest-to-purge-up-to-800000 -voters-from-pa-s-rolls/ [https://perma.cc/YN8S-5ZC5] (describing efforts of Judicial Watch). On the potential interactions between a right-to-vote amendment and the issue of decentralized administration of elections, see Richard Briffault, *Three Questions for the "Right to Vote" Amendment*, 23 Wm. & Mary Bill Rts. J. 27, 39–40 (2014).

23. Alexander Keyssar et al., *Shoring Up the Right to Vote for President: A Modest Proposal*, 118 Pol. Sci. Q. 181, 200 (2003) (comments of Rick Pildes).

24. For a recounting of the scandal, see Hasen, *Election Meltdown* 96–101 (2020); see also Leigh Ann Caldwell, Rich Gardella, and Ben Kamisar, "In N.C. Election Fraud Case, Witness Says Operative Held Onto 800 Absentee Ballots," NBC News, December 11, 2018, https://www.nbcnews.com/politics/politics-news/n-c-election -fraud-case-witness-says-operative-held-800-n946831; Richard Fausset, Alan Blinder, Sydney Ember, Timothy Williams, and Serge F. Kovaleski, "North Carolina's 'Guru of Elections': Can-Do Operator Who May Have Done Too Much," *New York Times*, December 8, 2018, https://www.nytimes.com/2018/12/08/us/politics/north -carolina-election-fraud-dowless.html.

25. Joe Malinconico, "No 'Political Witch Hunt:' What Mendez Losing Ruling in Paterson Election Fraud Case Means," *Paterson Press*, September 29, 2022, https://

www.northjersey.com/story/news/paterson-press/2022/09/29/paterson-nj
-election-fraud-alex-mendez-selective-prosecution/69527759007/ [https://perma
.cc/MKK6-ZSCZ]; Joe Malinconico, "Paterson Councilmen Michael Jackson, Alex
Mendez Indicted in Voting Fraud Case, Grewal Says," *Paterson Press*, March 3, 2021,
https://www.northjersey.com/story/news/paterson-press/2021/03/03/paterson
-nj-councilmen-michael-jackson-alex-mendez-indicted-voting-fraud/6908946002
/ [https://perma.cc/PA7Q-V9PF]; Joe Malinconico and Ed Rumley, "AG: Paterson
Councilman, Councilman-Elect and 2 Others Charged with Election Fraud," *Paterson Press*, June 25, 2020, https://www.northjersey.com/story/news/paterson-press
/2020/06/25/paterson-nj-councilman-councilman-elect-arrested-election-fraud
/3259649001/ [https://perma.cc/F5Q7-AH2U] ("In early May, the Passaic
County Board of Elections discounted about 900 ballots that officials said were illegally bundled, or mailed together, a sign they said of likely wrongdoing. Those 900
allegedly bundled ballots were among a total of more than 3,200—or 20% of those
submitted—rejected by the county election board for various reasons, including
questionable voter signatures."); Anna Sturla, "Judge Invalidates Paterson, NJ, City
Council Election after Allegations of Mail-In Voter Fraud," CNN, August 20, 2020,
https://www.cnn.com/2020/08/20/politics/paterson-new-jersey-city-council
-voter-fraud/index.html [https://perma.cc/3Z2E-KXRP].

26. Press Release, *Former Rensselaer County Elections Commissioner Pleads Guilty
to Identity Theft in Connection with Ballot Fraud Scheme*, U.S. Department of Justice,
January 11, 2023, https://www.justice.gov/usao-ndny/pr/former-rensselaer-county
-elections-commissioner-pleads-guilty-identity-theft [https://perma.cc/2M9V
-ZZ2B]; Brendan J. Lyons, "Rensselaer County Elections Commissioner Will Plead
Guilty to Federal Criminal Charges," *Albany Times-Union*, December 28, 2022,
https://www.timesunion.com/state/article/Rensselaer-elections-commissioner-to
-plead-guilty-17681350.php [https://perma.cc/983P-2P3Z].

27. The National Conference of State Legislatures posts a list of each state's ballot
collection laws. See *Table 10: Ballot Collection Laws*, NCSL, May 17, 2022, https://
www.ncsl.org/research/elections-and-campaigns/vopp-table-10-who-can-collect
-and-return-an-absentee-ballot-other-than-the-voter.aspx [https://perma.cc/9KN3
-9EM2].

28. 141 S. Ct. 2321 (2021). Although I focus here on Native American voters, some
Hispanic voters appear to face similar difficulties. See *id.* at 2370 n. 12 ("Certain Hispanic communities in Arizona confront similar difficulties. For example, in the bor-
der town of San Luis, which is 98% Hispanic, '[a]lmost 13,000 residents rely on a post
office located across a major highway' for their mail service. The median income in
San Luis is $22,000, so 'many people [do] not own[ ] cars'—making it 'difficult' to
'receiv[e] and send . . . mail.'"). (Citation omitted.)

29. See 52 U.S.C. § 10301(b) (Violation of statute when "the political processes leading to nomination or election in the State or political subdivision are not equally open to participation" by members of a protected class "in that its members have less opportunity than other members of the electorate to participate in the political process and to elect representatives of their choice."). On vote denial claims generally before *Brnovich*, see Nicholas O. Stephanopoulos, *Disparate Impact, Unified Law*, 128 Yale L. J. 1566 (2019); Joshua S. Sellers, *Election Law and White Identity Politics*, 87 Fordham L. Rev. 1515, 1546–51 (2019); Jamelia N. Morgan, *Disparate Impact and Voting Rights: How Objections to Impact-Based Claims Prevent Plaintiffs from Prevailing in Cases Challenging New Forms of Disenfranchisement*, 9 Ala. C.R. & C.L.L. Rev. 93 (2018); Pamela S. Karlan, *Turnout, Tenuousness, and Getting Results in Section 2 Vote Denial Claims*, 77 Ohio St. L. J. 763 (2016); Daniel P. Tokaji, *Applying Section 2 to the New Vote Denial*, 50 Harvard Civil Rights—C.L.L. Rev. 439 (2015); Janai Nelson, *The Causal Context of Disparate Vote Denial*, 54 Boston Coll. L. Rev. 579 (2013); Christopher S. Elmendorf, *Making Sense of Section 2: Of Biased Votes, Unconstitutional Elections, and Common Law Statutes*, 160 U. Pa. L. Rev. 377 (2012).

30. Thornburg v. Gingles, 478 U.S. 30 (1986) (construing the 1982 amendments to Section 2).

31. Veasey v. Abbott, 830 F.3d 216 (5th Cir. 2016) (en banc).

32. For my statement about why Democrats should not have pushed the *Brnovich* litigation in the current Supreme Court, see Richard Hasen, *A Partisan Battle in an Overreach of a Case*, SCOTUSBlog, February 22, 2021, https://www.scotusblog.com/2021/02/a-partisan-battle-in-an-overreach-of-a-case/ [https://perma.cc/9ZP9-EY7W].

33. I explain how Justice Alito's opinion deviated from text, history, and precedent in my testimony before a subcommittee of the Senate Judiciary Committee. *Hearing on "Restoring the Voting Rights Act after Brnovich and Shelby County" before the Subcomm. on the Const. of the S. Comm. on the Judiciary*, 117th Cong. 4–5 (2021), https://electionlawblog.org/wp-content/uploads/hasen-testimony-senate-brnovich-final.pdf [https://perma.cc/N9EC-TJ42] (statement of Richard L. Hasen, Chancellor's Professor of L. and Pol. Sci., UC Irvine School of Law). See also Richard L. Hasen, "The Supreme Court is Putting Democracy at Risk," *New York Times*, July 1, 2021, https://www.nytimes.com/2021/07/01/opinion/supreme-court-rulings-arizona-california.html [https://perma.cc/Q64S-M4CV].

34. *Brnovich*, 141 S. Ct. at 2346–48. Justice Alito quoted from the district court in explaining the lack of statistical evidence as to the scope of the problem: "[B]allot collection was used as a [get-out-the-vote] strategy in mostly low-efficacy minority communities, though the Court cannot say how often voters used ballot collection, *nor can it measure the degree or significance of any disparities in its usage*" (emphasis added by Justice Alito). *Id*. at 2347 n.19 (citation omitted).

35. Justice Alito wrote:

> The dissent's primary argument regarding HB 2023 concerns its effect on Native Americans who live on remote reservations. The dissent notes that many of these voters do not receive mail delivery at home, that the nearest post office may be some distance from their homes, and that they may not have automobiles. We do not dismiss these problems, but for a number of reasons, they do not provide a basis for invalidating HB 2023. The burdens that fall on remote communities are mitigated by the long period of time prior to an election during which a vote may be cast either in person or by mail and by the legality of having a ballot picked up and mailed by family or household members. And in this suit, no individual voter testified that HB 2023 would make it significantly more difficult for him or her to vote. Moreover, the Postal Service is required by law to "provide a maximum degree of effective and regular postal services to rural areas, communities, and small towns where post offices are not self-sustaining." Small post offices may not be closed "solely for operating at a deficit," and any decision to close or consolidate a post office may be appealed to the Postal Regulatory Commission. An alleged failure by the Postal Service to comply with its statutory obligations in a particular location does not in itself provide a ground for overturning a voting rule that applies throughout an entire State.

Id. at 2348 n.21 (citations omitted).

36. *Id.* at 2370 (Kagan, J., dissenting) (citations omitted).

37. *Id.*

38. *Id.* at 2371, 2371 n.14.

39. *Id.* at 2371–72 n.15.

Chapter 5. Safeguarding American Democracy

1. Carl Hulse, "Obama Is Sworn in as 44th President," *New York Times,* January 20, 2009, https://www.nytimes.com/2009/01/21/us/politics/20web-inaug2.html.

2. Rick Hasen, *Inauguration Day,* Election Law Blog, January 20, 2009, https://electionlawblog.org/?p=11905 [https://perma.cc/BW2T-JDPP].

3. UCI Law, Ad Hoc Comm. For 2020 Election Fairness and Legitimacy, *Fair Elections During a Crisis: Urgent Recommendations in Law, Media, Politics, and Tech to Advance the Legitimacy of, and the Public's Confidence in, the 2020 U.S. Elections,* April 2020, https://www.law.uci.edu/news/press-releases/2020/2020ElectionReport.pdf [https://perma.cc/C3X5-URGJ]. For details on the Safeguarding Democracy Project, see http://safeguardingdemocracyproject.org/.

4. Danielle Kurtzleben, "Questioning If an Election Will Be 'Rigged' Strikes at the Heart of Democracy," NPR, August 7, 2016, https://www.npr.org/2016/08/07

/488893858/questioning-if-an-election-will-be-rigged-strikes-at-the-heart-of
-democracy [https://perma.cc/EQ84-6H8N] (quoting Gore); Bush v. Gore, 531 U.S.
98. On that controversy, see Richard L. Hasen, *The Voting Wars: From Florida 2000 to
the Next Election Meltdown* (New Haven: Yale University Press, 2012), 11–40.

5. Kurtzleben, *supra* note 4; Patrick Healy and Jonathan Martin, "Donald Trump
Won't Say if He'll Accept Result of Election," *New York Times,* October 19, 2016,
https://www.nytimes.com/2016/10/20/us/politics/presidential-debate.html.

6. Donald J. Trump (@realdonaldtrump), Twitter, February 3, 2016, https://
twitter.com/realDonaldTrump/status/694879900256354304 [https://perma.cc
/M68V-T5NX].

7. Transcript, "President Trump Defends Response to COVID Crisis in Exclusive
Interview with Chris Wallace," Fox News Sunday, July 19, 2020, https://www.foxnews
.com/transcript/president-trump-defends-response-to-covid-crisis-in-exclusive
-interview-with-chris-wallace [https://perma.cc/TRX2-JNR9].

8. Hasen, *supra* note 4, 41–73; Richard L. Hasen, *Election Meltdown: Dirty Tricks,
Distrust, and the Threat to American Democracy* (New Haven: Yale University Press,
2020), 15–46 (describing lawsuit against Kansas law requiring documentary proof of
citizenship to register to vote and former Kansas Secretary of State Kris Kobach's
characterization of the evidence of noncitizen voting to support such a law as the "tip
of the iceberg," *id.* at 24); *id.* at 24 (quoting the federal district court examining the
evidence put forward by Kobach that concluded: "There is no iceberg . . . only an
icicle, largely created by confusion and administrative error" (quoting Fish v. Kobach,
309 F.3d 1048, 1103 (D. Kan. 2018)).

This section draws from Richard L. Hasen, *Identifying and Minimizing the Risk of
Election Subversion and Stolen Elections in the Contemporary United States,* 135 Harv.
L. Rev. F. 265, 267–82 (2022) (Hasen, *Identifying*), as updated by the January 6th Committee's report. Select Committee to Investigate the January 6th Attack
on the U.S. Capitol, Final Report, H.R. 117–663 (2022), https://www.govinfo.gov
/content/pkg/GPO-J6-REPORT/pdf/GPO-J6-REPORT.pdf [https://perma.cc
/A7K7-S3SC] (hereafter, *January 6th Final Report*).

9. See Aaron Blake, "Donald Trump Claims None of Those 3 to 5 Million Illegal
Votes Were Cast for Him. Zero.," *Washington Post,* January 26, 2017, https://www
.washingtonpost.com/news/the-fix/wp/2017/01/25/donald-trump-claims-none
-of-those-3-to-5-million-illegal-votes-were-cast-for-him-zero [https://perma.cc
/E7UM-S635] ("Of those [supposed three-to-five million fraudulent] votes cast,
none of 'em come to me. None of 'em come to me. They would all be for the other
side. None of 'em come to me."). Alana Abramson, "Hillary Clinton Officially Wins
Popular Vote by Nearly 2.9 Million," ABC News, December 22, 2016, https://abcnews
.go.com/Politics/hillary-clinton-officiallywins-popular-vote-29-million/story?id
=44354341 [https://perma.cc/UQG4-BQQC]; Rob Griffin, Ruy Teixeira, and John

Halpin, Ctr. For Am. Progress, *Voter Trends in 2016* at 1 (2017); Steven Porter, "Clinton Wins US Popular Vote by Widest Margin of Any Losing Presidential Candidate," *Christian Science Monitor*, December 22, 2016, https://www.csmonitor.com/USA /Politics/2016/1222/Clinton-wins-US-popular-vote-by-widest-margin-of-any -losing-presidential-candidate [https://perma.cc/N9ZG-ECMP].

10. Hasen, *Election Meltdown, supra* note 8, at 16, 25–32.

11. For a detailed chronology, see Richard L. Hasen, *Cheap Speech: How Disinformation Poisons Our Politics—and How to Cure It* (New Haven: Yale University Press, 2022), 1–19. See Reid J. Epstein, "Democrats' Vote-by-Mail Effort Won in Wisconsin: Will It Work Elsewhere?" *New York Times*, September 14, 2020, https://www .nytimes.com/2020/05/10/us/politics/Wisconsin-election-vote-by-mail.html [https://perma.cc/A4FJ-3K7K] ("In Georgia, more than 1.2 million people have requested absentee ballots for the state's June 9 primary—compared to just 36,200 requests for the 2016 presidential primary."); Drew DeSilver, *Mail-in Voting Became Much More Common in 2020 Primaries as COVID-19 Spread*, Pew Research Center, October 13, 2020, https://www.pewresearch.org/fact-tank/2020/10/13/mail-in -voting-became-much-more-common-in-2020-primaries-as-covid-19-spread [https://perma.cc/H3U8-XH9X]; Emily Bazelon, "Will Americans Lose Their Right to Vote in the Pandemic?" *New York Times*, July 18, 2021, https://www.nytimes .com/2020/05/05/magazine/voting-by-mail-2020-covid.html [https://perma.cc /W3V8-SP9K]; Eric McGhee, Jennifer Paluch, and Mindy Romero, Pub. Pol'y Inst. Of Cal., *Vote-By-Mail and Voter Turnout in the Pandemic Election* 5–6, 9–10 (2021); Miles Parks, "Trump, While Attacking Mail Voting, Casts Mail Ballot Again," NPR, August 19, 2020, https://www.npr.org/2020/08/19/903886567/trump-while -attacking-mail-voting-casts-mail-ballot-again [https://perma.cc/U462-VVSX]; see Christina A. Cassidy, "Far Too Little Vote Fraud to Tip Election to Trump, AP Finds," AP, December 14, 2021, https://apnews.com/article/voter-fraud-election -2020-joe-biden-donald-trump-7fcb6f134e528fee8237c7601db3328f [https:// perma.cc/TFP7-HXWZ]; Pam Fessler, Miles Parks, and Barbara Sprunt, "As Trump Pushes Election Falsehoods, His Cybersecurity Agency Pushes Back," NPR, November 14, 2020, https://www.npr.org/sections/live-updates-2020-election-results /2020/11/14/934220380/as-trump-pushes-election-falsehoods-his-cybersecurity agency-pushes-back [https://perma.cc/6XS7-SSLW]. (Citing joint statement signed by prominent government officials concluding that the 2020 election was "the most secure in American history . . . [with] no evidence that any voting system deleted or lost votes, changed votes, or was in any way compromised.") Samantha Putterman, Amy Sherman, and Miriam Valverde, "Rudy Giuliani, Trump Legal Team Push Conspiracy Theories, Baseless Claims about 2020 Election," *Politifact*, November 20, 2020, https://www.politifact.com/article/2020/nov/20/giuliani-trump -legal-team-push-conspiracy-theories [https://perma.cc/B9GA-54HU].

12. *January 6th Final Report, supra* note 8, at 195–202, 213–30; Hasen, *Cheap Speech, supra* note 11, at 1–19; see William Cummings, Joey Garrison and Jim Sergent, "By the Numbers: President Donald Trump's Failed Efforts to Overturn the Election," *USA Today*, January 6, 2021, https://www.usatoday.com/indepth/news/politics/elections/2021/01/06/trumps-failed-efforts-overturn-election-numbers/4130307001 [https://perma.cc/79U5-44T4]; Alex Hern, "Trump's Vote Fraud Claims Go Viral on Social Media Despite Curbs," *The Guardian*, November 10, 2020, https://www.theguardian.com/us-news/2020/nov/10/trumps-vote-claims-go-viral-on-social-mediadespite-curbs [https://perma.cc/8458-PVJY]; Greg Sargent, "Trump Just Repeated His Ugliest Claim About the Election. Why Isn't It Bigger News?" *Washington Post*, September 15, 2020, https://www.washingtonpost.com/opinions/2020/09/15/trump-just-repeated-his-ugliest-claim-aboutelection-why-isnt-it-bigger-news [https://perma.cc/7Y7Z-QAYV]; Karen Yourish and Larry Buchanan, "Since Election Day, A Lot of Tweeting and Not Much Else for Trump," *New York Times*, November 24, 2020, https://www.nytimes.com/interactive/2020/11/24/us/politics/trump-twitter-tweets-election-results.html [https://perma.cc/LZN4-RUV2]. ("In total, the president attacked the legitimacy of the election more than 400 times since Election Day, though his claims of fraud have been widely debunked.")

13. See generally *January 6th Final Report, supra* note 8, at 195–576. On the unprecedented nature of the claims of a stolen election, see Ned Foley, *How Best to End "Electoral McCarthyism"?*, Election Law Blog, September 13, 2021, https://electionlawblog.org/?p=124540 [https://perma.cc/75QN-C4PZ]. ("Based on the research I did for *Ballot Battles*, I'm not aware of a historical example (prior to 2020) in which a serious dispute over counting votes was accompanied by the kind of blatant falsification of reality that is the mark of McCarthyism-style demagoguery. Not even the Hayes-Tilden dispute, in my judgment, was of that nature.")

14. Martin Pengelly, "Trump Aide Asked DOJ to Investigate Bizarre 'Italygate' Claim Votes Were Changed by Satellite," *The Guardian*, June 6, 2021, https://www.theguardian.com/us-news/2021/jun/06/donald-trump-mark-meadows-doj-italygate [https://perma.cc/5CHD-M48E]; Donald J. Trump (@realDonaldTrump), Twitter, November 27, 2020, https://twitter.com/realDonaldTrump/status/1332352538855747584 [https://perma.cc/E2YV-HFJQ].

15. Linda So and Jason Szep, "Reuters Unmasks Trump Supporters Who Terrified U.S. Election Officials," Reuters, November 9, 2021, https://www.reuters.com/investigates/special-report/usa-election-threats [https://perma.cc/HX2Y-EMQ3]; Linda So and Jason Szep, "Special Report, Terrorized U.S. Election Workers Get Little Help from Law Enforcement," Reuters, September 8, 2021, https://www.reuters.com/legal/government/terrorized-us-election-workers-get-little-help-law-enforcement-2021-09-08 [https://perma.cc/5MTG-JHSJ]; John Kruzel,

"Threats of Violence Spark Fear of Election Worker Exodus," *The Hill*, August 2, 2021, https://thehill.com/homenews/campaign/565722-threats-of-violence-spark-fear -of-election-worker-exodus [https://perma.cc/V8VE-6EZ2]; Nick Corasaniti, Jim Rutenberg, and Kathleen Gray, "Threats and Tensions Rise as Trump and Allies Attack Elections Process," *New York Times*, February 1, 2021, https://www.nytimes .com/2020/11/18/us/politics/trump-election.html [https://perma.cc/887Q -3YXD].

For example, Claire Woodall-Vogg, the executive director of the Milwaukee Election Commission, "received voicemails calling for her hanging" in August 2021, nine months after the end of the election. One angry caller railed: "You motherfucker. You rigged my fucking election, you fucking piece of shit. We're going to try you, and we're going to fucking convict your piece-of-shit ass, and we're going to hang you. You fucking piece—you get the fuck out of my country, you pile of shit." Rob Kuznia, Bob Ortega and Casey Tolan, "In the Wake of Trump's Attack on Democracy, Election Officials Fear for the Future of American Elections," CNN, September 13, 2021, https://www.cnn.com/2021/09/12/politics/trump-2020-future-presidential -elections-invs [https://perma.cc/G348-8D8D]. The audio of the call may be accessed directly at: https://pmd.cdn.turner.com/cnn/2021/images/08/27 /threatening-call-wi.mp3 [https://perma.cc/QT7Z-F8Z2].

16. See Michael Wines, "After a Nightmare Year, Election Officials Are Quitting," *New York Times*, July 2, 2021, https://www.nytimes.com/2021/07/02/us/politics /2020-election-voting-officials.html [https://perma.cc/RG2P-B7S9]; Fredreka Schouten, "Personal Threats, Election Lies and Punishing New Laws Rattle Election Officials, Raising Fears of a Mass Exodus," CNN, July 21, 2021, https://www.cnn.com /2021/07/21/politics/election-officials-exodus [https://perma.cc/7F7T-22Y7]; Press Release, Brennan Center for Justice, *One in Three Election Officials Report Feeling Unsafe Because of Their Job*, June 16, 2021, https://www.brennancenter.org/our -work/analysis-opinion/one-three-election-officials-report-feeling-unsafe-because -their-job [https://perma.cc/8BNH-5WGV]. For the report itself, see Brennan Center for Justice and Bipartisan Pol'y Ctr., *Election Officials Under Attack* (2021).

17. Cummings et al., *supra* note 12; Adam Liptak, "Supreme Court Rejects Texas Suit Seeking to Subvert Election," *New York Times*, January 15, 2021, https://www .nytimes.com/2020/12/11/us/politics/supreme-court-election-texas.html [https://perma.cc/AW9V-NEPC] (discussing Texas v. Pennsylvania, 141 S. Ct. 1230, 1230 (2020) (mem)). See also Russell Wheeler, *Trump's Judicial Campaign to Upend the 2020 Election: A Failure, But Not a Wipe-Out*, Brookings Inst., November 30, 2021, https://www.brookings.edu/blog/fixgov/2021/11/30/trumps-judicial-campaign -to-upend-the-2020-election-a-failure-but-not-a-wipe-out [https://perma.cc/E2RP -W288] ("Trump . . . lost all but one case—and the great majority of judicial votes

in all cases disfavored his claims."); Rosalind S. Helderman and Elise Viebeck, "'The Last Wall': How Dozens of Judges across the Political Spectrum Rejected Trump's Efforts to Overturn the Election," *Washington Post*, December 12, 2020, https://www .washingtonpost.com/politics/judges-trump-election-lawsuits/2020/12/12 /e3a57224-3a72-11eb-98c4-25dc9f4987e8_story.html [https://perma.cc/YBD3 -H2FC] ("In a remarkable show of near-unanimity across the nation's judiciary, at least 86 judges—ranging from jurists serving at the lowest levels of state court systems to members of the United States Supreme Court—rejected at least one post-election lawsuit filed by Trump or his supporters . . .").

18. *January 6th Final Report, supra* note 8, at 263–272; Anita Kumar and Gabby Orr, "Inside Trump's Pressure Campaign to Overturn the Election," *Politico*, December 21, 2020, https://www.politico.com/news/2020/12/21/trump-pressure -campaign-overturn-election-449486 [https://perma.cc/H5MB-RU4V] ("In total, the president talked to at least 31 Republicans, encompassing mostly local and state officials from four critical battleground states he lost—Michigan, Arizona, Georgia and Pennsylvania. The contacts included at least 12 personal phone calls to 11 individuals, and at least four White House meetings with 20 Republican state lawmakers, party leaders and attorneys general, all people he hoped to win over to his side. Trump also spoke by phone about his efforts with numerous House Republicans and at least three current or incoming Senate Republicans."); Maria Polletta, "Trump Lashes Out at Gov. Doug Ducey Following Certification of Arizona Election Results," *AzCentral*, December 1, 2020, https://www.azcentral.com/story/news /politics/elections/2020/11/30/president-trump-slams-arizona-gov-ducey-after -election-certification/6472784002 [https://perma.cc/39NC-LMGE]; Kyle Cheney, "Trump Calls on GOP State Legislatures to Overturn Election Results," *Politico*, November 21, 2020, https://www.politico.com/news/2020/11/21/trump -state-legislatures-overturn-election-results-439031 [https://perma.cc/UNT9 -K3RV]; Amy Gardner, "'I Just Want to Find 11,780 Votes': In Extraordinary Hour-Long Call, Trump Pressures Georgia Secretary of State to Recalculate the Vote in His Favor," *Washington Post*, January 3, 2021, https://www.washingtonpost.com /politics/trump-raffensperger-call-georgia-vote/2021/01/03/d45acb92-4dc4-11eb -bda4-615aaefd0555_story.html [https://perma.cc/ZF8M-9JS6].

19. *January 6th Final Report, supra* note 8, at 341–72.

20. *Id.* at 373–426; Katie Benner, "Report Cites New Details of Trump Pressure on Justice Dept. over Election," *New York Times*, November 6, 2021, https://www .nytimes.com/2021/10/06/us/politics/trump-election-fraud-report.html [https:// perma.cc/3JBS-Q8V2]; Katie Benner, "Former Acting Attorney General Testifies about Trump's Efforts to Subvert Election," *New York Times*, August 7, 2021, https:// www.nytimes.com/2021/08/07/us/politics/jeffrey-rosen-trump-election.html

[https://perma.cc/993B-AF7X]; Katherine Faulders and Alexander Mallin, "DOJ Officials Rejected Colleague's Request to Intervene in Georgia's Election Certification: Emails," ABC News, August 7, 2021, https://abcnews.go.com/US/doj-officials -rejected-colleagues-request-intervene-georgias-election/story?id=79243198 [https://perma.cc/EAE4-AC4D].

21. *January 6th Final Report, supra* note 8, at 427–498; Jamie Gangel and Jeremy Herb, "Memo Shows Trump Lawyer's Six-Step Plan for Pence to Overturn the Election," CNN, September 21, 2021, https://www.cnn.com/2021/09/20/politics /trump-pence-election-memo [https://perma.cc/DM92-SABH]; see also Kevin Breuninger, "Trump Ally Jim Jordan Forwarded Mark Meadows Argument for Mike Pence to Reject Biden Electoral Votes," CNBC, December 16, 2021, https://www .cnbc.com/2021/12/15/jim-jordan-texted-mark-meadows-argument-for-mike -pence-to-reject-biden-electoral-votes.html [https://perma.cc/J763-ULMK].

22. *January 6th Final Report, supra* note 8, at 427–98; Deanna Paul, "Trump Campaign Wants States to Override Electoral Votes for Biden. Is that Possible?" *Wall Street Journal*, November 21, 2020, https://www.wsj.com/articles/trump-campaign -wants-states-to-override-electoral-votes-for-biden-is-that-possible-11605973695 [https://perma.cc/SD9D-FU36]. A federal district court reviewing a challenge by John Eastman to a subpoena from a House committee investigating the January 6 insurrection concluded that Eastman and Trump's actions "more likely than not constitute attempts to obstruct an official proceeding." Eastman v. Thompson, 594 F. Supp. 3d 1156, 1190 (C.D. Cal. March 28, 2022). The court concluded: "If Dr. Eastman and President Trump's plan had worked, it would have permanently ended the peaceful transition of power, undermining American democracy and the Constitution. If the country does not commit to investigating and pursuing accountability for those responsible, the court fears January 6 will repeat itself." *Id.* at 1198–99.

23. *January 6th Final Report, supra* note 8, at 499–666; Maggie Haberman and Annie Karni, "Pence Said to Have Told Trump He Lacks Power to Change Election Result," *New York Times*, September 14, 2021, https://www.nytimes.com/2021/01 /05/us/politics/pence-trump-election-results.html [https://perma.cc/QZY9 -PJY5]; Lisa Mascaro, Eric Tucker, Mary Clare Jalonick, and Andrew Taylor, "Biden Win Confirmed after Pro-Trump Mob Storms US Capitol," AP, January 7, 2021, https://apnews.com/article/joe-biden-confirmed-0409d7d753461377ff2c5bb91ac4 050c [https://perma.cc/F4GN-YGSD]; Harry Stevens, Daniela Santamariña, Kate Rabinowitz, Kevin Uhrmacher, and John Muyskens, "How Members of Congress Voted on Counting the Electoral College Vote," *Washington Post*, January 7, 2021, https://www.washingtonpost.com/graphics/2021/politics/congress-electoral-college -count-tracker/ [https://perma.cc/AN8W-Q93K]; "Tempers Flare as Congress Rejects Objections to Pennsylvania Electoral Votes," 6ABC, January 7, 2021, https://6abc

.com/conor-lamb-morgan-griffiths-house-confrontation-pennsylvania-electoral
-votes/9430160 [https://perma.cc/L25K-39KP]; Jonathan Tamari, "Eight Pennsylvania Republicans in Congress Will Join a Push Today to Reverse Trump's Election
Loss," *Philadelphia Inquirer*, January 6, 2021, https://www.inquirer.com/politics
/election/electoral-college-certification-congresspennsylvania-republicans
-20210106.html [https://perma.cc/HG7R-MNT6].

24. *January 6th Final Report, supra* note 8, at 499–576; Dan Barry and Sheera
Frenkel, "'Be There. Will Be Wild!': Trump All but Circled the Date," *New York
Times*, July 27, 2021, https://www.nytimes.com/2021/01/06/us/politics/capitol
-mob-trumpsupporters.html. For a detailed chronology, see Trial Memorandum of
the United States House of Representatives in the Impeachment Trial of President
Donald J. Trump at 20–22, In re Impeachment of President Donald J. Trump (U.S.
Sen. February 2, 2021), https://judiciary.house.gov/uploadedfiles/house_trial_brief
_final.pdf [https://perma.cc/6SWZ-TEST].

25. *January 6th Final Report, supra* note 8, at 637–688; Michael S. Schmidt and
Luke Broadwater, "Officers' Injuries, Including Concussions, Show Scope of Violence at Capitol Riot," *New York Times*, July 12, 2021, https://www.nytimes.com/2021
/02/11/us/politics/capitol-riot-police-officer-injuries.html ; Jack Healy, "These Are
the 5 People Who Died in the Capitol Riot," *New York Times*, February 22, 2021,
https://www.nytimes.com/2021/01/11/us/who-died-in-capitol-building-attack
.html; Jan Wolfe, "Four Officers Who Responded to U.S. Capitol Attack Have Died
by Suicide," Reuters, August 2, 2021, https://www.reuters.com/world/us/officer
-who-responded-uscapitol-attack-is-third-die-by-suicide-2021-08-02 [https://
perma.cc/TH7B-TXGD]; Peter Hermann, "Two Officers Who Helped Fight the
Capitol Mob Died by Suicide. Many More Are Hurting," *Washington Post*, February 21, 2021, https://www.washingtonpost.com/local/public-safety/police-officer
-suicides-capitol-riot/2021/02/11/94804ee2-665c-11eb-886d-5264d4ceb46d
_story.html [https://perma.cc/5E22-XZPA]; Peter Baker and Sabrina Tavernise,
"One Legacy of Impeachment: The Most Complete Account So Far of Jan. 6," *New
York Times*, February 13, 2021, https://www.nytimes.com/2021/02/13/us/politics
/capitol-riots-impeachment-trial.html [https://perma.cc/VBE5-UYSY].

26. Jackie Salo, "US Capitol Building Invaded for the First Time Since War of
1812," *New York Post*, January 6, 2021, https://nypost.com/2021/01/06/us-capitol
-building-invaded-for-first-time-since-war-of-1812 [https://perma.cc/93YK
-5ZZH]; Ashley Parker, Carol D. Leonnig, Paul Kane, and Emma Brown, "How the
Rioters Who Stormed the Capitol Came Dangerously Close to Pence," *Washington
Post*, January 15, 2021, https://www.washingtonpost.com/politics/pence-rioters
-capitol-attack/2021/01/15/ab62e434-567c-11eb-a08b-f1381ef3d207_story.html
[https://perma.cc/QZ8X-6D5F]; Adam Goldman, John Ismay, and Hailey Fuchs,

"Man Who Broke into Pelosi's Office and Others Are Charged in Capitol Riot," *New York Times*, January 8, 2021, https://www.nytimes.com/2021/01/08/us/politics /capitol-riot-charges.html [https://perma.cc/XT3K-RMLC]; "New Timeline Shows Just How Close Rioters Got to Pence and His Family," CNN, January 15, 2021, https://www.cnn.com/videos/politics/2021/01/15/mike-pence-close-call-capitol -riot-foreman-vpx.cnn [https://perma.cc/7R2D-KHCP]; Dan Lamothe, Karoun Demirjian, and Devlin Barrett, "Generals Cast Military Response to Capitol Riot as an 'Unforeseen' Change in Mission," *Washington Post*, June 15, 2021, https://www .washingtonpost.com/politics/generals-cast-military-response-to-capitol-riot-asan -unforeseen-change-in-mission/2021/06/15/5201dcbe-ce0a-11eb-a7f1-2b8870bef7c _story.html [https://perma.cc/P3KC-HJDF]; Mascaro, Tucker, Jalonick, and Taylor, *supra* note 23.

27. Ayesha Rascoe, "For 1st Time in 150 Years, Outgoing President Doesn't Attend Inauguration," NPR, January 20, 2021, https://www.npr.org/2021/01/20/958905703 /for-1st-time-in-150-yearsoutgoing-president-doesnt-attend-inauguration [https:// perma.cc/C37L-W5RU]; Michael D. Shear, Maggie Haberman, Nick Corasaniti, and Jim Rutenberg, "Trump Administration Approves Start of Formal Transition to Biden," *New York Times*, November 24, 2020, https://www.nytimes.com/2020/11/23 /us/politics/trump-transition-biden.html. On the deplatforming of President Trump by Facebook and Twitter, see Hasen, *Cheap Speech*, *supra* note 11, at 2, 15–16, 123, 145– 57. On Elon Musk's replatforming of Trump on Twitter, see Shannon Bond, "Elon Musk Allows Donald Trump Back on Twitter," NPR, November 19, 2022, https:// www.npr.org/2022/11/19/1131351535/elon-musk-allows-donald-trump-back-on -twitter [https://perma.cc/4SYQ-K7JN]. On Meta's replatforming, see Shannon Bond, "Meta Allows Donald Trump Back on Facebook and Instagram," NPR, January 25, 2023, https://www.npr.org/2023/01/25/1146961818/trump-meta-facebook -instagram-ban-ends [https://perma.cc/QLX5-PGKQ].

28. Michael Wines, "Half a Year after Trump's Defeat, Arizona Republicans Are Recounting the Vote," *New York Times*, September 23, 2021, https://www.nytimes .com/2021/04/25/us/Election-audit-Arizona-Republicans.html; Nicholas Ricca- rdi, "Experts or 'Grifters'? Little-Known Firm Runs Arizona Audit," AP, May 23, 2021, https://apnews.com/article/donald-trump-arizona-businesstechnology-election -recounts-c5948f1d2ecdff9e93d4aa27ba0c1315 [https://perma.cc/4LMS-2RS9]; Jack Healy, Michael Wines, and Nick Corasaniti, "Republican Review of Arizona Vote Fails to Show Stolen Election," *New York Times*, September 30, 2021, https:// www.nytimes.com/2021/09/24/us/arizona-election-review-trump-biden.html [https://perma.cc/D7NW-28LD]; Andrew Seidman, "Pennsylvania GOP Leaders Face Growing Pressure to Pursue an Arizona-Style 2020 Election 'Audit,'" *Philadel- phia Inquirer*, June 4, 2021, https://www.inquirer.com/politics/pennsylvania

/pennsylvania-republicans-election-audit-legislature-arizona-20210604.html [https://perma.cc/9A2G-2MPJ]; Nick Corasaniti, "Republicans Seek Pennsylvania Voters' Personal Information as They Try to Review the 2020 Results," *New York Times*, October 14, 2021, https://www.nytimes.com/2021/09/15/us/politics /pennsylvania-election-audit-republicans.html; Scott Bauer, "Wisconsin Election Clerks Say GOP Investigator's Inquiry Landed in Junk Folders," *Pioneer Press*, September 14, 2021, https://www.twincities.com/2021/09/14/wisconsin-election -clerks-say-gop-investigators-inquiry-landed-in-junk-folders [https://perma.cc /GMP7-62UW]; Reid J. Epstein, "Wisconsin Republicans Push to Take Over the State's Elections," *New York Times*, November 19, 2021, https://www.nytimes.com /2021/11/19/us/politics/wisconsin-republicans-decertify-election.html.

29. Eugene Scott, "What Happened to the 10 Republicans Who Voted to Impeach Trump?" *Washington Post*, November 23, 2022, https://www.washingtonpost .com/politics/2022/11/23/gop-trump-impeachment-house/ [https://perma.cc /7SGX-3RAZ]; Michelle L. Price, "Nevada GOP Censures Election Official Who Defended Results," AP, April 11, 2021, https://apnews.com/article/donald-trump -barbara-cegavskenevada-elections-bccf4ffe9a52dd6ebbe6e93ad0285e5a [https:// perma.cc/W7UH-VHE7]; Lisa Lerer, "Republicans in Two Rural Georgia Counties Censure Gov. Brian Kemp and Others," *New York Times*, August 30, 2021, https:// www.nytimes.com/2021/04/14/us/politics/georgia-kemp-raffensperger-trump -republicans.html; Dave Boucher, "Whitmer Appoints New Member to Elections Board after GOP Wanted Replacement," *Detroit Free Press*, January 19, 2021, https:// www.freep.com/story/news/politics/elections/2021/01/19/tony-daunt-whitmer -gop-michigan-board-state-canvassers/4210262001 [https://perma.cc/U3R4 -6WG9]; Jonathan Martin, "Ohio House Republican, Calling Trump 'a Cancer,' Bows Out of 2022," *New York Times*, November 2, 2021, https://www.nytimes.com /2021/09/16/us/politics/anthony-gonzalez-ohio-trump.html [https://perma.cc /2Q4V-Q6VZ]; Reid J. Epstein, "Adam Kinzinger, Republican Trump Critic, Won't Seek Re-election in House," *New York Times*, October 29, 2021, https://www.nytimes .com/2021/10/29/us/politics/adam-kinzinger-illinois-election.html.

30. Nick Corasaniti and Reid J. Epstein, "What Georgia's Voting Law Really Does," *New York Times*, August 18, 2021, https://www.nytimes.com/2021/04/02/us /politics/georgia-voting-law-annotated.html [https://perma.cc/4WWL-DXB5].

31. States United Democracy Ctr., Protect Democracy & Law Forward, *A Democracy Crisis In The Making: How State Legislatures Are Politicizing, Criminalizing, And Interfering With Election Administration* 1 (2021), https://s3.documentcloud.org /documents/20688594/democracy-crisis-report-april-21.pdf [https://perma.cc /3HBS-XAS2]; *id.* at 26 (citing Act of March 8, 2021, ch. 12, 2021 Iowa Acts Reg. Sess. 22 (codified at scattered sections of Iowa Code)); see Iowa Code §§ 39A.2(1)(g),

39A.6(3)(a), 53.2(1)(c), 53.8(4) (2022); States United Democracy Ctr., Protect Democracy & Law Forward, *Democracy Crisis Report Update: New Data and Trends Show the Warning Signs Have Intensified in the Last Two Months* 1 (2021), https://statesuniteddemocracy.org/wp-content/uploads/2021/06/Democracy-Crisis-Part-II_June-10_Final_v7.pdf [https://perma.cc/7SM2-BDEE]; Sean Morales-Doyle, *We're Suing Texas over Its New Voter Suppression Law*, Brennan Center for Justice, September 7, 2021, https://www.brennancenter.org/our-work/analysis-opinion/were-suing-texas-over-its-new-voter-suppression-law [https://perma.cc/9TBM-83GE] (describing new Texas law that "threatens poll workers with criminal prosecution if they try to stop partisan poll watchers from harassing or intimidating voters"); Lawrence Norden, "Protecting American Democracy Is No Crime: New Laws Could Make Election Officials Legal Targets," *Foreign Affairs*, April 7, 2021, https://www.foreignaffairs.com/articles/united-states/2021-04-07/protecting-american-democracy-no-crime [https://perma.cc/5RCD-D7UK].

32. Isaac Arnsdorf, Doug Bock Clark, Alexandra Berzon, and Anjeanette Damon, *Heeding Steve Bannon's Call, Election Deniers Organize to Seize Control of the GOP—and Reshape America's Elections*, ProPublica, September 2, 2021, https://www.propublica.org/article/heeding-steve-bannons-call-election-deniers-organize-to-seize-control-of-the-gop-and-reshape-americas-elections [https://perma.cc/JJ5J-Z3FF]. See Wines, *supra* note 16; Schouten, *supra* note 16.

33. Bente Birkeland and Megan Verlee, "Colorado Clerk is Indicted for Election Tampering and Misconduct," NPR, March 9, 2022, https://www.npr.org/2022/03/09/1085452644/colorado-clerk-indicted-on-13-counts-of-election-tampering-and-misconduct [https://perma.cc/8V6E-TJVF]; Nick Corasaniti, "G.O.P. Election Reviews Create a New Kind of Security Threat," *New York Times*, October 27, 2021, https://www.nytimes.com/2021/09/01/us/politics/gop-us-election-security.html; Lawrence Norden and Derek Tisler, *Addressing Insider Threats in Elections*, Brennan Center for Justice, December 8, 2021, https://www.brennancenter.org/our-work/analysis-opinion/addressing-insider-threats-elections [https://perma.cc/KMR3-8HMP].

34. CNN Poll Conducted by SSRS 10 (September 12, 2021), http://cdn.cnn.com/cnn/2021/images/09/12/rel5c.-.partisanship.pdf [https://perma.cc/D5EZ-53SH]; Jennifer Agiesta and Ariel Edwards-Levy, "CNN Poll: Most Americans Feel Democracy Is Under Attack in the US," CNN, September 15, 2021, https://www.cnn.com/2021/09/15/politics/cnnpoll-most-americans-democracy-under-attack/index.html [https://perma.cc/MTE5-YX6M].

35. John Danforth, Sen., et al., *Lost, Not Stolen: The Conservative Case that Trump Lost and Biden Won the 2020 Presidential Election* (July 2022) [https://perma.cc

/U2CG-4YR7]; Cybersecurity & Infrastructure Security Agency, *Joint Statement from Elections Administrator Governing Council & the Elections Infrastructure Sector Coordinating Executive Committees*, November 12, 2020, https://www.cisa.gov/news /2020/11/12/joint-statement-elections-infrastructure-government-coordinating -council-election [https://perma.cc/EF8ENVQL] ("The November 3rd election was the most secure in American history."); Christina A. Cassidy, "Far Too Little Vote Fraud to Tip Election to Trump, AP Finds," AP, December 14, 2021, https:// apnews.com/article/voter-fraud-election-2020-joe-biden-donald-trump-7fcb6f13 4e528fee8237c7601db3328f [https://perma.cc/8QR5-Q9VH] ("An Associated Press review of every potential case of voter fraud in the six battleground states disputed by former President Donald Trump has found fewer than 475—a number that would have made no difference in the 2020 presidential election."); Nathaniel Persily and Charles Stewart III, *The Miracle and Tragedy of the 2020 Election*, 32 J. Democracy 159, 159, 165–170 (2021).

36. *January 6 Final Report, supra* note 8.

37. Lindsay Whitehurst, Alanna Dunkin Richer, and Michael Kunzelman, "Oath Keepers' Rhodes Guilty of Jan. 6 Seditious Conspiracy," AP, November 29, 2022, https://apnews.com/article/oath-keepers-founder-guilty-of-seditious-conspiracy-42affe1614425c6820f7cbe8fd18ba96 [https://perma.cc/MYL6-PPHN]; Spencer S. Hsu, Devlin Barrett, and Tom Jackman, "The Jan. 6 Investigation Is the Biggest U.S. History. It's Only Half Done," *Washington Post*, March 18, 2023, https://www .washingtonpost.com/dc-md-va/2023/03/18/jan-6-investigation-2000-charged/ [https://perma.cc/RT9G-B6DU]; U.S. Attorney's Office: District of Columbia, *Capitol Breach Cases*, Justice.gov, https://www.justice.gov/usao-dc/capitol-breach -cases [https://perma.cc/L6MR-AN9B] (listing all pending charges from January 6).

38. Alan Feuer and Maggie Haberman, "Trump Is Indicted in His Push to Overturn Election," *New York Times*, August 1, 2023, https://www.nytimes.com/2023/08 /01/us/politics/trump-indicted-election-jan-6.html [https://perma.cc/HA3S -WR3H]. In addition to the Georgia charges for election subversion, Trump has been charged federally with mishandling classified documents and in New York State for falsifying business records. "Keeping Track of the Trump Investigations," *New York Times*, last updated August 14, 2023, https://www.nytimes.com/interactive/2023 /us/trump-investigations-charges-indictments.html [https://perma.cc/BMX6 -382A].

39. See H.R. 2617, 117th Cong., Second Sess., Division P—Electoral Count Reform and Presidential Transition Act (2022), https://thehill.com/wp-content /uploads/sites/2/2022/12/JRQ121922.pdf [https://perma.cc/AAL7-EMYU]; "Read the Full 4,155-Page, $1.7 Trillion Spending Bill Released by Congress," *The Hill*,

December 20, 2022, https://thehill.com/policy/finance/3781758-read-the-full-4155
-page-1-7-trillion-government-funding-bill-released-by-congress/ [https://perma
.cc/K6VH-WDZX]; Derek T. Muller, "Congress Passes Legislation That Will Close
Off Presidential Election Mischief," *The Conversation*, December 12, 2022 (updated
December 23, 2022), https://theconversation.com/congress-passes-legislation-that
-will-close-off-presidential-election-mischief-and-help-avoid-another-jan-6-196204
[https://perma.cc/Y2EK-X2CR].

40. Jonathan J. Cooper, "Lake Refuses to Concede in Arizona Race She Lost,"
AP, November 17, 2022, https://apnews.com/article/2022-midterm-elections
-arizona-phoenix-government-and-politics-bcea98345ee81ec1b8fa6a5364bc296f
[https://perma.cc/RFR7-YMZA]; Charles Homans, Jazmine Ulloa, and Blake
Hounshell, "How the Worst Fears for Democracy Were Averted in 2022," *New York
Times*, December 24, 2022, https://www.nytimes.com/2022/12/24/us/politics
/democracy-voters-elections-2022.html [https://perma.cc/B7LN-ZSHW]; Richard L. Hasen, "I've Been Way More Worried about American Democracy Than I Am
Right Now," *Slate*, November 14, 2022, https://slate.com/news-and-politics/2022
/11/arizona-midterm-results-2022-democracy-good.html [https://perma.cc
/VW5K-6X77].

41. Select Comm. to Investigate the January 6th Attack on the U.S. Capitol,
117th Congress (2022), at 20–21(dep. of Cleta Mitchell on May 18, 2022), https://
january6th.house.gov/sites/democrats.january6th.house.gov/files/20220518
_Cleta%20Mitchell.pdf [https://perma.cc/JRB8-6J2R]; see also *id.* at 136–39 (dis-
cussing Mitchell being on the call between Trump and Raffensperger); Gardner,
supra note 18 (discussing Mitchell's participation on call between Trump and
Raffensperger). On Mitchell's broader views against student voting and against expansion of the electorate, see Rick Hasen, *Cleta Mitchell's Fear of Democracy*, Election
Law Blog, May 16, 2023, https://electionlawblog.org/?p=136227 [https://perma.cc
/B8JV-VAZ2]:

> As Mitchell described the upcoming 2024 U.S. presidential election contest,
> she repeatedly complained about states making it too easy for people to vote.
> And these claims were not primarily about cheating, although there was
> plenty of innuendo about that too. They were instead complaints that the
> United States has too much democracy.
>
> She railed against private foundations such as Mark Zuckerberg providing
> money to election officials to run fair and safe elections during the 2020 pan-
> demic, after Congress failed to come up with adequate funding to do so. Par-
> ticipation itself is bad in Mitchell's view, especially if resources are directed to
> places where Democrats may vote.

Mitchell also complained about the activity of charitable foundations being used to motivate more people to vote: "Civic engagement, who could be against that? Expanding the electorate? When they are talking about expanding the electorate, they're not talking about voter registration drives. They're talking about how came we literally manufacture voters from people who don't really have any interest in voting and how can we do that most easily without having what they call 'voter suppression' is anything that would protect the integrity of the outcome. . . ." She further lamented outreach to "underserved" communities because she said that those people would vote "90 to 95 percent" for the Democrats.

Her reference to "literally manufacturing" voters is not a claim of voter fraud, to be clear. It is a claim that these groups are motivating people to vote who otherwise would not vote. Mitchell appears to believe that if voting is too easy, the wrong people will be voting. And this is what she wants to fight against.

42. Moore v. Harper, 143 S. Ct. 2065 (2023); Bush v. Gore, 531 U.S. 98, 104 (2000) ("When the state legislature vests the right to vote for President in its people, the right to vote as the legislature has prescribed is fundamental; and one source of its fundamental nature lies in the equal weight accorded to each vote and the equal dignity owed to each voter"). It would violate the Due Process Clause of the Fourteenth Amendment for a state legislature to seek to retroactively disenfranchise its own voters. See the sources cited in chapter 2, footnote 31. On the scope and limit of *Moore*, see Richard L. Hasen, *There's a Time Bomb in Progressives' Big Voting Case Win, Slate*, June 27, 2023 [https://perma.cc/4JC8-7DTK].

In addition, a legislature's appointment of its own electoral slate after Election Day would violate 3 U.S.C. § 1, which establishes a uniform day for the appointment of electors on the first Tuesday after the first Monday in November. See National Task Force on Election Crises, *A State Legislature Cannot Appoint Its Preferred Slate of Electors to Override the Will of the People after the Election 2*, https://bit.ly/3CPYI4M [https://perma.cc/X7B7-PNAS].

43. On the lack of a constitutional duty on the part of the state to protect a child from abuse by his father, see *DeShaney v. Winnebago County Department of Social Services*, 489 U.S. 189 (1989).

44. Wholly electronic voting machines raise risks to the integrity of the process by failing to provide a mechanism by which people can verify the accuracy of election results tabulated by a machine. (Such machines also raise risks of undermining voter confidence in the election system, because there is no physical evidence that doubting voters can verify an election result's accuracy.) On the need for a paper trail for voting see Hasen, *Identifying, supra* note 8, at 294–97.

45. See *id.* at 297–99 (discussing other legislation Congress could enact to minimize the risk of election subversion).

Chapter 6. How to Get a Real Right to Vote

1. Alexander Keyssar, *The Right to Vote: The Contested History of Democracy in the United States* (New York: Basic Books, rev'd ed. 2009), 82 ("Ratification of the [Fifteenth A]mendment was made a condition for readmission to the union for four southern states."); J. Morgan Kousser, *The Shaping of Southern Politics: Suffrage Restriction and the Establishment of the One-Party South, 1880–1910* (New Haven: Yale University Press, 1974). The Supreme Court first upheld the power of Congress to impose remedies such as preclearance in the Voting Rights Act in *South Carolina v. Katzenbach*, 383 U.S. 301 (1966). It rejected that power in *Shelby County v. Holder*, 570 U.S. 529 (2013). See the discussion in chapter 1.

2. *Report of the United States Commission on Civil Rights* 144 (1959) [https://perma.cc/WJG2-MMAM]. On the constitutional amendment being supported by northerners on the Commission, see Keyssar, *supra* note 1, at 209.

3. 105 Cong. Rec. A7949 (September 10, 1959) (statement of Rep. Bademas); see also 105 Cong. Rec. 18878–79 (September 10, 1959) (Senator Humphrey comments on the report: "The argument in favor of such an amendment to the Constitution, as presented in the Commission's report, is to me most persuasive and logical."). But see 105 Cong. Rec. 19446 (September 14, 1959) (Senator Hill criticizes the Commission and the proposed voting amendment: "Not satisfied with the recommendation to substitute a Federal registrar for State and local registrars, three of the Commissioners go even further and recommend a constitutional amendment which would destroy the rights of States to set any qualifications for voters, except age and residence requirements.").

4. Joint resolutions "To Establish a Free and Universal Franchise throughout the United States," were introduced in the House between 1959 and 1963: H.R.J. Res. 524, 86th Cong. (1959) (Brademas); H.R.J. Res. 3, 87th Cong. (1961) (Dingell); H.R.J. Res. 658, 87th Cong. (1962) (Lindsay); H.R.J. Res. 231, 88th Cong. (1963) (Minish); H.R.J. Res. 3, 88th Cong. (1963) (Dingell). Others were introduced as "Proposing an amendment to the Constitution of the United States with respect to the right of citizens to vote": S.J. Res. 141, 86th Cong. (1959) (Humphrey); H.R.J. Res. 535, 86th Cong. (1959) (Green). On Katzenbach's proposed constitutional amendment, see Bruce Ackerman and Jennifer Nou, *Canonizing the Civil Rights Revolution: The People and the Poll Tax*, 103 Nw. U. L. Rev. 63, 91–98 (2009). As recounted in *id.* At 91, the key part of the proposed amendment read: "The right of citizens of the United States to vote shall not be denied or abridged by the United States or by any State for any cause except

(1) inability to meet residence requirements not exceeding sixty days or minimum age requirements, imposed by State law; (2) conviction of a felony for which no pardon or amnesty has been granted; (3) mental incompetency adjudicated by a court of record; or (4) confinement pursuant to the judgment or warrant of a court of record at the time of registration or election."

5. H.R.J. Res. 72, 107th Cong. (2001). As Keyssar, who was involved in these efforts, explains, "the text of the amendment also included other provisions that varied over the years (and were understood to be negotiable): these addressed issues such as the establishment of national performance standards for the conduct of election, election day registration, and the allocation of electoral votes in presidential elections." Keyssar, *supra* note 1, at 291 n.107.

6. Keyssar, *supra* note 1, at 292–93; Jamin Raskin, "A Right to Vote," *The American Prospect* 10, August 7, 2001; Alexander Keyssar et al., *Shoring Up the Right to Vote for President: A Modest Proposal*," 118 Pol. Sci. Q. 181 (2003).

7. Jamin B. Raskin, *Overruling Democracy: The Supreme Court vs. the American People* (New York: Routledge, 2003), 43–44. See also Jamin Raskin, *A Right-to-Vote Amendment for the U.S. Constitution: Confronting America's Structural Democracy Deficit*, 3 Election L. J. 559 (2004); *id.* at 573 (containing text of Raskin's proposed right-to-vote amendment). For some other calls from this period for a right-to-vote amendment, see John Nichols, "Time for a 'Right to Vote' Constitutional Amendment," *The Nation*, March 5, 2013, http://www.thenation.com/article/173200/time -right-vote-constitutionalamendment# [https://perma.cc/S89V-67WC]; Norm Ornstein, "The U.S. Needs a Constitutional Right to Vote," *The Atlantic*, October 31, 2013, http://www.theatlantic.com/politics/archive/2013/10/the-us-needs-a -constitutional-right-to-vote/281033/ [https://perma.cc/WN6N-CD75]; Jonathan Soros, *The Missing Right: A Constitutional Right to Vote*, Democracy J. Ideas (Spring 2013), http://www.democracyjournal.org/28/the-missing-right-a-constitutional -right-to-vote.php [https://perma.cc/CUW7-9ZZR].

8. H.R.J. Res. 74, 115th Cong.(2017).

9. On FairVote's support for reform, see FairVote, *Right to Vote Amendment*, Fair-Vote, https://fairvote.org/archives/reform_library-right_to_vote_amendment/ [https://perma.cc/NGT8-JH3Z]. Advancement Project, *In Pursuit of An Affirmative Right to Vote: Strategic Report* 7 (July 2008), https://perma.cc/H63R-L7KA.

10. Laura Williamson and Brenda Wright, Demos, *Right to Vote: The Case for Expanding the Right to Vote in the U.S. Constitution* (2020), https://perma.cc/DY23 -WU48. The text of the proposed constitutional amendment appears on pages 27–28 of the report.

11. David Schleicher, *The Seventeenth Amendment and Federalism in an Age of National Political Parties*, 65 Hastings L. J. 1043, 1044–45 (2014); Ron Elving, "Is

America a Democracy or a Republic? Yes, It Is," NPR, September 10, 2022, https://www.npr.org/2022/09/10/1122089076/is-america-a-democracy-or-a-republic-yes-it-is [https://perma.cc/KC3E-GNSX]; Heather K. Gerken, *The Right to Vote: Is the Amendment Game Worth the Candle?*, 23 Wm. & Mary Bill Rts. J. 11, 14–15 (2014).

12. Shannon Najmabadi and Mandi Cai, "Democrats Hoped High Turnout Would Usher in a Blue Wave Across Texas; It Didn't," *Texas Tribune*, November 4, 2020, https://www.texastribune.org/2020/11/04/texas-voter-turnout-democrats/ [https://perma.cc/K4YN-GQYQ]; Mike Snyder, "Record Turnout Helped Texas Republicans. So Why Are They Still Pushing to Make It Harder to Vote?" *Texas Monthly*, November 23, 2020, https://www.texasmonthly.com/news-politics/voter-restrictions-texas-gop-2022/ [https://perma.cc/LR7D-HCR3]; "After Increase in 2020 Turnout, Texas Republicans Attempt to Restrict Voting Laws," PBS News Hour, May 14, 2021, https://www.pbs.org/newshour/show/texas-lawmakers-who-said-the-2020-election-was-rigged-want-to-change-state-election-laws [https://perma.cc/BG8X-337V].

13. Daron Shaw and John Petrocik, *The Turnout Myth: Voting Rates and Partisan Outcomes in American National Elections* (Oxford: Oxford University Press, 2020), 4.

14. On the partisan split in early voting options during the pandemic, with Democrats generally favoring more voting by mail and Republicans generally favoring more in-person early voting, see Paul Herrnson and Charles Stewart III, *COVID-19 and Voter Turnout and Methods in the 2020 U.S. General Election* (draft dated December 29, 2022), https://papers.ssrn.com/sol3/papers.cfm?abstract_id=4314257; see also Michael P. McDonald, *From Pandemic to Insurrection: Voting in the 2020 Presidential Election* (Berlin: De Gruyter, 2022); Michael P. McDonald, Juliana K. Mucci, Enrijeta Shino, and Daniel A. Smith, *Mail Voting and Voter Turnout*, Election L. J. (June 1, 2023), https://doi.org/10.1089/elj.2022.0078.

15. Charles Homans, Alexandra Berzon, Jim Rutenberg, and Ken Bensinger, "Kari Lake Claims Her Voters Were Disenfranchised. Her Voters Tell a Different Story," *New York Times*, November 19, 2022, https://www.nytimes.com/2022/11/19/us/politics/maricopa-voter-complaints.html.

16. On the expansion of early voting in Kentucky, see Jessica Piper, "New Data Shows the Folly of Trump's Crusade against Early Voting," *Politico*, January 2, 2023, https://www.politico.com/news/2023/01/02/trump-early-voting-new-data-00075611 [https://perma.cc/MXH4-87T6].

17. Richard L. Hasen, *The Voting Wars: From Florida 2000 to the Next Election Meltdown* (New Haven: Yale University Press, 2012), 197–201.

18. See Joseph Fishkin and David E. Pozen, *Asymmetric Constitutional Hardball*, 118 Colum. L. Rev. 915 (2018); David E. Pozen, *Hardball and/as Anti-Hardball*, 21 N.Y.U. J. Legis. & Pub. Pol'y 949 (2019).

19. Fishkin and Pozen, *supra* note 18, at 981 (original emphasis).

20. Cong. Rsch. Serv., RL30360, *Filibusters and Cloture in the Senate* (updated April 7, 2017), https://crsreports.congress.gov/product/pdf/RL/RL30360.

21. Carl Hulse, "Here's Why Republicans Can't Filibuster President Biden's Supreme Court Nominee," *New York Times*, January 26, 2022, https://www.nytimes.com/2022/01/26/us/politics/biden-scotus-nominee-filibuster.html.

22. Elizabeth Rybicki, Cong. Rsch. Serv., RL31980, *Senate Consideration of Presidential Nominations: Committee and Floor Proceedings* (updated February 21, 2023), https://crsreports.congress.gov/product/pdf/RL/RL31980.

23. Hulse, *supra* note 21; Jordain Carney, "Bitter Fight over Barrett Fuels Calls to Nix Filibuster, Expand Court," *The Hill*, October 27, 2020, https://thehill.com/homenews/senate/523050-bitter-confirmation-fight-fuels-calls-to-nix-filibuster-expand-court/ [https://perma.cc/9MBP-SUY8]. On the emergence of the so-called "Biden rule," see David M. Herszenhorn and Julie Hirschfield Davis, "Joe Biden Speech from 1992 Gives G.O.P. Fodder in Court Fight," *New York Times*, February 22, 2016, https://www.nytimes.com/2016/02/23/us/politics/joe-biden-speech-from-1992-gives-gop-fodder-in-court-fight.html.

24. Jonathan Weisman, "In Voting Rights Fight, Democrats Train Ire on Sinema and Manchin," *New York Times*, January 19, 2022, https://www.nytimes.com/2022/01/19/us/politics/democrats-filibuster-sinema-manchin.html.

25. I first advanced this argument in Richard L. Hasen, "How Democrats Can Reverse Years of Voter Suppression," *Slate*, October 30, 2018, https://slate.com/news-and-politics/2018/10/democrats-2020-election-voting-reform-nuclear-option.html [https://perma.cc/P4ZF-RZGM].

26. The push to expand the number of Supreme Court justices is gaining some traction on the left, but so far the position has not become a dominant one in the Democratic Party. Marianne Levine, "Liberal Push to Expand Supreme Court Is All But Dead among Hill Dems," *Politico*, April 26, 2021, https://www.politico.com/news/2021/04/26/liberals-expand-supreme-court-democrats-484562 [https://perma.cc/QVP7-RSFV].

27. Richard L. Hasen, "No One Is Coming to Save Us from the 'Dagger at the Throat of America,'" *New York Times*, January 7, 2022, https://www.nytimes.com/2022/01/07/opinion/trump-democracy-voting-jan-6.html ("If Republicans have embraced authoritarianism or have refused to confront it, and Democrats in Congress cannot or will not save us, we must save ourselves."). See also Alex Keyssar, *Constitutional Amendments and the Right to Vote: Some Reflections on History*, 9–14 (manuscript prepared for the Claiming Democracy conference, Washington, D.C., November, 2003, and posted at https://archive.fairvote.org/media/rtv/keyssar.pdf [https://perma.cc/8L8Y-J8FT]), discussing strategies and tactics throughout American history to expand the right to vote; Steve Cobble, *The Right to Vote: A*

Constitutional Amendment Strategy (unpublished draft) (October 2003) (posted at https://fairvote.app.box.com/v/cobble-rtv-amendment [https://perma.cc/V497 -X34N]); but see Gerken, *supra* note 11, at 21–25, expressing skepticism that a social movement can arise from organizing around a barebones and vague right-to-vote amendment when many people already possess the rights that would be protected.

INDEX

2000 U.S. presidential election, 25, 113; reform efforts spurred by problems with, 135–36

2016 U.S. presidential election, 113–15

2020 U.S. presidential election, 4, 7–8, 12, 116–31; January 6, 2021, insurrection following and investigation of, 121–22, 125–26; reform efforts spurred by problems with, 125–26

absentee balloting. *See* vote-by-mail

Ackerman, Bruce, 30, 167n28, 210n4

Adams, J. Christian, 116

adulthood voting requirement. *See* voting qualifications, adulthood

Advancement Project, 137

affirmative right to vote: lack in existing constitution of, 1, 8; history of proposing amendment guaranteeing, 12–13, 17–18, 28, 132–38

affirmative right to vote amendment, contents of, 54–66

—assuring equal voting opportunities and limiting burdens on voting rights, 61–64, 154

—automatic voter registration and unique voter identification numbers, 60–61, 154

—Congress's broad enforcement powers, 65–66, 155

—constitutionalizing protection of minority voting rights, 64–65, 154–55

—equal weighting of votes, 59–60, 153

—extensions beyond basic version (felons, residents of U.S. territories, Electoral College repeal, Senate repeal), 155–58

—positive right to vote, 57–59, 153

African American voting rights. *See* U.S. Constitution, Fifteenth Amendment; voting rights, of African Americans

Alabama, treatment of voting rights in, 9–10, 22–24

Albert, Richard, 187n49

Alito, Samuel, 33, 107–11

Allen, Jayla, 48–49

Allen v. Milligan, 163n15

Amar, Vikram, 159n8

Anderson-Burdick balancing, 64

Arizona, treatment of voting rights in, 24, 106–11, 121–23

Aronowitz, Jacob, 47–48

Article I. *See* U.S. Constitution, Article I

Article II. *See* U.S. Constitution, Article II

Asian American voting rights. *See* voting rights, of Asian Americans

Bademas, John, 135, 138

Baker v. Carr, 32–33

ballot harvesting. *See* vote-by-mail

Barrett, Amy Coney, 33, 147

Basic Law of the Federal Republic of
Germany, 27

Bennett, Robert, 180n4

Biden, Joe, 8, 85–86, 117, 124, 147

Blais, André, 176n30

Bland, Sandra, 49

Brakebill v. Jaeger, 191nn12, 13, and 15,
192nn16, 17, 18, and 20

Breedlove v. Suttles, 3

Briffault, Richard, 53, 162n9, 175n27,
193n22

*Brnovich v. Democratic National Com-
mittee*, 106–11, 163n15, 168n39

Brown v. Board of Education, 32

Brudney, James, 169n42, 171n48

Bush, George W., 112–13, 142

Bush v. Gore, 25–26, 58, 101–2

California, treatment of voting rights in,
7, 105

Camacho, Leevin, 81

campaign finance law, 138, 172n3

Campbell, Matthew, 96

Canadian Charter of Rights and
Freedoms, 26–27

Caraley, Demetrio James, 176n32

Carrington, Herbert, 19–22, 24–25, 40,
41–47

Carrington v. Rash, 19–22, 24–25, 32,
41–50

Cázares-Kelly, Gabriella, 93

Celler, Manny, 30

cheap speech, 52, 116–17

Chemerinsky, Erwin, 168n35

citizenship. *See* voting qualifications,
citizenship

Civil War, 12, 22–23, 27, 133

Clark, Jeffrey, 119

Clinton, Hillary, 86, 113, 115

Cobble, Steve, 213n27

Codrington, Wilfred, III, 30, 167nn26,
27, 29, 30, and 31, 184n30

Coker, Ruth, 169n42, 171n48

Colorado, treatment of voting rights
in, 105, 110

Congress's power over voting rights,
10–12, 14–15, 23–24, 34–39, 65–66,
129–30, 143

Connor, Geoffrey, 46

Constitution. *See* U.S. Constitution

constitutional hardball and anti-
hardball, 145–46

courts, role of in protecting voting
rights, 8–9, 10, 118, 150–51. *See also*
Supreme Court

COVID-19 pandemic and voting, 4,
91–95, 105, 114, 116, 139

*Crawford v. Marion County Election
Board*, 26, 63, 97–98, 101, 178n42

Crum, Travis, 165n22

Cruz, Ted, 114

Cusick, John, 49

Cyber Ninjas, 122

Danforth, John, 206n35

De León, Jacqueline, 94

Democratic Party, stance on voting
rights of, 7, 11, 18, 29–30, 136

Demos, 137–38

DeSantis, Ron, 70–71, 76

documentary proof of citizenship
laws, 5

Dominion Voting Systems, 123

Douglas, Joshua, 180n5

Dred Scott case. See *Scott v. Sandford*

Dubois, Ellen Carol, 2, 165n24

early voting, 62

Eastman, John, 119, 125, 202n22

election administration in the United States, 6; decentralized nature of, 6; partisan nature of, 6

election denialism. *See* election subversion risk

election fraud allegations. *See* voter fraud allegations

Election Law Blog, 112–13

Elections Clause. *See* U.S. Constitution, Elections Clause

election subversion risk, 8, 12, 15, 17, 66, 112–31, 140–43, 150

Electoral College, 8, 16, 29, 51, 55, 58–59, 84–89, 119–20, 130, 132, 137, 143–44, 156–67; National Popular Vote compact as alternative to constitutional amendment abolishing, 186n48

Electoral Count Act, 88, 120, 125–27

Electoral Count Reform Act, 125–26, 142

Elmendorf, Christopher, 195n29

Equal Rights Amendment, 161n22

Eskridge, Charles, 48

Evenwel v. Abbott, 32–33, 51, 177n36

FairVote, 137

federalism and affirmative right to vote, 17, 60, 100–101, 103, 143

felon voting rights. *See* voting rights, of felons

Fifteenth Amendment. *See* U.S. Constitution, Fifteenth Amendment

Fishkin, Joseph, 145, 177n36

Fitisemanu, John, 82–83

Fletcher, Matthew, 190n8

Florida, treatment of voting rights in, 69–79

Foner, Eric, 163n12

For the People Act, 14, 147

Fourteenth Amendment. *See* U.S. Constitution, Fourteenth Amendment

Freedom to Vote Act, 147

Garland, Merrick, 147

Georgia, treatment of voting rights in, 122–23, 128–29

Gerken, Heather, 139, 160n21, 211n11, 213n27

gerrymandering. *See* redistricting

Giles, Jackson, 9–10, 22–23

Giles v. Harris, 22–23, 28

Ginsburg, Ruth Bader, 34–35, 38–39, 66, 98

Goldberg, Jonah, 54

Gore, Al, 113

Gorsuch, Neil, 33, 82–83, 147

Gray, Iris, 76

Guam voting rights. *See* voting rights, of people living in U.S. territories

Halstead, Joan, 72

Harlan, John Marshall, 20–21

Harper v. Virginia State Board of Elections, 3, 31

Heitcamp, Heidi, 95–96

Herrnson, Paul, 212n14

Holland, Spessard, 29–30

House of Representatives, U.S., 8–9, 21

independent state legislature theory, 128

informed voters, 52

Insular Cases, 82–83

Jackson, Jesse, Jr., 135–36

John R. Lewis Voting Rights Advancement Act, 14, 147

Johnson, Lyndon, 135

Kagan, Elena, 98, 107–11, 168n39

Kansas, treatment of voting rights in, 5–6

Karlan, Pamela, 171n51, 195n29

Katz, Ellen, 163n15

Katzenbach, Nicholas, 135

Kavanaugh, Brett, 33, 81–82, 147

Keating, Kenneth, 29

Kelly, Jane, 98

Kentucky, treatment of voting rights in, 141

Keremidchieva, Zornista, 165n24

Keyssar, Alexander, 27–28, 87–88, 103, 136, 163n12, 165nn21 and 22, 171n51, 175n25, 186n44, 193n23, 210n1, 211nn5 and 6, 213n27

Kobach, Kris, 5, 116

Kolbert, Steve, 159n4, 165n24

Kousser, J. Morgan, 163n14, 169n31, 210n1

Kowal, John, 30, 167nn26, 27, 29, 30, and 31, 184n30

Koza, John, 186n48

Kraditor, Aileen, 165n24

Kramer, Morris, 21–22, 24, 32, 40

Kramer v. Union Free School District No. 15, 21–22, 24–25, 50

Ladd, Jonathan, 89–90

Lake, Kari, 126, 140–41

Lash, Kurt, 163n12

Lassiter v. Northampton County Board of Elections, 19–20, 24, 50–51

Latino American voting rights. *See* voting rights, of Latino Americans

Lee, Mike, 139

Legal Defense Fund (LDF), 49

Levinson, Sanford, 161n22, 179n1

Levitt, Justin, 177n36

Lindell, Mike, 123–24

literacy tests for voting, 19–20, 24, 50–52

litigation over election rules, 10–12, 17, 91–111, 118, 141–42, 150

Litman, Leah, 159n4, 165n24, 170n45

living constitutionalism, 33

Lowenstein, Daniel Hays, 164n17, 168n38, 171n3, 177nn35 and 36, 179nn45 and 1

mail balloting. *See* vote-by-mail

Manchin, Joe, 14, 147

Massicotte, Louis, 176n30

Mastriano, Doug, 126

May, Gary, 163n15

Mazo, Eugene, 162n8

McCaul, Michael, 47

McConnaughy, Corrine, 161n23, 165n24

McConnell, Mitch, 147

McDonald, Michael, 212n14

McGhee, Eric, 198n11

mental competency and voting rights. *See* voting rights, of mentally incompetent

Meta (Facebook), 122

Michelman, Frank, 179n1

military members, voting rights of. *See* voting rights, of military members

Minor, Virginia, 1–3, 9, 22

Minor v. Happersett, 1–3, 9, 29

Miranda v. Arizona, 32

Mitchell, Cleta, 127–28

Moore v. Harper, 128, 209n42

Morgan, Jamelia, 195n29

Mucci, Juliana, 212n14

Muller, Derek, 160n19, 193n21, 207n39

Musk, Elon, 122

NAMUDNO v. Holder, 37

National Association for the Advancement of Colored People, 30

National Voter Registration Act, 74
Native American voting rights. *See* voting rights, of Native Americans
Nelson, Janai, 195n29
Nevada, treatment of voting rights in, 92–93
New York, treatment of voting rights in, 21–22
Nineteenth Amendment. *See* U.S. Constitution, Nineteenth Amendment
noncitizen voting, 5
nonfelon status. *See* voting qualifications, nonfelon status; voting rights, of felons
North Dakota, treatment of voting rights in, 95–101
Northern Mariana Islands voting rights. *See* voting rights, of people living in U.S. territories
Northwest Austin Municipal Utility District Number One v. Holder. See *NAMUDNO v. Holder*
Nou, Jennifer, 30, 167n28, 210n4

Obama, Barack, 112–13, 146–47, 178n51
O'Neill, Kathyn, 159n7
one-person, one-vote rule. *See* redistricting
Oregon v. Mitchell, 31, 167n31
originalism, 33

Paluch, Jennifer, 198n11
partisan gerrymandering. *See* redistricting
Patterson, Tony, 72, 75
Paul, Rand, 88
Pence, Mike, 116, 119–21
Perry, Rick, 139
Persily, Nathaniel, 169nn41 and 43, 188n1, 206n35

Peters, Tina, 123–24
Petrocik, John, 140
Pildes, Richard, 103, 163n13, 169n41
Pocan, Mark, 137
political equality and voting rights, 11–12, 17, 41–66, 132
poll taxes, 29. *See also* U.S. Constitution, Twenty-Fourth Amendment
Pozen, David, 145, 187n49
Prairie View A&M University, 17, 45–50
president, voting for. *See* Electoral College
Pryor, Jill, 74–75
Puerto Rico voting rights. *See* voting rights, of people living in U.S. territories

Racine, Karl, 81
Raffensperger, Brad, 118, 120, 127, 142
Raskin, Jamin, 136, 160n10, 164n16, 179n1, 211n7
redistricting, 32–33, 51, 55, 59–60, 138, 145, 148, 177nn33 and 36
Republican Party, stance on voting rights of, 6–7, 11, 15, 18, 49–50, 55, 69–79, 88–89, 102–3, 114–18, 138–52
residency. *See* voting qualifications, residency
Reynolds v. Sims, 32–33, 51, 59
Richardson v. Ramirez, 77
Roberts, John, 37–38
Roberts Court. *See* Supreme Court, Roberts Court era of
Roe v. Wade, 32
Romero, Mindy, 198n11
Rosen, Jeffrey, 119, 120
Rosenberg, Jonas Hultin, 175nn23 and 2

Safeguarding Democracy Project, 113

Samoa voting rights. *See* voting rights, of people living in U.S. territories

Scalia, Antonin, 139, 147

Schiffler, Courtney, 180n6

Schleicher, David, 165n25, 211n11

Schmidt, Thomas, 187n49

Schofield, Jason, 105

Schroedel, Jean, 94

Schwartz, Bernard, 162n7

Scott v. Stanford, 22

Seaton, Henry, 3–4

Sellers, Joshua, 195n29

Senate, U.S., 8–9, 16, 27, 29, 51, 55, 59–60, 89–90, 132, 143–44, 157–58; filibuster rules in, 14, 146–48

Seventeenth Amendment. *See* U.S. Constitution, Seventeenth Amendment

Shaw, Daron, 140

Shelby County v. Holder, 10, 14, 23–24, 34–39, 51, 66, 109, 133, 148, 168n39, 210n1

Shino, Enrijeta, 212n14

Siegel, Mike, 47

Siegel, Reva, 165n24

Sinema, Kyrsten, 14, 147

Smith, Daniel, 212n14

Snyder Act, 94

Sotomayor, Sonia, 82

South Carolina v. Katzenbach, 35, 168n39, 210n1

South Dakota, treatment of voting rights in, 94–95

special purpose district elections, 177n35

Stephanopoulos, Nicholas, 195n29

Stewart, Charles, III, 188n1, 206n35, 212n14

strategy for enacting constitutional amendment, 39–40, 55–56, 132–51

student voting rights. *See* U.S. Constitution, Twenty-Sixth Amendment; voting rights, of students

Supreme Court, 2, 9–10, 12, 16, 21–39, 53, 148–49; Roberts Court era of, 9, 36–39; Warren Court era of, 9, 15–16, 21–25, 31–32, 40, 42–45, 87–88, 150

Symm, Leroy, 45–46

Symm v. United States, 46

Taylor, Miles, 80

Terborg-Penn, Rosalyn, 165n24

territories, voting rights of residents of U.S. *See* voting rights, of people living in U.S. territories

Texas, treatment of voting rights in, 4, 16–17, 19–22, 41–50, 61, 92, 106, 118, 139, 161n1, 188n2

Thirteenth Amendment. *See* U.S. Constitution, Thirteenth Amendment

Thomas, Clarence, 33, 37–38

Thornburg v. Gingles, 106, 163n15

Tokaji, Daniel, 167n34, 195n29

Tolson, Franita, 39, 171n50

transgender voting rights. *See* voting rights, of transgender people

Trump, Donald, 7–8, 79, 85–86, 88, 92, 112–31, 138, 140, 147

Twenty-Fourth Amendment. *See* U.S. Constitution, Twenty-Fourth Amendment

Twenty-Sixth Amendment. *See* U.S. Constitution, Twenty-Sixth Amendment

Twenty-Third Amendment. *See* U.S. Constitution, Twenty-Third Amendment

Twitter, 122

United States Commission on Civil Rights. *See* U.S. Commission on Civil Rights

United States Constitution. *See* U.S. Constitution

United States Supreme Court. *See* Supreme Court

United States v. Vaello Madero, 81–82

U.S. Commission on Civil Rights, 134–35

U.S. Congress. *See* Congress's power over voting rights; House of Representatives; Senate

U.S. Constitution
—amendment procedures, 14–16, 17–18
—Article I, 8–9, 27, 29, 34, 39, 59, 129, 146
—Article II, 25–26, 27, 58, 127–28
—Article V, 89, 160n22
—Elections Clause, 39, 129
—Fifteenth Amendment, 10, 12, 22–23, 27, 34, 65, 133, 134, 144, 163n15
—First Amendment, 138
—Fourteenth Amendment, 2, 4, 9–10, 19–25, 27–28, 32, 34, 40, 49, 59, 64, 74, 77, 97–98, 128, 172n6, 176n31, 209n42
—"necessary and proper" clause, 34
—Nineteenth Amendment, 1–4, 15, 22, 29, 34, 133, 142, 144
—Seventeenth Amendment, 9, 29, 133, 139, 144, 166n25
—Tenth Amendment, 34
—Thirteenth Amendment, 22
—Twenty-Fourth Amendment, 29–31, 34, 74, 133, 135
—Twenty-Seventh Amendment, 161n22
—Twenty-Sixth Amendment, 4, 14, 31, 34, 46, 49, 133, 135, 144, 167n31, 172n11
—Twenty-Third Amendment, 29–30, 84, 133–36, 144

U.S. House of Representatives. *See* House of Representatives

U.S. Senate. *See* Senate

U.S. Supreme Court. *See* Supreme Court

Vaello Madero, José Luis, 81

Vietnam War, 31

Virgin Islands voting rights. *See* voting rights, of people living in U.S. territories

von Spakovsky, Hans, 116

vote-by-mail, 4, 7, 24, 62, 91–95, 104–11, 114, 116, 140

voter fraud allegations, 6–8, 26, 105–11, 114–18, 140–41, 149–50

voter identification laws, 3–4, 26, 46–47, 60–61, 95–101, 106, 141

voter registration, 12, 60–61, 92–93, 95–103, 141

voter suppression allegations, 6, 99, 115, 142, 149–50

voting qualifications, 9, 11–12, 55–56, 132; adulthood, 9, 68–69; citizenship, 9, 67–68; mental competency, 67–69, 176n30, 180n6; nonfelon status, 9, 69–9; residency, 9, 21–22, 41–50, 67–68, 171n2, 172n6

voting rights: of African Americans, 1, 4–5, 9–10, 22–23, 29–31, 34–39, 49–50, 64, 150–51; of Asian Americans, 64; of felons, 17, 24, 55, 69–79, 137, 143, 148, 155; of Latino Americans, 64, 194n28; of mentally incompetent, 67–69, 176n30, 180n6; of military members, 16, 19–22, 41–47, 50; of Native Americans, 5, 24, 64, 91–111; of people living in U.S. territories, 16–17, 24, 29–30, 55, 79–85, 143, 148, 156; of students, 17, 24–25, 45–50, 67; of transgender people, 3–4; of

voting rights (*continued*)
women, 1–4, 22, 29, 142, 150–51; of
young Americans, 4, 24, 25, 31, 45–50
Voting Rights Act, 4–5, 8, 10, 14, 23–24,
28, 32, 34–39, 50–51, 64–65, 77, 106–11,
133, 135, 163n15, 178nn43 and 44,
183n24, 195n29, 210n1
voting wars, 8, 12, 17, 66, 91–111, 143

Waldman, Michael, 167n38
Wallace, Chris, 114
Warren Court. *See* Supreme Court,
Warren Court era of
Washington, D.C., voting rights. *See* U.S.
Constitution, Twenty-Third Amend-
ment; voting rights, of people living
in U.S. territories

Weare, Neil, 186n41
Wegman, Jesse, 87–88, 186nn45, 46,
and 48
Wejryd, Johan, 175nn23 and 27
Wirls, Daniel, 166n25
women, voting rights of. *See* U.S.
Constitution, Nineteenth Amend-
ment; voting rights, of women

Yoshinaka, Antoine, 176n30
young adult voting rights. *See* U.S.
Constitution, Twenty-Sixth
Amendment; voting rights, of
young Americans

Zamora, Manny, 47
Zwicki, Todd, 166n25

A NOTE ON THE TYPE

This book has been composed in Arno, an Old-style serif typeface in the classic Venetian tradition, designed by Robert Slimbach at Adobe.